Reading the Bible in Faith

Reading the Bible in Faith

THEOLOGICAL VOICES
FROM THE PASTORATE

Edited by

William H. Lazareth

WILLIAM B. EERDMANS PUBLISHING COMPANY
GRAND RAPIDS, MICHIGAN / CAMBRIDGE, U.K.

© 2001 Wm. B. Eerdmans Publishing Co.
All rights reserved

Wm. B. Eerdmans Publishing Co.
255 Jefferson Ave. S.E., Grand Rapids, Michigan 49503 /
P.O. Box 163, Cambridge CB3 9PU U.K.

Printed in the United States of America

06 05 04 03 02 01   7 6 5 4 3 2 1

Library of Congress Cataloging-in-Publication Data

Reading the Bible in faith: theological voices from the pastorate /
edited by William H. Lazareth.
         p.   cm.
Includes bibliographical references.
ISBN 0-8028-4877-X (pbk.: alk. paper)
1. Bible — Evidences, authority, etc.   2. Protestant churches — Doctrines.
3. Theology, Doctrinal.   I. Lazareth, William Henry, 1928-

BT89.R39 2001
230'.044'0973 — dc21

00-069196

www.eerdmans.com

CONTENTS

CONTENTS

PART TWO: HOLY CHURCH

IV. TRINITARIAN DOCTRINE

V. DIVINE WORSHIP

CONTENTS

PREFACE

THE RECOVERY OF THEOLOGY
IN THE SERVICE OF THE CHURCH

The presupposition underlying this research project is that the so-called "crisis of the church," specifically the crisis of the churches of the American Protestant mainline, is neither organizational nor programmatic, but theological. The crisis *of* the church is simply the public face of the crisis *in* the church, which is essentially a crisis of faith.

The Crisis in the Church

There are many studies by social scientists of the phenomenology of the crisis in the church. These studies have been useful and suggestive as to the dimensions and proportions of the problem, but they have seldom touched the heart of the matter. The heart of the matter is the loss of the church's identity as a theological community, occasioned by the distance at which the church lives from the source and sources of its faith and life. The heart of the matter, in the language of faith, is the apparent inability of the contemporary church to answer the question that Jesus put to his disciples long ago, "But who do you say that I am?"

The renewal of the church, now as always, is accomplished by the power of the Holy Spirit and is received as a gift of God. If history is any indication, however, the gift of renewal is most frequently given when the church places itself within the realm of possibility, in the context of those means of grace by which, according to the Old and New Testaments, the Spirit works. Thus the renewal of the church begins, at least on the human level, with the recovery of those sources and practices that historically have enabled people to encounter and to be encountered by "the grace of our Lord Jesus Christ, the love of God, and the communion of the Holy Spirit."

The renewal of the church may be anticipated when witness is borne through preaching, teaching, pastoral care, and church administration to the gospel of what God has done in and through Jesus Christ. The persuasiveness of the Christian message, when accompanied by the power of the Spirit, is in the power of its articulation to render a more convincing account of the facts of life, to make more sense out of life, and to give more meaning to life than do other alternatives.

The church is often assisted but never renewed by such things as management skills, goal-setting processes, reorganization, public relations, or conflict management. The church waits most faithfully for the gift of new life when it recovers its identity as a theological community and attends to those sources and practices which are the promised means by which God creates, sustains, and preserves the church.

The Separation of Theology and Church

A significant part of the current crisis in the church is the hiatus between academic theology as an intellectual discipline and ecclesial theology as a confessional stance. The achievement of a high level of competence and specialization in theological education requires a certain degree of proficiency in rational analysis, as well as the mastery of languages, texts, ideas, cultures, and extensive bibliographies. It also requires the maintenance of a certain critical distance in order to distinguish the more from the less true. The bridging of the gap between the academic study of theology and the confessional theology of the church, between the critical distance that rational analysis requires and the profound commitment that Christian witness requires, is not easy and is accomplished only with great skill.

Furthermore, there is a tendency on the part of many denominational theological seminaries, which live in proximity to secular institutions of higher education, to become centers of religious studies. Seminary faculty are increasingly educated in graduate schools of secular universities and are often called to teaching positions in denominational institutions of whose theological tradition they have little knowledge. Seminary teachers increasingly write not for the church, but for other professionals in the "guild." Thus the primary purpose of the theological seminary, i.e. to prepare pastors for the theological vocation of preaching, teaching, and pastoral care, is undercut by the guild, the priority of which is not that of maintaining the identity of the Christian church.

As might be expected given these circumstances, there has been a sharp decline of the pastor-scholar both in seminary faculties and in the ministry of congregations. The movement from seminary faculty to the ministry of a congregation, and conversely from congregation to classroom, has all but ceased. The result is a relatively new phenomenon in American church life, namely, the profound separation between serious theological work and congregational life.

The Trivialization of the Church

One of the legacies of continental Protestant Christianity is the subordination of questions concerning polity and program to convictions concerning the essence of the church. It began not simply with the question, "How can I find the gracious God?" or "What is the meaning of life?" but with questions concerning the nature of the church, such as "What is the essence of the true church?" and "What are the marks by which it may be recognized?" Questions about polity and boundaries were always secondary to the conviction that the church is the people of God, constituted by the Word of God. Other ecclesiologies approach the essence of the church in other ways, e.g. the Roman Catholic, Anglican, and representatives of the Anabaptist tradition. But in one way or another, each would confess that the church, unique among all other constructs, is a profoundly theological reality.

The Protestant Reformers also had a clear understanding of the ordained minister. None would have suggested that the ordained ministry as such is essential to the church, only the Word of God heard in faith and obeyed in love. But they knew full well that the minister fulfilled an important office for the well-being of the church, namely that of preaching, teaching, and exercising pastoral care in the context of a Christian congregation. The task of the minister was the theological task of the proclamation, explication, and application of the Word of God. The expectation was that, through such service, God would act to gather, establish, and empower the church. Once again, other ecclesiologies would confess that the ordained ministry is essential to the existence of the church. But all would agree that the minister's task is theological in nature, not merely organizational or primarily institutional.

A striking fact about the church in our time is that where ministers pursue their calling as church theologians with energy, intelligence, imagination, and love, the church lives . . . and where they do not, the church tends to be trivialized and languishes. A vital church possesses an institutional sense of self that distinguishes it from a civic club, social agency, political party, or self-help organization, and it does not confuse its minister with a social change agent, therapist, or entertainer. One might well document the fact that the crisis in the church parallels the loss of theological identity by the church and the shift in its understanding of the minister from that of pastor-theologian to that of chief executive officer. Hence the recovery of a substantive doctrine of the ordained ministry as a theological vocation, and a strategy for the formation and support of the pastor as theologian and scholar in preaching, teaching, pastoral care, and administration, are crucial for the renewal of the church and for the revitalization of contemporary Christian communities.

The Center of Theological Inquiry as Servant of the Church

The proposal to establish a center for advanced theological research was first advanced by President James I. McCord at a meeting of the Board of Trustees of Princeton Theological Seminary in 1962. "If the age in which we are living is one of transition and revolution, and if the shape of things to come cannot be predicted," he said, "surely the church ought to have some men and women who are giving intense thought at the deepest level to the church's theology, strategy, and mission in the age that is evolving."

After fifteen years of discussion and planning, a Center of Theological Inquiry was established in Princeton, New Jersey as a separate corporation, not under the control of any denomination or institution, to inquire at the post-graduate level into the relationship between theological and non-theological disciplines, including both the human and natural sciences; to inquire into the relationship between diverse religious traditions, particularly the Christian and non-Christian, Western and non-Western; to inquire into the present state of religious and quasi-religious consciousness in the modern world; and to examine other facets of religion in the modern world as may be appropriate to supplement these inquiries.

It was not intended that the Center should focus on religion in general or that it should undertake its task apart from the faith and life of the ecumenical church. To the contrary, the Center was intended as an expression of the claims and commitments of catholic Christianity to the uniqueness of Jesus Christ; the biblical concern for the redemption of individuals, societies, and the entire creation; and the service of God with the life of the mind. The assumption underlying its existence is that God is the source and author of all truth; that truth arrived at in any discipline is not inimical to faith in God; that where faith and reason seem to clash, either reason has been distorted or faith misunderstood and misrepresented.

Over one hundred Protestant, Catholic, and Jewish scholars, representing various non-theological as well as the traditional theological disciplines, have undertaken periods of residency at the Center to pursue their research projects. A like number have been involved in consultations, conferences, and seminars sponsored by the Center on such topics as theology and science, Calvin and the visual arts, eschatology, globalization, and biblical authority. The Center seeks to fulfill its founders' vision by being a context in which people think ahead for the church in order to identify the ideas and issues with which theology will have to cope in the coming years, and to explore the resources upon which theology may call for so doing.

One issue yet to be addressed, however, is that of dissemination. The Center of Theological Inquiry is committed to the proposition that theology is not true to itself when it is simply an academic discipline; that Christian theology, being by definition incarnational, cannot be done in isolation from the church or the world. It seeks to foster interdisciplinary theological research whereby the faith of the church engages and is engaged by the various forces that shape the culture of which it is a part, such as science, other philosophies of life, and different religious traditions.

How might interdisciplinary dialogue, such as that fostered by the Center, gain access to the mind and heart of the church, broaden its theological horizons, and inform its mission in the world? How is the church to recover its identity as a theological community of faith and hope as well as love? What can be done about the separation of theology and church? What role might the Center play in the renewal of the church in our time?

The Pastor-Theologian Program

Assisting us to address this current crisis in the church and in theology, the Lilly Endowment made a major grant to the Center of Theological Inquiry in support of a new venture in ecumenical theological education. A *Pastor-Theologian Program* would seek to focus attention on the ordained ministry as a theological vocation and on the church as a theological community. We were acting on the conviction that in all denominations there are pastors of exceptional theological scholarship, who lack only the time, context, and encouragement for such pursuits; and that on their emergence as a formative influence the renewal of the church depended. They would be further equipped, while in the church's active service, to obey the apostolic admonition to be ready to answer all who ask about "a reason for the hope" that gives life to the church (I Pet. 3:15).

The Center's grant proposal rested on the assumption that a ministry of theological substance is of crucial importance for the renewal of the church. It fully acknowledged the role and place of theological seminaries and divinity schools in preparing men and women for the ordained ministry, but it also contended that additional structures of intellectual development must also be in place if the pastor-theologian model of ministry is to be an instrument of the continuing reformation and renewal of the church. Participating pastors, as recommended by church and seminary leaders, would therefore be drawn ecumenically from congregations of various churches throughout the country.

"Reading the Bible in Faith" (1998-99)

It was further determined that the research of the first year of the program would focus on the theme of "Reading the Bible in Faith." Special attention would be given to the interpretation of two key texts: the binding of Isaac (Gen. 22) and the Passion of Christ (Matt. 26-27). The texts were chosen because they direct attention to theological issues that are crucial for the church's preaching and teaching in our time: theology of the cross, faithful suffering and death, obedience, the relation of the Old and New Testaments, and the identity, purpose, and action of the Triune God.

We believed that the church's current confusion is related to its loss of the capacity to read biblical texts such as these in profound engagement with church tradition. We hoped to help promote the recovery of practices of "Christian reading." Moreover, we expected that these conversations would generate a range of teaching and writing projects that could eventually be shared with one another and the wider public.

During the ensuing academic year, the group completed fifteen regional seminars, comprising three sessions of three days duration each in different locations within five regional areas (Northeast, Southeast, North Central, South Central, Far West). All five groups expressed a growing sense of common purpose and mutual trust as the three parallel rounds of seminars progressed. The circulation of academic resource persons provided variety; thematic continuity was achieved through the critical group analyses of the provided common texts:

Braaten, Carl, and Jenson, Robert. *Reclaiming the Bible for the Church.* Grand Rapids: Eerdmans, 1995.

Brown, Raymond Edward. *The Death of the Messiah: From Gethsemane to the Grave. A Commentary on the Passion Narratives in the Four Gospels.* New York: Doubleday, 1994.

Carroll, John T. *The Death of Jesus in Early Christianity.* Peabody, Mass.: Hendrickson, 1995.

Childs, Brevard S. *Biblical Theology of the Old and New Testaments: Theological Reflection on the Christian Bible.* Minneapolis: Fortress, 1993.

Demson, David E. *Hans Frei and Karl Barth: Different Ways of Reading Scripture.* Grand Rapids: Eerdmans, 1995.

Levenson, Jon Douglas. *The Death and Resurrection of the Beloved Son: The*

Transformation of Child Sacrifice in Judaism and Christianity. New Haven: Yale University Press, 1993.

Given the distinctive subject matter of Genesis 22 and Matthew 26–27, the calendar coincidence of Lent and Holy Week between the second and third rounds of seminars provided both ecclesial reinforcement and immediate applications for the budding pastor-theologians. In an unsolicited affirmation afterward, one pastor gratefully declared in public seminar, "This was the most meaningful Lent in my ministry, thanks to this program."

The annual program climaxed with the holding of its first national conference in Princeton in July 1999. Participants included all sixty pastor-theologians, six resource theologians, six Center Scripture Project theologians, six denominational executives in the continuing education of pastors, along with some observers from the Lilly Endowment and cognate bodies.

As in the regional seminars, the national conference program was built around alternate seminars of worship and group presentations, both in plenary and in small-group exchanges. This time, however, the five discussion groups were intentionally composed of three subgroups made up of persons from all five geographical regions. This volume contains excerpts from their written projects.

Expanding the Discussions

A complete roster of all clergy participants in the year's program activities is provided at the end of the book. Included in their number are the authors of all the excerpted articles edited for publication in this work. While these blocs of material are admittedly both short and taken out of context, they nevertheless do contribute far more to a lively, multivoiced discussion than would the total arguments of their authors' much longer original essays. Each chapter here is opened with an editor's introduction that briefly summarizes and integrates the excerpts. We intentionally have retained the authors' diversity in style and structure. In short, the total format allows for more pastor-theologians to make their distinctive contributions to what is essentially an ecumenical group effort.

We publish this book, therefore, both as a record of the Center's initial stewardship and as a cordial invitation for readers, especially other pastor-theologians in local congregations, to join us by extension in this and other similar publications of annual discussions already projected for future years. We do so with deep gratitude to the Lilly Endowment for its generous financial assistance and helpful staff support in our joint endeavor to strengthen outstanding pastor-theologians for leading the people of God in the mission of the church of Jesus Christ in and for the world.

Wallace M. Alston, Jr.
Director, Center of Theological Inquiry

William H. Lazareth
Program Associate, Pastor-Theologian Program

PART ONE

HOLY SCRIPTURE

CHAPTER I

HERMENEUTICAL CHALLENGES

Introduction

The opening collection of excerpts from six of our authors' essays centers on preliminary issues of hermeneutics, the art of interpretation. This is one of the major issues in contemporary theology that is organically related to the current crisis in biblical authority. "Do you understand what you are reading?" asked Philip of an Ethiopian with a copy of Isaiah in his hands. "How can I," he replied, "unless someone guides me?" The Lukan witness then describes Philip's response: "beginning with this scripture [of Isaiah], he told him the good news of Jesus" (Acts 8:30-35). While acknowledging the contemporary reader's similar plight, our own authors suggest significantly different approaches to its solution. Knowing more and more about the Bible and its historical composition does not necessarily make the church's interpretive task any easier today. It demands pastor-theologians of extraordinary skills.

The first selection, "Why Christian Faith Is Often Impossible," is graphically descriptive of a local congregation in which the pastor serves. The self-critical reader is invited to compare the features of this ethos with his or her own parish situation. What is the same and what are the differences? Here is a local case study of America's growingly influential trends of pluralism, consumerism, pragmatism, relativism, and biblical illiteracy. How do they impact current ministry?

Seeking pastoral assistance from the Jewish tradition, the second selection advocates the theory and practice of "midrash" to assist us in the "recovery of biblical authority" in the Christian faith. Disavowing both fundamentalism and deconstruction, the author asks us whether Scripture does not contain "multiple meanings" within itself that need to be explored, compared and contrasted with differing and even conflicting views. Jesus Christ, the crucified Messiah and risen Lord, is both proclaimed and obeyed with different voices in different lives. What are the likely benefits and risks of seeking such reconciled diversity within an "ecclesial hermeneutic"?

In the third excerpt, "life and death" is proposed as the ultimate frame of reference for the church's pastoral theology. The current crises in both theology and church are grounded in postmodernism, which highlights historical consciousness and a pluralistic cultural awareness. This post-Enlightenment mindset calls for a "thoroughgoing theological reformulation of the Christian faith," which self-critically acknowledges and rectifies its own absolutized historical and cultural conditioning. Scripture's essential nature as "witness" repudiates all defensive claims of inerrancy or infallibility. Can such a "serviceable theology" for a new age truly remove the "intellectual millstones" in our Scriptural interpretation that are barriers to Christian faith in the living God?

Reflecting a similar spirit, the next selection, "The Word of God and the Authority of Scripture," challenges the false dichotomy posed between the alleged hermeneutics of Athens and Jerusalem, the ideology-ridden academy and the grace-inspired community of faith. Such a view underrates the persisting capacity for ignorance and idolatry within the imperfect church itself. Is it not true that every hermeneutic "operates out of an ideological framework which demands criticism in light of the gospel"? The key is not where the biblical interpretation takes place, but rather whether it is properly geared to alleviating the plight of the suffering and the dehumanized.

A fifth excerpt concentrates on the nature of Holy Scripture as the "book of the church," which contains the revelation of God for human salvation and the obedience of faith. The Scriptures provide the "foundational authority" for the life of the church. Indeed, they are to be read and studied because their "divine Author and many human authors" seek through the Holy Spirit to provide believers, and their preachers, with "guidance, wisdom, truth, correction, and purpose to enable faithful attempts to follow God in Christ." Since the Bible was composed to create and sustain faith, must not its final home as "Holy Scripture" be within the community of faith, and not the secular temples of autonomous human reason?

The final selection begins to develop a "Christian Reading of the Bible" as the professed Scriptures of the church. This nuanced approach disavows any purely historical approach that avoids all canonical norms, a sectarian reading that eliminates the acknowledged human element in transmission, and a secular stance that rejects the Bible's uniqueness as the Word of God. What is presented here is concentrated thematic form in a "Christian reading" that coherently interrelates the Scriptures' central symbols of (1) Jesus Christ (Lord of the church confessed in the church's canon), (2) church (community of the faithful who confess the lordship of Christ in the Scriptures), (3) canon (the Old and New Testaments, which prepare and fulfill God's salvific event in Christ), and (4) confession (affirmation of faith in the Triune God as the Christ-centered content of the witness of God's people).

1. Why Christian Faith Is Often Impossible, Always Difficult, and Yet Sometimes Happens in Contemporary, Pluralistic, Postmodern American Suburban Life

RICHARD R. CROCKER

I am the pastor of a mainstream Protestant parish in suburban New Jersey, twelve miles west of New York City. My parish is an ethnically and economically diverse town of 40,000 people, but its median income definitely places it above average in the United States. It is the home of some established wealthy people, of many of the "new class" of media and cultural elite who have chosen it as a place to settle and raise their families while earning their living in New York City, and of some average employees in the service economy.

Most of the families in my church are well-educated, dual-career, dual-income families. If they have young children, they are apt to have nannies for child care. (On the other hand, several members of the con-

5

gregation are child-care providers, immigrants from the Caribbean, mainly.) The congregation has a large number of retired persons: one-third of the members are over seventy years of age. However, this part of the congregation is declining due to deaths and to relocation to less expensive areas for retirement. The *average* home in this town is assessed at $250,000, and the average local property tax is $12,000 per year.

My congregation, like most Protestant parishes in this town, has declined dramatically in numbers over the last forty years. In 1955, the church membership was approximately 1000. In 1995, it was 200. Today it is 210, but many names are kept on the roll for nostalgic reasons. Worship attendance averages about 100. There are 25 children enrolled in Sunday school. The congregation is 85 percent white, 5 percent African-American, 2 percent Asian, 3 percent Hispanic, and 5 percent Caribbean-American. About 20 percent of the members are in interreligious families, either Christian and Buddhist or Christian and Jewish. Part of the numerical decline is due to changing demographics. Formerly mainly Protestant, our town now has many more Roman Catholics, Jews, Hindus, Buddhists, and Muslims than in years past.

But the decline is not due entirely to changing demographics. Rather, it is an illustration of the fact that the fastest-growing segment of the American population is not Protestant or Catholic or liberal or conservative, but "religiously unaffiliated." The combined membership figures of all forty-four religious institutions in this town amount to less than half of the population. Enrollment of children in Sunday school or other religious education programs is less than one-third of the enrollment of the public elementary schools. (These figures are not exact — they are based upon rough calculations supplied by an imprecise sampling of my colleagues.) At the same time that traditional religious affiliation has decreased, this town shares the burgeoning interest in "spirituality" that leads to many organized meditation groups, several religious and New Age book stores, multitudes of twelve-step programs and other support groups. In order to maintain and use its large physical plant, my congregation has rented space during the last twenty years to a daycare facility for the frail elderly, a nursery school, the YMCA, a Baptist congregation (the remnants of Harry Emerson Fosdick's first congregation, which, five years ago, sold its huge building to an interracial independent Pentecostal congregation, which draws members from a wide area and is now the largest Protestant church in town, although it has scarcely any interaction with other churches), a Reconstructionist Jewish congregation, and three AA groups (all of which average more than 100 persons in attendance).

My thesis is that most of my parishioners (and potential parishioners) have a *vague awareness* of certain facts and issues that make the practice of Christian faith problematic, difficult, impossible, or irrelevant for them. Usually these issues are unarticulated. They exist on the fringe of consciousness but act powerfully to inhibit Christian faith, not just in the professional critical community (academics) but also in middle-class Western culture. And yet, Christian faith still is possible, though sometimes it leads to disaffiliation from the church.

The problem that many people in my town have with religious beliefs is that many of them — indeed, more and more of them — find it impossible to believe anything like the more explicit orthodox Christian doctrines summarized, for example, in the Apostles' Creed. I believe that this is true not only for these residents but also for many others in postmodern American culture. The effect of their education, experience, lifestyle, and interaction with others makes it impossible for them to believe. Usually their lack of faith is not fully articulated; rather, it exists as a vague awareness, a sense of discomfort, and the experience of alienation from Christian practice.

The vague awareness I hypothesize is due to a combination of intellectual, sociological, existential, and ethical challenges, which, in combination, have served to undermine the credibility of orthodox Christian faith. Adults in this town are well educated. While most of them are not experts in theology or philosophy or history or science, the residue of their education is a series of challenges to naive faith. The legacy of Galileo and Darwin and Freud has led them to a general suspicion of the simpler forms of Christian faith, at least in its attempts to articulate a doctrine of cosmology or providence. Their college courses in religion taught them that the historical method of studying Scripture has raised many questions about Scripture's uniqueness and consistency. Most of my potential parishioners are vaguely interested in Scripture, but not well acquainted with it and not interested in serious study of it. They find a strong interest in the Bible no more and no less compelling than a strong interest in anything else. Although the Bible does occupy a place of historic and cultural honor, it is not of much genuine personal interest now.

7

Why the lack of interest in the Bible? Not only is there the feeling remembered from college classes that experts have dissected the Bible and found it wanting, but there is also the fact that there are few compelling interpreters. Theology, for most of my congregation and would-be congregation, is the most boring subject imaginable. They simply do not connect with it. Although a group of twenty-five to thirty adults gathers on Sundays before worship for "Adult Ed," they want topical study that shifts quickly and does not require any preparation. Having the occasional theologian speak or having a short course of Bible study is all well and good, but forty-five minutes per week is the maximum amount of time available, and the preferred topics of discussion include current events, issues like health care, aging, parenting, grandparenting, and presentations about world religions. A group of about six retirees, mainly women, do gather for weekly Bible study with the pastor. A recent study of Genesis and Exodus revealed two things: first, their unfamiliarity with the Bible, and second, their moral distaste for some of the reported actions of God. They can maintain their Christian faith only by supposing that the Bible recounts stories that are limited in their perceptions of the divine. The effect of the systematic Bible study was to alienate them from many parts of the text.

The challenges to faith — or even to interest in faith — are not all intellectual; they are also sociological. My parishioners are intensely aware of the fact of religious pluralism. Since many of them are married to persons of another faith, or have children who are married to persons of a different faith or no faith, they hold their own religious claims more loosely than do people who are surrounded by a society of like-minded believers. Religious pluralism is a fact in America — but it is more of a fact in suburban New Jersey than it is in some other regions. Being surrounded by people who hold strong but opposing convictions necessarily challenges one's own convictions. It can lead either to a fierce particularism, as we see in some parts of the world, or to a kind of benign but paralyzing relativism, which is the case here. Valuing tolerance means that all claims are seen as less than absolute, and the deep claims of faith are hard to understand or practice in such a context. Rituals of community building, which can occur in church or synagogue, are considered valuable, but the faith underlying those communities must be minimized to avoid a lack of social cohesion.

New Jersey is the future. With its variety of piety, its cacophony of competing confessions, and its established indifference, New Jersey is much more what the U.S. is coming to — much more than Utah, with its dominant Mormonism, or Mississippi, with its Baptist near-establishment, or Rhode Island, with its Catholic monopoly. In New Jersey we confront the fact, finally, that Christendom is dead. The Christendom that Kierkegaard derided, the establishment that made genuine faith so hard to distinguish from its counterfeits, no longer exists. Christian faith is no longer compelled, presupposed, supported, or encouraged by any governmental or cultural establishment. It is therefore not surprising that, in New Jersey, the public manifestations of Christian faith and practice should have diminished. What is surprising is that, despite the factors mitigating against it, some people continue to believe. But it is also a fact that some of those who are drawn to Jesus will not be able to believe in the church. Like Tolstoy, they will believe — but they will believe outside the church. Some of them are the people who affirm spirituality but oppose organized religion. And it is also the case that there may be people who are church members for reasons totally extraneous to Christian faith. I think there are considerably fewer of those in our town than there used to be.

Paradoxically, the church makes Christian faith possible — and, for many, almost impossible.

2. Midrash and the Recovery of Biblical Authority

CYNTHIA A. JARVIS

The question for Christian readers of Scripture, readers who face crises in biblical authority and the collapse of traditional structures and tenets, is first of all a question concerning the legitimacy of *midrash* (exegesis) in relation to our understanding of Scripture. Clearly midrash would not have the status of serious biblical criticism and scholarship. But could the imaginative engagement with Scripture embodied in *haggadah* (non-prescriptive interpretation) be reclaimed — or tried out by Christians for the first time — as a strategy for listening to Scripture in community, for hearing the reality of Scripture as it lends meaningfulness to the reality of our lives, and for allowing multiple readings to exist side-by-side in this time of polarized and politicized readings of biblical texts?

The Theory of Midrash

David Stern asks the question: "Is there a logic to interpretation in midrash, a set of rules or exegetical conventions governing the free play of its commentators?"[1] The logic, in the end, would seem to be precisely the lack of singular logic! What characterizes the habit of midrash and what undergirds the practice of midrash is the belief that Scripture contains within itself multiple meanings. This is marvelously illustrated by two sayings from the Talmud cited by Stern:

> Abbaye [a fourth-century Babylonian sage] said: The verse says, "Once God has spoken, but twice I have heard" (Ps. 62:11). A single verse has several senses, but no two verses ever hold the same meaning.

> It was taught in the school of Rabbi Ishmael [a second-century Palestinian sage]: "Behold, my Word is like fire — declares the Lord — and like a hammer that shatters rock" (Jer. 23:29). Just as this hammer produces many sparks [when it strikes the rock], so a single verse has several meanings.[2]

"The idea of Scriptural polysemy presented in these two sayings," according to Stern, "represents a virtual ideological cornerstone of midrashic exegesis."[3] From this cornerstone, Stern goes on to note that "The notion of Scriptural polysemy raises several questions. If every verse has several meanings, what did the Rabbis believe was the meaning of Scripture? Did the Bible even have a determinate sense for the Rabbis, or did they consider it essentially an open text, an unbounded

---

1. David Stern, *Midrash and Theory: Ancient Jewish Exegesis and Contemporary Literary Studies* (Evanston: Northwestern University Press, 1996), p. 15.
2. Stern, *Midrash and Theory*, p. 17.
3. Stern, *Midrash and Theory*, p. 18.

field for the unlimited play of interpretation? If so, was my interpretation of Scripture valid? Or did there exist exegetical criteria, constraints upon the free activity of Scriptural interpretation, and if so, what were they? In the case of contradictory, mutually exclusive, or opposed exegeses, what criteria existed for resolving conflicts of interpretation?"[4]

Stern's questions are our questions. On the surface, they are questions characteristic of an approach to Scripture that would major less in certitude than in an ongoing engagement with the reality of the narrative as it lends meaningfulness to the reality of human existence. Yet they are questions asked out of a time and a culture gone mad over subjective truth and the indeterminacy of texts: it means what you want it to mean and, finally, it means nothing. This is precisely where midrash does not go! Rather midrash presupposes that all contradictory interpretations come from the speech of God himself. Different houses of interpretation hear the legitimate voice of God in contrary ways such that "even if they contradict each other, [differing interpretations] are considered equally true; identically alive to Torah's meaning, to the words of the living God."[5]

The Recovery of Midrash for the Church

At the heart of this current crisis of biblical authority, there is the crisis of a meaningful, helpful, challenging, and life-giving conversation atrophied by a multitude of factors: the political and ideological agendas that have emerged out of a society's profound dislocation from its religious and moral underpinnings; the growth of para-camps within denominations that vie for influence and power more profoundly than they seek the purposes of the living God; the secular world bettering the church as the church defines herself in competition with the same; the explosion of communications that, paradoxically, has threatened the gathered community and privileged the virtual community; the fascination with a free-floating phenomenon referred to as *spirituality*, which, for the most part, is self-referential; and the pluralism wherein

4. Stern, *Midrash and Theory*, p. 18.
5. Stern, *Midrash and Theory*, p. 22.

truth is subjective, no text is common, and every text is read through the lens of one's own "accident" of birth. We could go on. Suffice it to say, the concept of authority itself has fallen on hard times. The more authority is asserted, the less authoritative the church becomes in the real lives of people. In many ways, I do not weep for the effect this has had on the moribund institutional church of our day, but I do mourn the loss of the biblical narrative authoritatively heard at the center of our common life. This is the most tragic loss of all to people whose lives are desperate for the very meaning awaiting them through its words.

The coincidence of crises has led me to investigate midrash as a means for our reengagement of Scripture's reality with the reality of human experience, by conceding the significance of the latter more magnanimously and carefully than much current scholarship will allow. At this point, I will simply list some of what I think we may find helpful from midrashic theory and practice for our current ecclesial morass vis-à-vis biblical authority:

- The understanding of Scripture as a prism, a lens through which we may view our own world;
- The way midrash listens to the reality of Scripture through the reality of human experience, gleaning the term of reference from Scripture wherein our lives are given new meaning, reclaiming the vocabulary of Scripture as a vocabulary through which to articulate feelings and thoughts;
- The resistance of midrash to ideology and politics, granting that this unfortunately arose from a distrust of history as any longer revelatory of God's purposes;
- The playfulness with which midrash engages Scripture, reminding us not to take ourselves as interpreters too seriously;
- The conversation prolonged through the stories told from the stories of Scripture, which claim only to be conversations with the God whom we meet in the biblical narrative;
- The polysemy of Scripture and scriptural interpretation, which could lead us out of the hierarchy necessary to orthodoxy's claims and the indeterminacy of postmodern pluralism.

Luke Timothy Johnson offers for consideration "A Midrashic Model for an Ecclesial Hermeneutic." He suggests that the church today should seek to imitate the process by which the New Testament writings came into being, namely the process of midrash. He merely skims the surface, but his points underline the potential fruitfulness of such an exploration.

Johnson contends that "as midrash is a category that enables us to understand the process of the text's creation, so it is a category that enables us to move in the direction of a properly ecclesial hermeneutic."[6] He likens the prism through which the Talmud throws light upon Torah to the New Testament as the prism through which "the light of the experience of Jesus the crucified Messiah and risen Lord" is thrown upon Torah.[7] Further, he underlines the significance for our times of the rabbis' insistence on listening to multiple voices, "in all their conflicts and disagreements, for it is precisely in those elements of plurality and even disharmony that the texts open themselves to new meaning, so that they are allowed to speak to the disharmonies and disjunctions of contemporary life."[8]

Significant problems await us, however. First, we have no common understanding of Scripture that would coincide with the earliest rabbis' absolute clarity concerning Scripture's perfect Author and perfect authority. We as Christians have no comparable communal claim to make about Scripture's perfect Author short of the claim that leads us toward the straitjacket of inerrancy. Those Christians who "love" the Bible tend toward a latter-day biblicism while those who may thrill to its "stories" are wary of making communal claims concerning the truth contained therein. We have no schools of rabbis reading between the lines in such a way that our lives are taken seriously. There are only scholars interpreting texts whose primary referent tends to be the academy rather than the congregation.

The only Word we have been given as both limit and license in our response to Scripture's truth is Jesus Christ. He is enough. In a sense, the story we are told of his life, death, and resurrection is God's eternal midrash made flesh on the law and the prophets. In addition, we may look at Jesus' "take" on the Scripture of his community and learn from

---

6. Luke Timothy Johnson, *Scripture and Discernment: Decision Making in the Church* (Nashville: Abingdon Press, 1996), p. 39.

7. Johnson, *Scripture and Discernment,* p. 39.

8. Johnson, *Scripture and Discernment,* p. 39.

him the questions to ask, the silences to hear, the contradictions to notice which will call forth our own midrash. He will be our teacher for the stories we may truthfully and playfully tell out of the story we have been told in him.

Further, a model of *how* Jesus Christ is limit and license, in relationship to some recovery of the midrash as interpretive genre, is given us in the synoptic gospels, the Gospel of John, and the Pauline letters. There is surely some degree of polysemy in the New Testament itself. In fact, that part of the canon could be said positively to glorify polysemy. Still, there are limits and there is a limit set by the canon that must not be lightly overstepped. The model of New Testament writers coupled with the stories and sayings of Jesus also may act as limit and license, as teacher who alone can guide us through his midrash to the midrash of our time and community.

His church, as it is given to be a living hermeneutic of the gospel, ought to incarnate a midrashic gathering of motivations, feelings, and thoughts unexpressed in Scripture but acted out in the ongoing story that is our human response to Scripture. If the church could be guided by pastor-theologians studying Scripture across denominational lines or within denominations across theological camps, and led by scholars studying Scripture among diverse theological faculties as well as across academic disciplines, then perhaps the resulting midrashim could be used in congregations as a means of reengaging the reality of people's lives with the reality, power, and authority of Scripture. As midrash was written only in community and by those who loved Torah, so would the Christian community look to those whose learned love of Jesus Christ would be limit and license as together they listen to Scripture in faith, telling those stories which, in response to Scripture's silence and inconsistencies, bear witness to the same Christ therein revealed.

We *could* be in the perfect situation, because of Jesus Christ, to play in the fields of midrash with some degree of discipline and abandon. How this would affect the study of Scripture among seminarians, or the centrality of Scripture within the life of congregations, or the authority of Scripture as it reorders the common life is not in our hands but God's. First, however, we must return to Scripture *together*, to the primary place where Christ meets us, as God's eternally relevant Word. Then whatever by grace we may venture in his name, we can be sure that God is able to do exceedingly more than we can ask or imagine.

3. In Life and in Death

BYRON C. BANGERT

Introduction

The Pastor-Theologian Program has assumed, and I myself have assumed, that there is a crisis in theology and the church. This past year our focus has been on the crisis in biblical authority. In my previous essays I have tried to indicate, both implicitly and explicitly, that this is a theological crisis of the first order. That is to say, if any resolution of this crisis is to be found, it must include a newly reformulated theology of Scripture. While the emergence of the present crisis in biblical authority can hardly be understood apart from the widespread acceptance of historical-critical methods of biblical study, this crisis will not be resolved by some new hermeneutic or methodology of interpretation. This crisis is not to be resolved by resort to literary or narrative approaches, for example, whether or not these approaches are bolstered by the claims of a canonical biblical theology.

In the first place, the crisis in theology and the church is part of a much larger intellectual and spiritual crisis in the West that can hardly be understood apart from what academics call postmodernism. Postmodernism may be characterized as marked by the rise of historical consciousness and an increasingly pluralistic global cultural awareness. Less obviously, but possibly even more importantly, it is marked by the growing awareness that all social reality is not only historically and culturally conditioned, but also humanly constructed. We are not only the projects of our times and circumstances, we are also in some sense the makers of these times and circumstances. We contribute to the construction of the social worlds of ideas, beliefs, artifacts, and institutions that we inhabit.

In this context there is hardly anything of the Christian tradition that is not called into question or rendered problematic. The situation calls for thoroughgoing theological reformulation of the Christian faith. Attempts to finesse the intellectual challenges of postmodernism by reassertion of the Christian tradition without such reformulation

15

can only lead to more insular and authoritarian expressions of Christianity, which may well survive but will hardly be able to offer compelling moral and spiritual guidance to the contemporary world.

In the second place, the biblical witness is inherently unsuitable for resolving the crisis in theology and the church, insofar as that crisis is generally conceived to be a crisis of authority resulting from a lack of unity and consensus. Far from providing a uniform theological standard, the biblical witness is multivoiced, multifaceted, and multifarious. One might even say that it is pluralistic. The so-called "unity of the Bible" can be claimed, if at all, only as a theological conviction.

There is first the question of which Bible. The Hebrew Bible? The Tanakh? The Roman Catholic Bible, with the Apocrypha? The Protestant Bible, without? There is also the question of which text or texts are the most original or authentic of the available manuscripts, as well as the question of translation. But even if one could finally and satisfactorily settle the canonical, textual, and translation questions, there would remain the fact that, by any objective descriptive account, the Bible is really a collection of writings, not a single book. These writings are of different genres, dating from different historical periods, reflecting different historical circumstances and problems, with differing theological outlooks and sometimes contrasting theological formulations, not to mention certain inconsistencies in the reporting of what are ostensibly the same facts and events.

Meaningful and convincing claims to the authority of the Bible cannot depend on assertions of unity of content. Moreover, there is no methodology of interpretation that guarantees convergence and consistency. Any number of biblical texts yield differing and sometimes markedly contrasting interpretations at the hands of faithful interpreters. This is true whether the interpreters rely primarily upon historical-critical methods or literary methods of interpretation, whether they believe in working as canonical theologians or not, whether they assume a unity of the Bible or not.

This is not to say that one can find no convergences in interpretation of biblical texts either at particular times and places or over certain extended periods of history. There are schools of thought (for example, today's "Yale" school, or the "Chicago" school from early in this century) and there are traditions of interpretation (Lutheran, Reformed, and others). Neither is it to say that the "truth" of Scripture can never be proclaimed. It is to say that whatever truths come to expression through the Scriptures cannot be distilled without remainder to a univocal set of propositions or coherent systematic doctrines. It is to say that a single universal and enduring consensus regarding what constitutes the proper or correct interpretation of most passages of Scripture, and perhaps also of Scripture as a whole, would seem to lie beyond our grasp.

The Nature of Scripture

Is this situation a problem for biblical interpretation? Is it a problem for theology? It all depends upon what one thinks the tasks of biblical interpretation and theology are. Here I would like to stress the nature of Scripture as witness.

All ministers, elders, and deacons to be ordained and installed in the Presbyterian Church must answer the following question in the affirmative: "Do you accept the Scriptures of the Old and New Testaments to be, by the Holy Spirit, the unique and authoritative witness to Jesus Christ in the Church universal, and God's Word to you?" That the Scriptures of the Old and New Testament are unique and authoritative witness seems to me relatively unproblematic and true. In fact, it is as witness that I believe they are best understood — witness by individuals and communities, born of experience and faith, to divine reality in their history and in their midst. Even so, one must have a broad understanding of witness to include within this rubric such biblical works as Esther, where there is no mention of God nor any allusion to matters divine, and Ecclesiastes, in which human experience seems to be characterized more by uncertainty, ambiguity, vanity, and theological agnosticism than by witness to divine reality.

Other particulars of the ordination "vow," specifically the identification of Jesus Christ as the referent of Old as well as New Testament Scriptures, and the identification of these Scriptures as "God's Word," are wholly contingent upon the crucial qualification, "by the Holy Spirit." Without the Holy Spirit, the Old Testament Scriptures have nothing to say about Jesus Christ. And without the Holy Spirit, the authoritative witness of both Testaments falls short of being "God's Word" to me or to anyone else. The other qualifying phrase, "in the

Church universal," is largely tautological. That is to say, the church universal can be defined or identified as existing only where the Scriptures actually function as the sort of witness here claimed, and where the Scriptures so function, the church exists.

All the same, it is clear that it was by means of an actual historical process that members of an institutionalized church made the decision over time to designate certain writings as Scripture and others not, presumably on the basis of judgments regarding the authoritativeness of their witness. Biblical authority, in this view, arises basically from a process of authentication through experience. There is no external warrant that can make Scripture authoritative, though there are teachings and doctrines that make such assertions. The final proof remains in the eating of the pudding.

Obviously, nothing in this understanding of Scripture requires the view that Scripture is infallible, either in its particular accounts of events or in its theological witness. To be authoritative, even uniquely so, and even "by the Holy Spirit," does not mean to be wholly without error. The Holy Spirit may be without error, but no one else in the transmission process is! To be authoritative is to claim my careful attention as a person of faith, but it is not to coerce my powers of intellect and spiritual discernment. Nothing in this understanding of Scripture requires the view that only those writings that have come to be regarded as Scripture can function authoritatively as witness to Jesus Christ or to divine reality, nor must one conclude that all the writings contained within the two Testaments are equally authoritative in any particular respect.

This is to say that the process by which certain writings have come to be regarded as Scripture and placed within the canon is not to be regarded as infallible any more than the contents of those writings must be considered so. It is also to say that even the best possible judgments of one historical period are not categorically immune to improvement. If it could be proved that some of the extrabiblical sayings in the Gospel of Thomas, for example, are authentic words of Jesus, such sayings would surely deserve our attention to such an extent that we might be led to revise our understanding of other teachings attributed to him. Moreover, if a third millennium shepherd were to discover a manuscript in an earthen jar in a cave near Qumran purporting, credibly upon careful scholarly examination, to be from the hand of Yeshua bar

Joseph of Nazareth, Christians would be obliged to regard its contents no less carefully and no less seriously than any other teachings attributed to Jesus in the New Testament.

The story is told about Paul Tillich that he, when asked what difference it would make for the Christian faith if Jesus' remains were to be found in a sealed tomb near Jerusalem, answered that it would make no difference at all. I quite agree; the resurrection is not about resuscitation. If some new teachings of Jesus were to be discovered, however, or if new sources came to light regarding Jesus' life and ministry, and if these were judged with a high degree of probability to be authentic teachings or reliable accounts of teachings, such a discovery conceivably would make a great difference. To argue otherwise, it seems to me, is to argue against the significance of what Christians have called the Incarnation.

The Authority of Scripture

As things now stand, what is required of the Scriptures for them to continue to be authoritative for the Christian faith is their capacity to continue to bear witness, by the Holy Spirit, to divine reality — most specifically to God, as we have come to know God through the person of Jesus whom we call the Christ. It is not possible to say, *a priori,* just exactly *how* authoritative the Scriptures are, in this view. We can say *that* they are authoritative, and that for Christians they are clearly more authoritative than any other collection of writings or texts. We can also say something about *how* they are authoritative. The following points seem to me to be sound:

a. There is no single, normative method for biblical interpretation. Biblical texts function, first of all, as sources for further reflection and conversation within communities that understand themselves to exist in historical continuity with the texts and their antecedent and interpretive traditions.

b. If it can be said that Scripture is normative, this statement must be understood to be descriptive of the biblical witness as it is appropriated in the life of the religious community. The meaning of the bare text of Scripture is hardly self-evident, nor would that meaning necessarily be normative for the religious community if evident. Scripture remains authoritative so long as it continues to be appropriated as a basic source for reflection, conversation, and identity within religious communities.

c. The truth of Scripture is to be found in its capacity — by the Holy Spirit — to mediate to us an apprehension or understanding of God, the universe, and human life. That Scripture possesses this capacity accounts for its continued appropriation and authority.

d. What is normative or truthful in Scripture is to be discerned within a narrative context, all the parts of which are not equally significant or normative or true. The truth of any scriptural text must be mined from its textual context — not taken out of context — by acts for which it is Scripture; such discernment of the truth of the text may not account for all of the particular features of the narrative.

e. Biblical interpretation is a profoundly theological undertaking.

This brings me to the threshold of the constructive project hinted at in the title of this essay. I would like to propose that the constructive task facing the church today is to articulate a theology that will serve us well in life and in death. I do not mean to imply by this that the purpose of theology is merely self-serving, or that human beings are the measure of all things. I do assume, however, that God desires our good. That is a momentous and unprovable assumption. It is a matter of faith — but not of blind faith. It is in many ways a conviction born of experience. It is also a reasonable conclusion to be drawn from the whole of the biblical witness as well as the tradition and teaching of the church. Nonetheless, it is anything but a demonstrable fact.

The crisis in theology and the church today is, at the very least, an intellectual crisis. One wonders how long the church will continue to insist on saying things that are no longer believable. We do not live in a three-story universe, there is no need to suppose that a virgin ever gave birth, and we are not to be herded into acceptable belief by the reassertion of exhausted claims of scriptural or creedal authority. Theological reformulation is necessary not to re-establish the claims of Christianity so much as to remove the intellectual millstones that are barriers to faith.

Even more basic to this crisis, however, is the unrelenting human quest for security, for validation, for certainty. We humans want to justify ourselves and save ourselves. We do not want to live in a world in which all that we can claim to know is provisional, tentative, subject to change. We do not want to have to depend upon appeals to authorities that are fallible, inconsistent, or unable to provide us final and un-equivocal answers to the disturbing questions of life (cf. I Cor. 13). We do not want to follow Paul's "more excellent way" (I Cor. 12:31). We do not want to live by faith — faith in a living God. Yet we have little choice. Protestant Christians especially should realize that in rejection of the conditions and limitations of our existence there is idolatry, but in acceptance of these conditions and limitations there is grace. That which limits us is also that which gives us our possibilities.

4. The Word of God and the Authority of Scripture

JEFFREY C. EATON

In their introduction to *Reclaiming the Bible for the Church,* Carl Braaten and Robert Jenson ask, "Which hermeneutic, then, is best qualified to understand the Scriptures: that of the autonomous scholar whose private ideological commitment is disguised as objective scientific research or that of a community of faithful memory that forthrightly acknowledges the Scriptures as divinely inspired authority?"[1] The question as posed seems a bit tendentious, and one might imagine those autonomous ideologues posing a question of their own: "Which hermeneutic is best qualified to understand the Scriptures? That of the investigator committed to scientific objectivity to the extent that such is possible, or that of a community that on the basis of the authority of Scripture has subordinated women to men inside and outside the Church, repressed the inquiries and findings of the sciences when they were seen to conflict with the prejudices of that community, and vilified and condemned those of other faith traditions for views that do

1. Carl Braaten and Robert Jenson, eds., *Reclaiming the Bible for the Church* (Grand Rapids: Eerdmans, 1995), p. xi.

not accord with those of the community?" It is not likely, I think, that questions of this sort are going to do much to inform anyone about the authority of Scripture or do justice to the venerable and perennial question of Tertullian, "What has Athens to do with Jerusalem?"

The impression that one gets from the essays assembled by Braaten and Jenson is that Athens doesn't have much at all to do with Jerusalem these days, that academic theology operates without regard for the inspiration of the Holy Spirit, whereas the church seeks out the inspiration of the Holy Spirit in its pursuit of theological understanding. The result is that the hermeneutics that comes out of the academy is detached from the Incarnation, and, as a consequence, treats the Bible merely as an ancient book and not Holy Scripture, takes the gospel as myth, sees the church as but one more human association, and deems the sacraments ineffectual.[2] Missing from this catalogue of ills cited by Braaten and Jenson that result from a dispirited hermeneutics is the denial of the Spirit's power to lead the church to a rethinking of ancient thoughts in such a way as to bring new visions of the gospel to light that would correct bias and remove irrelevance from the text. Are we not to look to the Holy Spirit for the critical testing of text, tradition, and the decreed teaching of the church, without which theology is only conservative?

It would no longer seem possible to maintain a privileged status for Christian theological claims such as would remove them from public accountability, and this would seem to be as true for the question of the authority of Scripture as it is for any other subject of Christian reflection. At the same time, the admission of public accountability of Christian claims does not mean that these claims must conform to the prevailing cultural norms in order to be acceptable or that one is operating with an Enlightenment standard of unconditioned reason in pursuing such accountability. We are, as Christopher Morse has argued, in a situation not unlike that faced by Thomas Aquinas, whose work is testimony to the need to balance the particularity of the Christian faith with the demands of scholarly inquiry. We are not, however, living in a time that admits of the magisterial syntheses Thomas put forward in his *Summae.* In addressing concrete historical struggles, the liberation theologies have argued that Christian teachings must be appraised in

---

2. Braaten and Jenson, *Reclaiming the Bible,* p. xii.

light of the consequences they have in particular social and cultural contexts. According to Morse, "no theology is creditable either as an ecclesial or an academic discipline unless it is accountable with respect to the situation of people whose humanity is currently in jeopardy."[3]

An apparent problem with the ecclesial approach to Scripture represented in Brevard Childs' canonical method of biblical interpretation is that, while it admits certain virtues of the historical-critical method, it stops short of examining the ideological structure of Christianity and the extent to which the gospel is a critique of Christian ideology. In the words of Dorothee Sölle, "whoever wants to proclaim the *solus Christus* cannot overlook the *Christus in ecclesia corruptus*."[4] Every hermeneutics, even one that claims to be simply canonical or ecclesial, operates out of an ideological framework that demands criticism in light of the gospel. Just as there are no kerygmatic truths and events that are unengaged from concrete historical praxis, so there is no mediation of kerygmatic truths or events that is unengaged and uncompromised by concrete historical praxis. It is not merely that there is no neutral academic stance from which to judge Scripture, but that there is also no neutral ecclesial stance on which to make the judgment.

Parish work puts one into contact with people whose lives are jeopardized in countless ways about which the Bible makes no specific reference. Some theological imagination is required to meet the situations in which contemporary Christians find themselves — not much, but some. The canonical warrant for this, in Brevard Childs' view, "lies in the conviction that Scripture itself has been shaped by . . . openness to the future generations of faith and to an anticipation of the eschatological in-breaking of God's reign."[5] In principle, at least, it seems that the canonical approach to Scripture leaves room for God to say new things in and through the proclamation of Scripture. The question is, what will this approach allow in practice?

If the authority of Scripture is to be defended, it must be defensible that the Word of God can be found within Scripture, that there is stuff in the Bible that has the look of holy inspiration, maybe quite a lot of

3. Christopher Morse, *Not Every Spirit: A Dogmatics of Christian Disbelief* (Valley Forge, PA: Trinity Press International, 1994), p. 29.

4. Dorothee Sölle, *Political Theology* (Philadelphia: Fortress Press, 1974), p. 17.

5. Brevard Childs, "On Reclaiming the Bible for Christian Theology," in Braaten and Jenson, *Reclaiming the Bible,* p. 9.

stuff, though certainly not all the stuff that is there. This stuff, the good stuff, is embedded in the canon for those who have eyes to see. Just as Jeremiah or Amos or St. Paul worked out their theologies in the particularity of their experience, so too must every generation that comes up against these texts seeking to find holy inspiration in them. For this daunting task we have the resources of the church and the academy, operating sometimes in harmony with each other, sometimes in tension, but in all cases accountable to the lives of people whose humanity is in jeopardy. It is such accountability that is at the heart of the gospel, which pronounces an end to human sacrifice in the story of the binding of Isaac, and which makes hope possible even when the forces of repression and death are allied against truth and life in the Passion of Jesus.

5. Why We Read It

SCOTT HOEZEE

Introduction

When we were called together for this pioneering year of the Pastor-Theologian Program, we were told up front that we would be confronting "the crisis in theology and the church." For this first year we have specifically been asked to focus on the crisis of biblical authority, with Genesis 22 and Matthew's Passion account as particular textual instantiations of the larger issues surrounding what it means to call Scripture the foundational authority for the life of the church. Not surprisingly, the study of these two texts has opened up wide vistas of discussion on topics ranging from homiletical concerns to historical-critical inquiries, from the inspiration of the texts to the unity of the two testaments, from the scandal of God's command to Abraham to the knotty Trinitarian questions surrounding Jesus' cry of dereliction from the cross.

Each text contains such a wealth of detail and curiosities that it would be easy to become enmeshed only in the texts per se without necessarily paying sustained attention to the wider theme of biblical authority, to which these passages were intended to give entrée. Whatever the delicious specifics of each passage, it is vital for us as *pastor*-theologians to address wider issues of how and whether these texts (and most any other biblical text) can and should speak to and make claims on congregations today. Genesis 22 and Matthew's Passion confront the modern reader and preacher (even as they have confronted readers and preachers through the ages) with difficult issues regarding the nature of God, the situation of fallen humanity, and the nature of salvation.

Are we willing and able to be confronted by these issues? Are we willing not just to learn *about* these texts but above all to learn also *from* them? For if the larger Scripture out of which these stories come does not bear decisive authority for congregations today, then neither do the Scripture's individual pericopae. But if Scripture as a whole makes some kind of authoritative claim upon the church, then our approach to individual texts like Genesis 22 and Matthew's Passion takes on a very different hue and purpose.

Why Read It?

A basic question to ponder regarding Genesis 22, Matthew's Passion, or really any biblical passage is this: Why do we read and study this text at all? Among the many people who have anything to do with the Bible there may be a bevy of answers to that question, including (but by no means limited to) those who study it as great literature, those who study it as a historical curiosity, those who study it for personal edification in the nurturing of piety, and those who study it in an attempt to open up Scripture for the building and education of the church.

As my congregation's minister of preaching, I am expected to be a student of Scripture. As such, it is also expected that I will be in touch with the many areas of scholarly inquiry into the Bible, but always with the goal of taking the fruits of these diverse areas of inquiry and packaging them in such a way that the resulting sermon will bring God's living Word into contact with the real lives of the congregation. This weekly message will then perhaps provide guidance, wisdom, truth, correction, and purpose to enable faithful attempts to follow God in Christ.

But why is it the Bible specifically that I am charged to explicate (as opposed to some other document of my own free-wheeling ideas)? What is it about the nature of this book in all its wild and rich diversity that makes it the most basic source for the sermon? Most of the people to whom I preach would say (and they would hope I also would say) that the reason the Bible occupies this place of prominence is that somehow *God* is revealed in that text in a way true of no other book. As such, the most basic assumption with which I approach, study, and finally proclaim Scripture is that it is the revelation of God, creation, and their relationship, and as such the larger Scripture hangs together as a meaningful whole. In the mystery of inspiration and through the myriad of human hands that had something to do with the composition, redaction, transmission, and preservation of these texts (and scholarly inquiry in recent centuries has increased our awareness of the process by which Scripture was composed and preserved), somehow it has finally been God through the Holy Spirit who has been active in unfolding some of the rich tapestry on which is embroidered the nature of God, creation, and their relationship.

The Church's Book

If we wish to speak of a "bottom line" to all of this, then it becomes clear that the Bible must continue to be viewed as the church's book. If I am correct that it is finally and properly a living faith that recognizes the authority of Scripture based on the authorship of God through the Spirit, then Scripture will achieve its truest purpose and do its best "work" among the community of the faithful. Recent centuries have demonstrated what can happen to the Bible when, in the name of free and objective intellectual inquiry, it is severed from the confessional community to be dissected on the tables of the academy. If the Bible is *a priori* treated like any other historical accident, it *a posteriori* remains a historical accident with no more necessary authority than Shakespeare, Gibbon, Horace, or Ovid. No matter how self-authenticating the believing community may claim the Bible to be, Scripture is not going to decisively prove itself divine in a laboratory setting.

If the Bible was written (by both the divine Author and its many human authors) for the creation and sustenance of faith — if that is the intended *nature and purpose* of Scripture — then its proper place is within the community of faith (or at the very least that is the place where its intended effect will most likely be experienced). To use an analogy: If a physician writes a jargon-laden, highly technical article for the *New England Journal of Medicine,* then it only makes sense that if I take this article into my den and try to read it by the fire while sipping a glass of wine, I am neither going to appreciate nor really understand what it is about. But then, it was not written for me and it does not belong in my den. The intended effect of the composition will be lost on me, but I would not for that reason have cause to upbraid the author, cast aspersions on her intentions or authenticity, or assert that this is clearly a piece of writing we need not take seriously because it fails to connect with a significant segment of the world. Even if doctors should always be intelligible to potential patients, they can still be expected to write for one another in a distinct genre that may not be intelligible to lay readers. Just because I *claim* (à la certain higher critics of Scripture) that a straightforward, objective reading of a passage *should* enable me to get a bead on it does not insure I will be successful (let alone that I was correct to make this claim in the first place). I am simply not an active, faithful member of the community for which the article was written. Naturally, therefore, it will likely not affect me as the author intended.

During this past year in the North Central region of the seminar, our resource theologians, Robert Jenson and Donald Juel, both pointed out that, theologically and philosophically, much that once bridged the present to the past (and so much which once lent unity and coherence to Scripture) has been eroded since the Enlightenment. It is now by no means clear to many what this ancient document could have to do with us today, and it is even less clear to many how or to what extent God could be conceived of as being involved in either the events on which the text reports or in the composition of that same text.

Even so, what keeps my congregation coming back to church each week is the belief that God himself (through the Spirit) provides the unity of, the bridge to, and the reliable content of Scripture. That the faith that informs this belief is difficult to maintain in the modern world is nothing against it. Despite the fact that one can find real-life examples of naive faith maintained largely by shutting out the contemporary setting, such a closing of the eyes is neither inevitable nor necessary. Instead, pastors and lay people (including a fair number of highly educated historians, scholars, scientists, and other Christians who are very much in touch with contemporary life) still struggle to hear God's distinctive voice even through the cacophony of the modern world.

Thus the weekly task of preaching, in my understanding, seeks faithful ways to echo the living voice of God's gospel, as that Word of life comes to us in God's Scripture, in ways that will allow the congregation to understand who they are and who they ought to be in the midst of a world of more competing claims to truth, more competing visions for what life should be, than many previous generations have experienced. The sermon, when based on as faithful an explication of God's Word as the preacher can muster, declares to the congregation how to see the world and God's relation to it. The sermon, rooted in Scripture, is how we see things.

In a morally confused society whose motto could well be the Nike slogan "Just Do It," God's Word comes to tell believers *what* to do, and also what not to do, according to the Creator's own good blueprint for the cosmos. In a consumer society whose motto could well be the Lays potato chip slogan, "Go Ahead: We'll Make More," God's Word comes to teach the meaning of sacrifice, of losing one's life in order to find it given back by grace.

In this sense the sermon, reflecting the inspired witness of God's Scripture, is a profoundly countercultural act. It cuts against the grain of the relativists who dispense with overarching truth. It flies in the face of the arrogance of the academy and the Jesus Seminar in their claims that they alone can tell the world precisely who Jesus was and who he definitively could not have been. It reverses our culture's excessive fascination with the present by suggesting that, in Wolfhart Pannenberg's understanding of the resurrection, the end of history has already appeared in our past, such that the deepest meaning of who we are and who we will yet become is not to be found in this present moment of scintillating technology and still less in some future evolutionary development of the human mind. Instead, preaching declares Scripture's contention that once upon a time the very Word of God became flesh, full of grace and truth, and that we have seen the glory of the One and Only.

The specific texts we studied this year confront the church with a God who commands and expects to be obeyed, with a Scripture bold enough to make the scandalous claim that God initiated a plan of global salvation millennia ago in a remote and dusty corner of the world with a childless retired couple named Abram and Sarai. The Scripture is bold enough to present us with a man named Jesus who was nothing less than Immanuel (God with us) and who, as such, climaxed the human story and filled up the Scripture through the horror of Golgotha.

These are not obvious or easy truths. They are not self-evident truths to which a person would tumble naturally through reason and logic. They are not ideas embraced by everyone — indeed, this is a picture of reality that offends many. But for the church to be the church in the deepest, most historical sense of the word, she must follow God's revelation and the view of reality it presents. To resist following, as increasing numbers do today, is not only to cut the church off from much of what she has been, but also to throw believers out into the wider marketplace of spiritual and moral ideas — a place where only the individual is his or her own epistemological referee.

6. On a "Christian Reading" of the Bible

JAMES L. MAYS

The following is a piece of work in progress. It needs development, correction, and clarification. It is an effort to order notes taken during our conversations in the seminar and during the reading done in connection with the sessions. It is offered as a stimulus and provocation as we think about the subject and as a target for critique. Drafting a normative and final description of a "Christian reading" of the Bible is probably an impossible task. It can be subject to the death of infinite correction and revision. And yet we read as Christians all the time in the practice of our vocation, unless we have come to think of hermeneutics as a discipline that is not properly qualified by the adjective "Christian." If one assumes that what we do as interpreters is qualified by what and why we interpret and who interprets, then the rudiments of

29

how we go about it ought to be subject to description, though more as assumptions and intentions than as method in a technical sense.

Probably the best way to exhibit the discipline is simply to do it. Composing a useful interpretation of a text and then reflecting analytically on what has been done is an illuminating procedure. If we undertake, however, to lay out the elements of a discipline of "Christian reading," we need to examine how we understand that discipline.

a. We could understand it in a *"history of interpretation"* sense, as concerning whatever Christians have done. It would include all the interpretive practices that have been employed in the course of Christian engagement with the Bible. This approach, of course, would not result in discerning a discipline that could be commended, but rather in a catalogue. It would desert any normative or critical intention. It is necessary, however, to note this understanding, because the variety in interpretive practice in the history of the community has been so rich that any particular discipline laid out must be conceived in a way that is open to variations rather than as structured and rigid rules.

b. One could understand the question in a *sectarian* sense. A Christian reading is one that is distinct from and exclusive of other ways of reading. This approach, of course, is on the face of it impossible, because the Bible as language and literature is embedded in ways of communicating and understanding that belong to general human culture and perhaps to basic human capacities. Furthermore, in every age Christians have employed hermeneutical strategies at home in the particular culture of their time and place to understand and speak about the Bible in and to their world. On the other hand, it is these strategies of the particular culture in a time and place that can garble and distort the biblical message in the process of reading, understanding, and communicating. So a way of reading that is coherent with the content and role of the Bible as the Scriptures of the Christian community is needed.

c. One could reject such a discipline as a false or *improper* topic. The objection might be that Christians should read the Bible in the same way that anyone reads any literature, subject to the general rules of reading and understanding. Otherwise the location of understanding in the reader becomes more important than what is there to be understood in what is read, and the authority of what is read is subverted. On the other hand, it can be claimed that all reading is informed by presuppositions, expectations, and information that constitute the possibility and reason of the relation of the reader to what is read. The question is whether the reading is informed and enabled by presuppositions and expectations that are consistent with the identity of the reader and what is being read.

d. One could construe this discipline as an issue in *Christology*. A "Christian reading" should be one that is ordered and informed by the reality of Christ. It would be an employment of the general rules of reading and understanding disciplined by following Jesus Christ. It would be understood as a dimension of the experience and practice resulting from being appointed, called, and commissioned by Christ.

The Christological Bases of the Discipline

a. A Christian reading of the Bible would be a way of understanding and communicating that is constrained by the reality represented by these interdependent symbols: Christ, church, canon, and confession.

b. Christ is the symbol for the One who is the basis of the identity and existence of the church, from whom the church receives its canon of Scripture, and who is the subject of the church's confession.

c. Church is the symbol of the community constituted by Christ, known through the canon of Scripture, and subject of the community's confession.

d. Canon is the symbol for the Old Testament and New Testament as the Scriptures of the church, on which the church depends for the knowledge of Christ that is acknowledged in the church's confession.

e. Confession is the symbol for the credo by which the church says it believes in the Triune God — Father, Son, and Holy Spirit — as the content of the canon's witness to Christ.

f. Each of these symbols in its interdependence with the others is a factor that disciplines understanding and speaking about the texts of the Bible.

Christ

a. We should read all biblical texts as part of a context whose critical center is Jesus Christ, the One who is the future and the past of the biblical witness.

b. We should read the Gospels in the confidence that the reality of Jesus Christ is presented to the reader through their scriptural account. (The Gospels' literary rendition of Jesus is the textual mediation of Jesus' revelatory reality, as by analogy the Old Testament story is the textual mediation of the revelatory reality of Israel's history.)

c. We should seek to understand and use the Scriptures in obedience to Christ's command to love God and neighbor beyond all else.

Church

a. We should seek to understand and expound the Scriptures as the church, knowing that the Bible is the possession of the whole people of God and not of any individual isolated within or from the community. So we interpret gratefully guided by the interpretations of the saints of the past, colleagues of the present, and the consensus of the confession, always seeking that sense of Scripture that makes sense for the church.

b. We should seek to understand and expound the Scriptures for the church, knowing that the Scriptures are given to the church for the purpose of evoking, sustaining and guiding its faith and life. So the leading question with which we take up any text is a quest to discern how the text illumines the continuity of our story with the story of the people of God in the Bible and how the text confronts us as people of God with the Word of God.

c. We should seek to understand and expound the Scriptures in lively awareness that the church is in the world, that the church is commissioned as a witness to the world, and that the world is in the church. So we must read the Bible with a critical responsiveness to the questions set by the world as environment and ingredient of the reading community.

Canon

a. We should read the biblical texts first and finally according to their defining genre as Holy Scripture, knowing and understanding that the defining genre subordinates and relativizes all other genres of writings incorporated in the canonical books.

b. We should read in confidence that the Scriptures in their canonical literary form are right and true witnesses to their subject (that to which they essentially refer), God and God's way with the world. So we seek to discern the verbal sense of texts, and that sense understood in the context of the book in which the text stands, and that sense understood and expounded in relation to other texts that deal with or bear on its particular witness.

c. We should read the Old Testament and the New Testament as two parts of one canon, seeking always to keep our understanding of the two parts in dialectical relation. The Old Testament provides the background without which the Christ cannot be properly known; and the New Testament witnesses to Jesus Christ as the critical center of the canon without which the Old Testament cannot be properly read as an authority for life and faith.

d. We should interpret biblical texts informed by and grateful for the knowledge, approaches, and questions of general secular scholarship while always giving priority to the canonical record and assigning only an explanatory and apologetic function to other presentations of the biblical content (such as a history of Israel, a reconstruction of the career of Jesus, or a critically reduced Paul).

Confession

a. We should open the Scriptures in the identity of believers seeking understanding — so enacting, rather than suspending, the confession of the church.

b. We should seek from the texts of Scripture illumination and critique of our understanding and use of the confession.

c. We should expect guidance from the confession in recognizing how texts deal with the agenda of faith and life.

d. We should read the variety and plurality of the Scriptures in the light of the single narrative of creation, redemption, and consummation discovered in the Scriptures by the confession.

e. We should seek an understanding of the texts guided by the dialectic of the Holy Trinity; where the verbal reference of texts concerns one person of the three, we may reflect on how that witness implies and engages the other persons.

CHAPTER II

THE PASSION OF CHRIST (MATT. 26-27)

Introduction

A second set of six selections from our authors' final reports concentrates on the Passion of Christ. Along with the binding of Isaac (Gen. 22), this New Testament text (Matt. 26-27) served as the generating core of the year's project on the research theme of "Reading the Bible in Faith." Christ's Passion was deemed of such great significance that the ancient church canonically organized the Bible into the Old and New Testaments. Moreover, the Gospels and Paul locate the usage of this rich, scriptural category of "testament/covenant" for the first time on the lips of Jesus himself, as he anticipated Calvary during the Lord's Supper on the last night of his earthly ministry: "This is my blood of the covenant" (Matt. 26:28; I Cor. 11:25).

The author of the first excerpt, "Looking to Follow," seeks to follow Matthew's witness in order to ground his own witness to the lordship of the crucified and risen Jesus. Along with all the writers and most of the readers of this book, our author is the pastor of a local congregation in a Christian denomination. It is by intentionally identifying with the public confession and mission of his own denomination's expression of the Christian faith that he finds, in the power of the Spirit, that the Bible is "the best, most reliable aid to living the Christian, God-formed, holy life." Therefore he preaches and teaches in light of his confident trust that God still speaks to the church today through the Holy Scriptures.

The second document on the "Interpretation of Matthew 27:32-54" serves to remind us of the wide variety of ways in which Matthew has been interpreted by biblical scholars through the centuries. This happens, not least, because the Scriptures are themselves testimonies of faith that convey both historical events and their theological meanings, all of which are then later "handed over" by other interpreters to still other persons living in other cultures in other generations. What remains historical and trustworthy in this complex process? The author affirms the unique guidance of the Holy Spirit in both the writing and the reception of the biblical texts for the inspired service of carrying out God's mission through the church in the world. By definition God's saving acts, as centered in Christ's Passion, both assume and yet transcend human history.

"Fulfilling All Righteousness" is next developed as the distinctive focus of the Gospel of Matthew's account of both Christ's teaching and his congruent Passion. Likely written between A.D. 80 and 90 as the work of a Hellenistic Jewish Christian community, the Matthean Gospel repeatedly aims to report to non-Jews about what happened in Jesus "to fulfill what had been spoken by the Lord through the prophet(s)" (1:22). Highlighted is the righteousness of the obedient Son of God while inaugurating the kingdom of heaven. From the Sermon on the Mount (Matt. 5–7) through the cross on Golgotha (Matt. 26–27), "God with us" (Emmanuel) reveals that our Savior is also God for us. As his teaching prepares for the Son of Man's final judgment of the nations (Matt. 25), so his cross precedes the risen Lord's glorification and the resultant church's commission to save and to serve (Matt. 27–28).

The next excerpt, "Where is the Triune God?" explores the mystery of what is taking place in Matthew's Gospel "between the dying Christ and his God." Once again, this critical personal relationship is decisively illumined by Matthew's understanding of Christ's fulfillment of the Old Testament Scriptures as they reveal "the purposive activity of God continuously in God's creation." In Jesus' cry from the cross, we hear the Son's anguished lament in a psalm (22) that is obediently addressed to "my God" in the power of the Spirit. Through Christ's fulfilled Passion, the Triune God is lovingly and effectively involved in the suffering, forgiveness, and renewal of humankind.

The selection "Overcoming Our Reality" defends the audacious claim that it is we who are called to conform to the scriptural reality revealed by God in Christ, and not vice versa. It is we who are in need of judgment, forgiveness, and renewal. Therefore it is God who is the almighty Actor in the Matthean narrative of Christ's Passion, as Immanuel ("God with us") from birth to death is pitted against the sinful unreality of the principalities and powers of this sin-broken world. In depicting the use and abuse of temporal authority by Herod, Pilate, Barabbas, the Sanhedrin, and the soldiers, Matthew employs these historical foils to glorify the transforming power of the Lord God who rules humankind effectively while incarnately hidden in Christ's voluntary and non-violent suffering and death. Paradoxically, invincible divine power is revealed on the cross as "the self-giving love that finds its most perfect expression in the Passion of Christ."

Our final selection analyzes the spiritual dynamics involved "When the Resurrection Community Reads the Passion Narrative" in the Gospel of Matthew. The author contends that "although lively with sensory effect and historical detail, the narrative's aim is neither to bewitch the senses nor to report what happened, but to interpret religious truth that is made concrete in the sensible and historical matter of life." In Christ, history is interpenetrated by a spiritual reality that eternally transcends it. This is, of course, a testimony of faith that can neither be proved nor disproved by historical-critical research as such, helpful as that is within its finite limitations. Concentrating on the trial of Jesus before Caiaphas the High Priest (26:57-75), the author contends that Matthew's faithful account is "intelligible only within the church, identified as resurrection community."

7. *Looking to Follow*

BARRY A. ENSIGN-GEORGE

It is a challenge to interpret the Passion narratives. They are so very familiar. Obviously they are of the utmost significance, but it is no simple matter to articulate that significance. In trying to shape an interpretation, I feel the pressure to offer insights that measure up to the significance of the passage. When that pressure combines with the familiarity of these words, I find that my thoughts begin to slide across the surface of the words. I have found myself looking for a place where I might begin to follow more deeply Matthew's telling of the crucifixion of Jesus Christ. As I seek to follow Matthew's lead, I must also attempt to make explicit some of the assumptions operative in the interpretative work I am doing.

I come to the Bible expecting that it will be my task to follow Scripture. I find the Bible to be the best, most reliable aid to living the Christian, God-formed, holy life. I did not discover Scripture's reliability as the result of independent inquiry. The church, into which I have been incorporated by Baptism, instructs me that the Bible is the most reliable guide for those pursuing that end that the baptized seek. The church has borne witness to this belief about the Bible by its millennia-long striving to be shaped by Scripture. It has communicated this belief to me both explicitly and implicitly, through what I have been taught and through practices into which it has initiated me or in which it has trained me (the creeds and confession of faith, worship, devotional Bible reading, seeking to live by biblical commands and examples). Clearly the Bible can be read for a variety of purposes. One's purpose will then direct what one seeks in Scripture. Those seeking to live the Christian life follow the church's instruction, turning to Scripture for guidance in living that life, seeking in Scripture knowledge of the Triune God and of the life shaped to the presence of this God.

So it is that I come to the Bible expecting that it will be my task to follow Scripture. I accept that task because of confidence that what Scripture makes available is deeply life-giving, in that Scripture reveals God. If I do not immediately see these depths in a passage of Scripture such as this, I presume the problem is mine, not Scripture's. I try to begin with the assumption that I will need to adapt myself to the text, rather than assuming that my understanding of the world is fixed and then seeking to adapt the text to my understanding of the world. Of course this is a notoriously difficult process, one that makes interpretation a back-and-forth process, a matter of refinements and revision. The incentive for such work is, again, the presumption that I find in Scripture (as I encounter it in the life of the church) that which gives life. I seek to follow Matthew's telling of these events because doing so aids me in following Jesus Christ — is in fact the best, most reliable aid.

It is also true that Scripture includes material that is not life-giving, and that anything in Scripture can be interpreted in ways that are not life-giving. Indeed, there are passages in Scripture itself that intentionally make us aware of this problem — for example, Jesus' intensification of the law in the Sermon on the Mount (Matt. 5:21-48). My belief is that Scripture, as interpreted in and by the church across time, and particularly as its interpretation is formulated in creeds and confessions of faith, provides what we need to sort the one from the other.

The church's affirmation that the Bible is the reliable guide to living the Christian life comes to me through the denomination in which I have been ordained to the ministry of Word and Sacrament — the Presbyterian Church (U.S.A.) (hereafter PCUSA). In its *Book of Confessions (BC)*, the PCUSA affirms that in the Bible, "all things necessary to be believed for the salvation of men are sufficiently expressed . . . we believe and confess the Scriptures of God sufficient to instruct and make perfect the man of God" (BC 3.18, 3.19). As our confession puts it elsewhere: "And in this Holy Scripture, the universal Church of Christ has the most complete exposition of all that pertains to a saving faith, and also to the framing of a life acceptable to God" (BC 5.002; cf. 6.007, 9.27). Scripture offers what is needed for salvation and for living the life made possible by salvation.

At first, of course, I took the claim about the Bible's reliability as guide to living the Christian life as a largely implicit assumption. I absorbed the assumption, awaiting the time when my life would bear out its validity as my life was ever more fully shaped to God's presence. I did not accept this claim about the Bible because I first demonstrated its validity to my own satisfaction. I was trained; I was led in a way of life that was built on the claim that the Bible is the best, most reliable guide to living the Christian life. Indeed, I believe I have been able to validate this claim precisely because I have been trained to live in ways shaped by the truth of this claim, a training that has nurtured an ability to hear God speaking in the words of Scripture even as I remain aware of the limits of my ability.

Ultimately, Scripture does not offer this guidance on its own. It is able to offer this guidance because in the words of Scripture God speaks to us: "For God himself spoke to the fathers, prophets, apostles, and still speaks to us through the Holy Scriptures" (BC 5.002). To live the Christian life we must hear and follow the Shepherd's voice (John 10:4-5, 27-28). We hear that voice in the words of the Bible.

The PCUSA's confession of faith affirms that in Scripture it is human words through which God speaks (BC 5.10; 9.29). We hear God's voice in and through the particular human words gathered together in Scripture (Nicholas Wolterstorff has recently offered a strong account of the claim that God speaks through human words in his book *Divine Discourse: Philosophical Reflections on the Claim That God Speaks* [Cambridge, 1995]; George Lindbeck has called attention to the potential fruitfulness of Wolterstorff's proposal). There is a parallel here to claims our confession makes about God's presence in the sacramental elements. It is God the Holy Spirit who makes sacramental elements and these particular Hebrew, Aramaic, and Greek words (and their English translations) the media of God's action among human beings. "What does it mean to eat the crucified body of Christ and to drink his shed blood? . . . it is to be so united more and more to his blessed body by the Holy Spirit dwelling both in Christ and in us that, although he is in heaven and we are on earth, we are nevertheless flesh of his flesh and bone of his bone, always living and being governed by one Spirit, as the members of our bodies are governed by one soul" (BC 4.076). Similarly, my denomination's confession of faith insists that only through the work of the Holy Spirit does Scripture reliably guide us in living the Christian life.

At the same time, this confession insists that the particular elements that are the media of God's action are not replaceable. Just as we cannot substitute pork chops for bread (even though pork chops are also food, and are also nourishing), so we cannot substitute other human words for the words of Scripture. Likewise the sacraments: "The author of all sacraments is not any man, but God alone. Persons cannot institute sacraments. For they pertain to the worship of God, and it is not for man to appoint and prescribe a worship of God, but to accept and preserve the one he has received from God" (BC 5.172; Robert Jenson called this point and its significance to my attention). With respect to Scripture, "The whole counsel of God, concerning all things necessary for his own glory, human salvation, faith, and life, is either expressly set down in Scripture, or by good and necessary consequence may be deduced from Scripture: unto which nothing at any time is to be added, whether by new revelations of the Spirit, or traditions of men" (BC 6.007; cf. 5.002).

I leave aside questions about the actual historical author(s) of the Matthean passion narratives. Such questions may be vital in some contexts, but they are secondary when those in the church seek in these words an introduction to the life lived with God. The meaning of this passage for the church is not determined by what the original composer(s) of these words had in mind in composing them. Our theories about what those composers might have intended to communicate, like our theories about how the "original" audience might have understood them, are secondary — useful, interesting supplements to what is available from the text.

Given the purpose of a churchly reading of Scripture outlined above, the work of interpretation will not reach a resting point until such insights are drawn. Matthew's concern for the followers of Jesus who come after Jesus' resurrection further invites us to the work of interpretation. By following Matthew's telling, I aim to find aid in following Jesus Christ. Thus the work of interpretation has not been completed until this point has been reached.

The fact that God works in such a way may make God's working hard to see. Like Jesus' contemporaries, we would prefer to see it whole, and to see this whole now, in unmistakable clarity. We yearn to be free of the constraints of time, among other constraints of finitude.

Sometimes we do not know God and God's work because of some failing on our part. John and those who mocked Jesus failed to know Jesus was the Messiah because of unwillingness to let God fulfill the scriptural sketch of the Messiah in an unexpected way. They fastened on some aspects of the sketch and lost hold of others. Eduard Schweizer makes this comment on those who stand at the cross as the eschatological signs unfold following Jesus' death: "While the bystanders look on unmoved, mocking and uncertain, the very rocks reel and shatter" (Matt. 27:51). We may think God is absent because we don't know whom we're looking for.

At other times we fail to know God and God's workings because we are overwhelmed by the conditions present in a world on the way. Jesus on the cross is such a moment. We soon afterward see that God has been at work even here. But in that moment (Matt. 27:45-50) it is difficult even for readers to see God at work. One can only begin to imagine what it would have been like for Jesus. The Christian life includes moments more or less deeply like this moment. Whatever the challenges, it remains for us to know God in and across time, taking Scripture as our key to identifying the God who is at work reuniting earth and heaven (11:28-30; 16:24-26).

41

Jesus' disciples are our examples in dealing with these problems. Thus, for example, confronted with Jesus' parables, they need help to understand (Matt. 13:36-43). Simon Peter perceives that "You are the Messiah, the Son of the living God" (16:16). However, in responding to this insight not only does he fail to fall in worship (in contrast to the disciples in 28:17), but he goes on to rebuke the Messiah (16:22)! God works redemption (in this case, specifically sanctification) in ways that are consistent with God's nature.

The fact that God works in such a way adds to the challenge of pastoring a congregation. God's work in a congregation is no more transparent than his other workings. Catching sight of this work in the life of a congregation whose life is not more obviously holy than my own requires a well-developed capacity to recognize the signs of God's work.

8. Interpretation of Matthew 27:32-54

BRUCE K. MODAHL

Raymond Brown makes the point a number of times that the events surrounding Jesus' death and resurrection are attempts by believers to describe the meaning of Jesus' dying and rising. What was passed on by tradition was shaped in such a way as to say what the core event means. For example, in his analysis of Matthew 27:51-53 and parallel passages, Brown says, "All the phenomena that we have discussed in this section represent a theological interpretation of the import of the death of Jesus."[1] Deciding what actually happened becomes a scholarly process that Brown labels "fragile";[2] it involves deciding on pre-Gospel sources. Secondly, uncovering the situation in the churches for which the evan-

---

1. Raymond Brown, *The Death of the Messiah: From Gethsemane to the Grave. A Commentary on the Passion Narratives in the Four Gospels* (New York: Doubleday, 1994), p. 1133.

2. Raymond Brown, *The Death of the Messiah*, Vol. II (New York: Doubleday, 1994), pp. 1133, 904.

gelists wrote is part of the process. Certainly those particulars influenced how events were presented in writing, and uncovering them involves a good deal of guesswork. Thirdly, a general rule for interpretation comes into play, one taught to me in a first-year seminary course called "Techniques of Biblical Exegesis": nothing happened then out of keeping with the way things happen now. Virgin births, rent rocks, opened tombs, and resurrected saints are all suspect. Those of us so taught were insulated from any numinous experience of our own. We certainly were handicapped when it came to dealing with any such experiences of our parishioners. The upshot of all of this when dealing with the text in question is that it is virtually impossible to decide by scholarly endeavor what actually happened. The best we can say is that these events are attempts at explaining the meaning of Jesus' death and resurrection.

Historical Necessities

The historical-critical apple is not going to be put back on the tree; a recourse to pre-critical exegesis is too unsatisfying. Earlier commentators spend too much time harmonizing and explaining away the critical problems. The post-Christian commentators leave us with not much more than a pocketful of mumbles about trying harder.

Perhaps a way through this is to be found by setting theology in service of history. Our theology can inform us about historical necessities. What must we insist on as Christians whose common faith is expressed by the Apostles' Creed? The Holy Scriptures of the Old and New Testaments were agreed to quite early on, with few additions or omissions by the early church, before any formal vote was taken on the issue. Is this not evidence of the guidance of the Holy Spirit? The canonical Holy Scriptures are constitutive for the life and faith of the church. While the Holy Spirit is the source of faith, the Holy Scriptures provide the norm for faith and life. Extra-canonical sources are helpful for understanding composition and the history of the early church, but the source of doctrine is the canon.

The clear passages of Scripture are those that exalt the benefits of Christ. The gospel alone, the good news concerning Christ, has the power to make new creatures out of us. The law demands obedience, but it cannot create obedient hearts. Only the gospel can create the obedient hearts demanded by the law. As Scripture is law and gospel, there are two historical necessities at work.

We confess a historical event, Jesus' death, and resurrection, impacting us with its benefits. This is not in the usual cause and effect of history. We are talking about a new era, one that transcends history and is not confined to the historical boundaries or criteria of the old era. The claim that Jesus' dying and rising should cause a new outcome for me is far beyond what we could expect of normal history. No event in the old era's history has the ability to give me life in place of inevitable death. Only the kingdom of God invading the old order has the power to do that. But this new order is not subject to the old order's historical criteria. We are out of bounds when we relegate the biblical story to human invention.

Theology does set the limits. That Jesus was crucified under Pontius Pilate, suffered death and was buried, and on the third day rose again in accordance with the Scriptures is not debatable for those who would call themselves Christians. What we confess is that the kingdom of God has breached the walls of the old order. These things are beyond the lens power of history's microscope to describe. Paul does his best in I Corinthians 15:42-44:

> So it is with the resurrection of the dead. What is sown is perishable, what is raised is imperishable. It is sown in dishonor, it is raised in glory. It is sown in weakness, it is raised in power. It is sown a physical body, it is raised a spiritual body. If there is a physical body, there is also a spiritual body.

When it comes to Scripture, therefore, we have the account of the new era impacting the old. We have a confluence of these two orders. One is bounded by sin and death and historical convention, but the new invading reality transcends all historical convention. We need not revert to pre-critical exegesis in an attempt to rationalize how the critical problems are not really problems and could have happened as described. I remember listening to a lecture on Jonah, claiming that he was actually swallowed by a whale since there was a newspaper account of a Japanese fisherman in the 1890s that survived such an incident. The lecture was long on the details of stomach acid and its effects. That approach does a disservice to the new era by putting around it the boundaries of the old. The post-Christian commentators actually have the very same approach to Scripture as the inerrantists. They also hold Scripture within the limits of the old order's history; only rather than arguing how it could really have happened that way, they disregard material deemed suspect according to the historical conventions of the old order.

There is another way, a way that testifies to what Scripture itself testifies — the advent of the redemptive reign of God in Christ Jesus, bringing a new prognosis to a death-bound old order. We live in the overlap of these ages. We get glimpses of the new, outcroppings showing us what will be. Baptism makes us citizens of God's commonwealth. The new invests the old when the Word reaches our ears and creates faith under the Holy Spirit's province. The Lord's Supper is an appetizer from the heavenly banquet table. God graces us with sightings of God's kingdom. People without faith have other explanations for these numinous experiences, but with eyes of faith, we know otherwise. These sightings are consistent with what God reveals in Scripture. Scripture remains the norm and rule, and again, theology sets the limits.

Let me illustrate what I think is the upshot of all of this for interpreting Scripture by addressing one of the details of the text in question (Matt. 27:32-54). Historically, what happened with the temple veil the day Jesus died? Was the veil torn in two from top to bottom? No, the veil was still intact the next day; it would take another forty years in our time before the temple veil was destroyed, when Roman legions destroyed the temple. That is old order history. But from the perspective of the new order of things, the temple veil was torn in two from top to bottom, because from that day on the veil did not wall off God. Which answer is reality? Those with eyes to see choose the second. We recognize it simply took the old order's story forty years to catch up with what had already happened.

ANITA R. WARNER

9. Fulfilling All Righteousness

ANITA R. WARNER

Matthew contains exactly twelve *formal fulfillment citations,* passages that claim that what is reported about Jesus happened "to fulfill what was written in the prophets" (1:22-23; 2:5-6; 2:15; 2:17-18; 2:23; 4:14-16; 8:17; 12:17-21; 13:14-15; 13:35; 21:4-5; 27:9-10). The number twelve often symbolizes Israel, since in the Old Testament Israel's offspring consisted of twelve tribes.[1]

The four times Jesus utters "fulfill" in Matthew without formal citation from Old Testament prophets all refer to Jesus himself bringing about God's fulfillment through participating in God's righteousness: at his baptism by John (3:15), the beginning of his teaching ministry (5:17), his betrayal (26:54), and his Passion (26:56).

Righteousness, an important theme throughout Matthew, is then *the obedience of the Son of God.* There are two large-scale inclusions in the Gospel of Matthew.

> After the notion of "God with us" has formed the outer brackets of the Gospel (1:23; 28:20), an inner bracket is added dealing with the obedience of the Son of God (3:13-4:11; 27:38-54). The same thought recurs in the middle of the Gospel. Once Peter has acknowledged the Son of God (16:16-17), Jesus points the disciples to the path of obedience, which is that of suffering (16:21 ff). It is precisely here that the disciples encounter failure. As the Matthean story will later show, God is present precisely by being with the obedient Son, whose path leads to suffering and death. He who, on the mountain, rejected the devil's offer of world domination (4:8-10), and chose the path of obedience, will for this very reason, again on a mountain, be granted all power in heaven and on earth at the end of his chosen path of obedience (28:16-20).[2]

1. Mark Allen Powell, *Fortress Introduction to the Gospels* (Minneapolis: Fortress Press, 1998), p. 72.
2. Ulrich Luz, *The Theology of the Gospel of Matthew,* trans. J. B. Robinson (Cambridge: Cambridge University Press, 1995), pp. 36-37.

This righteousness of the obedient Son of God stands in contrast to the righteousness of the religious leaders (5:20), who "have neglected the weightier matters of the law: justice and mercy and faith" (23:23). The religious leaders in Matthew's Gospel are unwilling to give this true righteousness its due.

This righteousness, this obedience of the Son of God, shows forth the *kingdom of heaven,* another important theme in Matthew. The kingdom of heaven has both a present and future aspect. Jesus inaugurates the kingdom of heaven through his public ministry, Passion, and resurrection. Moreover, every one of Jesus' thirty-six sayings about the kingdom of heaven (or of God) can be understood to be fulfilled in Matthew's Passion narrative.

Wisdom Is Vindicated by Her Deeds

Beginning with the Sermon on the Mount, and through the rest of the Gospel, Jesus the teacher of wisdom (13:54) is presented as the teacher of righteousness. In the Passion narrative in Matthew, Jesus actively fulfills his own teachings on the demands of righteousness. Jesus teaches his disciples not to swear at all (5:33-37); as he stands on trial before the high priest, who has put him "under oath before the living God, [to] tell us if you are the Messiah, the Son of God," Jesus answers, "You have said so" (26:64). Carroll and Green[3] point out that "the expression συ ειπας *(sy eipas)* here might be paraphrased, 'It is as you have said.' The reply tacitly affirms the question, yet returns to the speaker the burden of accepting the truth spoken." Thus Jesus answers the high priest (26:64) and Pilate (27:11), as well as Judas (26:25).

Jesus teaches, "Do not resist an evildoer" (5:38-39). When he is arrested by force, he rebukes the one who "resists," saying, "Put your sword back into its place; for all who take the sword will perish by the sword" (26:52). He teaches, "if anyone strikes you on the right cheek, turn the other also" (5:39); on the day of Jesus' death the governor's soldiers mock him by placing a reed in his right hand, as though a royal scepter, then take the reed and strike him on the head (27:29-30). Jesus' teaching

3. John T. Carroll and Joel B. Green, *The Death of Jesus in Early Christianity* (Peabody: Hendrickson, 1995), p. 44.

on righteousness includes, "if anyone wants to sue you and take your coat, give your cloak as well" (5:40); the governor's soldiers strip him twice, first of his clothes and then of the scarlet robe they put on him to mock him (27:28, 31). "And if anyone forces you to go one mile, go also the second mile," Jesus teaches his disciples (5:41). Jesus' last steps are a forced walk to his own crucifixion, along with Simon from Cyrene, who is compelled by the soldiers to carry Jesus' cross (27:31-32).

"Whenever you pray," Jesus teaches his disciples, "pray to your Father who is in secret" (6:6). In Gethsemane, Jesus says to his disciples, "Sit here while I go over there and pray" (26:36). Then he leaves them to pray (26:39). He teaches them to "Pray then in this way: Our Father . . . Your will be done" (6:9-10). In Gethsemane, Jesus prays, "My Father, . . . yet not what I want but what you want," and "My Father, . . . your will be done" (26:39, 42). He instructs his disciples to pray, "And do not bring us into the time of trial" (6:13); in Gethsemane, he reminds them again to "pray that you may not come into the time of trial" (26:41). Thus Jesus "fulfilled all righteousness," first by teaching on the righteousness of God, and then by enacting his own teachings on righteousness in his Passion.

For with the Judgment You Make You Will Be Judged

Jesus teaches on judging and on the judgment throughout Matthew. While his disciples are instructed not to judge, that they may not be judged (7:1), Jesus speaks several times of the coming day of judgment (10:15; 11:22, 24; 12:36, 41-42; 19:28). He ends his teachings in this Gospel with a scene describing the judgment of the nations (25:31-46), with the Son of Man sitting on his throne in glory.

This judgment scene is immediately followed by the Passion narrative, in which first the high priest, scribes, and elders sit in judgment on Jesus, then the Roman governor Pilate sits in judgment on Jesus (26:57-68; 27:1-2, 11-26). The reader is first struck with the deep irony of the religious leaders judging the Judge of the world — and then charging him with blasphemy. Writing after the destruction of the temple in Jerusalem, Matthew has witnessed, first, the judgment of the religious leaders and nation of Israel, and second, the beginning of the judgment of all nations according to righteousness, as the obedience to death of God's Son is shared among the Gentiles as well as the Jews.

When Jesus describes for his disciples the beginning of the end of the age, he mentions earthquakes as one of the signs of the beginning of the end (24:7). Upon the death of Jesus, there is an earthquake (27:54). The alert reader knows now: with the death of Jesus, the day of judgment is at hand. The day of judgment is signaled once again with Jesus' resurrection (28:2).

Thus, for all the talk of righteousness and judgment in Matthew, the final judgment, the final righteousness is the obedient Son of God's self-giving death, and God raising him from the dead. This connection between judgment, righteousness, and Jesus' death and resurrection is what finally keeps a theology of works righteousness from defining this Gospel. While Matthew's theology is indeed far different from Paul's, Matthew's final word of justification is not one of works righteousness inconsistent with Paul's message of grace through faith. However, it is important to hear Matthew's theology of judgment and the righteousness of the obedient Son of God on its own terms, without forcing it to match the Pauline theology of justification by grace. In the end, Matthew's theology of works righteousness is overshadowed by the stronger theology of forgiveness of sins through the righteousness of God's beloved Son.

This Is My Blood of the Covenant

The motif of the blood of Jesus "weaves its way as a bright red thread through the Matthean passion account, riveting readers' attention on the question of responsibility for the death of Jesus but at the same time enabling readers to probe the deeper layers of the event's meaning."[4] As Jesus shares the Passover cup with his disciples (26:27), he makes it clear that this is a death he accepted from his Father's hand (26:39). According to John Carroll and Joel Green, "The irony is thick here. The death of Jesus — precisely because it is the shedding of innocent, sacrificial blood, creates the possibility of forgiveness even for persons who bear responsibility for putting him to death."[5]

---

4. Carroll and Green, *Death of Jesus,* p. 39.
5. Carroll and Green, *Death of Jesus,* p. 48.

Poured Out for Many for the Forgiveness of Sins

When Jesus asserts that one of the twelve will betray him, Judas asks, "Surely not I, Rabbi?" Jesus responds, συ ειπας *(sy eipas)*, "You have said so." Thus, while tacitly affirming the question, he returns to Judas the burden of accepting the truth spoken. In Matthew's Gospel, Judas is not then dismissed but may be assumed to remain for Passover even after this disclosure, thus creating the possibility of forgiveness even for his betrayal of Jesus through the shedding of Jesus' innocent, sacrificial blood. In this way Jesus fulfills his own teaching, "Love your enemies and pray for those who persecute you" (5:44).

Sharing in this Passover meal also redefines the disciples, who all go on to fail Jesus. Judas fails him through his betrayal, Peter through denying him (26:70), and all fail Jesus by fleeing upon Jesus' arrest (26:56). In the Passover, the disciples are the first to receive Jesus' blood, "poured out for many for the forgiveness of sins" (26:28). Thus they are given the identity of forgiven people, who are to form inclusive communities of forgiveness (chapter 18; 28:16-20). This is the final meaning of discipleship in Matthew's Gospel.

And in His Name the Gentiles Will Hope

Through Matthew's use of the Old Testament to interpret Jesus' life, ministry and Passion; through his showing that the righteousness of God is the obedience of God's Son, which is the true fulfillment of the law and the prophets; through showing that the sacrificial death of Jesus and shedding his innocent blood are for the forgiveness of sins; through showing how Israel's rejection of God's Messiah opens the kingdom of heaven to all nations, Matthew's Gospel indeed shows that Jesus, the hope of Israel, is the Savior of the nations. Being his disciple means participating in a community defined by his death for the forgiveness of sins.

10. Where Is the Triune God?

F. HARRY DANIEL

What does Matthew's Passion narrative say about God? Where is God in the dynamics of the story, in the plot, in the actions, among the characters? Given the betrayals, the opponents, the agony of the mode of execution of God's Christ (Matt. 26–27), what is the meaning of Jesus' suffering for God's self? What is taking place between the dying Jesus and his God?

Even to begin to wrestle with these questions we need to grasp Matthew's understanding of Scripture *fulfillment* and the dynamics of the situation when Jesus quoted Scripture from the cross, something that Jesus had already done before during the temptation in Matthew 4 and on occasions during his ministry (9:13; 12:7). It is ironic that the latter two passages cite the same Old Testament text from Hosea, which desires mercy, not sacrifice.

For Matthew, Jesus' whole life, including the Passion, is comprehended and made intelligible by the Old Testament Scriptures. Nothing happens that catches God off guard. Any notion of historical contingency is excised. But what does it mean to say that "all this took place to fulfill what the Lord had spoken by . . ." (Matt. 1:22), or "so it is written by the prophet" (Matt. 2:5)?

I suspect that we often read Matthew anachronistically, as if he were like a twentieth-century fundamentalist who holds that once the Old Testament text is fulfilled it loses its value, unable to voice anything more about God and God's action, and who views the process of fulfillment as mechanical, with a transcendent God in heaven orchestrating the events and characters below in a tightly woven web of relationships (all the world's a stage and we are but the actors). The image of God that emerges is of one who pressures and arranges so that there is nothing new under the sun. The end result of such a process of understanding is to arrive at the conclusion that because God has already "seen" it all, any pain that occurs is already comprehended. The danger is that this trivializes the agony of Jesus' Passion and God in good Greek fashion remains unaffected. Then we are not far from the position that patripassionism is heretical. Thus dare we say that in this context Jesus' quotation of Scripture from the cross means "I thank you, O God, that even this is comprehended"? Then it is easy to see that the cry from the cross is not one of despair but of faith.

Matthew, I think, saw deeper and more profoundly, casting his work as that of a scribe (Matt. 13:52) who interprets ancient texts as revealing the purposive activity of God continuously in God's creation. For these texts speak of a God who is involved, who is characterized by verbs of action. These texts speak of a constancy in God, who guides the process and the minds and hearts of human beings, but they also speak of a God who adapts to existing conditions, conditions generated as a result of attitudes adopted by and situations created by human beings.

The Hebrew people learned this in many ways, superbly in the Exodus where God hears, sees, is moved, comes down, and acts. Far from muting these ancient texts, Matthew hears in them the eloquence of this acting God and sees in and through them this divine activity. Matthew reads the gospel in the context of the Old Testament God. The same God is at work now, in a crescendo of newness that is at the same time a profound oldness.

In Jesus' cry from the cross there is no statement of Scripture fulfillment, but there is the quotation of a text from Scripture, a quotation of a psalm already alluded to at least three times before in Matthew's Passion narrative. But his is a particular type of psalm — a lament (the works of Claus Westermann, Walter Brueggemann, Patrick Miller, and others have recovered the powerful impact and profound depth of this form for the faith of Israel). There were countless times in the life of Israel when the divine plan was hardly self-evident, when the God of the verbs was not experienced. There were poignant times when the pain of life, deserved or undeserved, was crushing and debilitating. A lament gave voice to all of that anguish. A lament knows that there is no way to live in this world without experiencing pain. Startlingly, a lament also knows that there is no way for God to be God without experiencing pain.

Matthew encourages us to understand the dynamics of the relationship between God and Jesus in the context of this ancient lament. I would not want to suggest that we cannot understand the psalm in the light of Jesus, but we do that already and easily. What I am suggesting is that we follow Matthew's lead and the fruitful insights it may suggest.

But we need to explore the dynamics of a lament. A lament is the expressing of pain in a time of darkness, blindness, silence, abandonment, and being lost. This is articulated within the full range of rhetorical techniques and devices. To what end? A lament is a reaching beyond for new answers, hoping that the present condition is not a final one, nor God's final intention. It asks whether what looks like a final situation is indeed so, and it asks that question out of a sense of enveloping total abandonment. But to speak a lament calls for a listener, another listener beyond the narrowing total focus on the agony that is threatening, which is consuming all reality other than its own painful one. A lament is desperate and yet hopeful. It is a crying out, desperate to be heard, and the addressee is God.

Matthew intensifies Jesus' lament when he takes Mark's translation of the cry into Greek *ho theos mou, ho theos mou* (a simple nominative singular) and changes it to a vocative that generates the plaintive *thee mou, thee mou.* But for Jesus to voice his pain through a lament even though he is calling for God to be faithful in no way lessens the intensity of depth of the pain — if anything, it intensifies it. Does Jesus know that God is there? No, he does not. But he is reaching beyond. God is being addressed. Who God is, is at stake.

The issues here are absolute. This is the consummate trusting one, innocent, brutalized, dying; where is the one trusted? That is the agony beyond our ability to grasp.

Who voices this agony? Now we must reflect back on the richness and diversity of Matthew's Christology. The "who" is the servant, chosen and bonded in love with God and God's people (Matt. 12:15-21); the "who" is the Wisdom of God, filled with insight, understanding, and active in creation (Matt. 12:41-42; 23:34; 11:19, 28-30); the "who" is the bearer of the Shekinah, the mediator of the presence of God (Matt. 17:1-9); the "who" is the Son in intimate, personal relationship with the Father and that identifies us as children of God (Matt. 11:27; 6:32); the "who" is the teacher of Israel and the church (Matt. 5–7). This is who is at stake! The lament is now translated onto a vastly higher plane that transcends and shatters the form itself. This is the lament to end all laments and lamenting.

What is at stake? The impact of a ministry of parables, miracles, debates, encounters, visions of the Satan falling from heaven, and blessed sight when what prophets and kings longed to see the disciples had seen. What is at stake? The kingdom reality experienced then and there, and the glorious, seen but not yet consummated, kingdom of heaven. *Thee mou, thee mou,* where is all of that? Is it lost?

Is the lament heard? The Exodus story answers yes: "we cried out, and God heard" (Ex. 2:23-25; 3:7, 8), as does Psalm 22:24: "For he has not despised or abhorred the affliction of the afflicted, and he has not hid his face from him, but has heard, when he cried to him." And this God will hear in the future (Ex. 22:27b). The Old Testament characterizes God as one who receives and takes seriously the cry of human pain. The godliness of God is defined in part as a hearing, listening compassion. God possesses a direct knowledge of the suffering of another. Knowledge means here an authentic, immediate, personal receiving. But such an act of receiving also calls to remembrance and touches the receiver's own pain. The receiver has lived it too. This means that God also has a direct experience of suffering, as the Exodus narrative demonstrates, a suffering of which texts such as Hosea 11:1-9 and Jeremiah 8:18-9:1 speak.

Thus characterizing the lamenter and the one who hears, we begin to sense the awesomeness of the pain in Matthew 27:46. Where is God? All of Matthew's scribal exposure of newness and oldness from the treasure of Scripture answers the question. God is there hearing, the God who remembers God's pain, and who now hears the lamenting pain of the Son, receiving and remembering. Matthew invokes all this richness of expression in his concept of Scripture being fulfilled. Here is Scripture, for you and me the Old Testament, interpreting experience.

In Matthew 26:64 at the hearing before the high priest, Jesus knows where God is: "you will see the Son of Man seated at the right hand of Power." He knows more: he knows God is with him. By the cross, that knowing is gone. But he is known, and his lament is heard, credited, taken seriously, and embraced in the most powerful sense of Scripture, which testifies, "we cried out, and God heard."

But experiencing pain, feeling pain with another is not enough, especially in the context of a lament. For it is a call to action. To be heard there must be resolution with attention to the structures and persons that define and cause the pain. A lament finally expresses relentless hope, the reaching trust that insists that no situation falls outside God's capacity to transform it. It bears, believes, hopes, endures, while reaching desperately toward healing.

Pain-generating institutions and persons, the pain-filled reality human beings have made, cannot long survive voiced, heard pain in the world of the lament, for the vision of an alternative future moves beyond promise to reality. This is the key to understanding Matthew's expansion of this Markan source in 27:52-54. The Power to which Jesus testified before the high priest acts in yet another way. The temple's capacity to function is shattered with the rending of the veil, implying the exposing of the divine self for all to see. The creation is shaken and wounded; the resurrected saints demonstrate the power of the cross to redeem. Even if the episode is an anachronism, it is a glorious one, with the Gentile centurion following the magi at the beginning of the story voicing the true confession. The final resolution of the lament waits for the first Easter morning and that appearance on the mountain.

And the Spirit? Where is the Spirit? The Spirit is in the power of the lament to create a new reality while embracing the pain caused by the old. The Spirit is the interpretative power of the treasure of Scripture from which come things both old and new. The Spirit vouches for the truth of the Passion, which is from many human perspectives in danger of being consumed by poignant, painful doubt. The Jesus who speaks the finest Christological confession in the gospel before the high priest utters his final human words in a lament reaching for God, waiting for God's response. The Spirit is in both. And when Jesus speaks again, it is on the mountain in the full power of the Spirit.

So what is Matthew 27:46? Is it a cry of despair or is it a cry of faith? It is far more than either. It is the final lament of human reality by the grace of the Triune God.

11. Overcoming Our Reality

ALLEN C. McSWEEN, JR.

The literary critic Erich Auerbach was not a biblical scholar or professional theologian, but his insights into the claims "the Scripture stories" press upon us, and the way in which they function in rendering "the only real world," point to an approach to the authority of Scripture that is rich with promise for the community of faith. Guided by this approach, we shall seek to reflect on the narrated world of the Gospel of Matthew in an attempt to let the narrative's own incarnation of doctrine and promise "overcome our reality," by reshaping our understanding of the power of God made manifest in Jesus the Christ.

As is true with all the great stories of Scripture, the Passion account of Jesus comes "fraught with background." Some of the background is provided by the events themselves, some by the interpretative framework of the Old Testament through whose symbols and language the deeper meaning of the events is set forth, and some by the concerns of the community to which each writer addressed his Gospel. But most of all for the faith community, the "background" with which the biblical narrative is "fraught" is the awesome reality of the Triune God, the subject and central character of the entire story.

If all the biblical narratives come "fraught with background," it is equally true that all are read and understood against the background of the particular context of the interpreter. Scripture is not written in a mythic vacuum or read in a social vacuum. The social-historical location of the reader provides the matrix in which certain features of the narrative come to the foreground of attention while others recede into the background. As an illustration, note the tremendous reserve of Matthew's crucifixion account. The Gospel is not fascinated by the "pornography of violence." The event itself is merely stated in a dependent clause ("they led him away to crucify him") with no glorification or sentimentality. There on the cross, Jesus is mocked by all. Yet once again, in the profound irony of the Gospel, their words of mockery nevertheless proclaim the hidden but effective truth. "He saved others; he cannot save himself" (Matt. 27:42). In addressing the delicate balance in the narrative between the power and powerlessness of Jesus, Hans Frei says that "Jesus is and remains powerful to the end, constraining all acts and words, even those of his opponents, to testify to him." But here in the words intended as mockery, Frei says that we find

> perhaps the most striking instance of the complex relation of efficacy and helplessness and of ironic reversal between them. In sum-

marizing and articulating his complete helplessness, the rulers are witness to his saving power.[1]

By the end of the passion account, Jesus is abandoned by all — even, it seems, by God. He dies in complete, utter powerlessness, crying out from the cross, "My God, my God, why hast thou forsaken me?" And yet, in the awesome irony of the Gospel, at the very moment of his greatest weakness, inconceivable power is released: "The curtain of the temple was torn in two . . . and the earth shook, and the rocks were split, and the tombs were opened, and many bodies of the saints who had fallen asleep were raised" (Matt. 27:51-52). In ancient apocalyptic images of both divine judgment and triumph, Matthew points to the power of God at work in the complete vulnerability of the Crucified One. The temple curtain is torn violently in two, the earth is shaken, and the rocks are split like the temple veil. The tombs of the saints are opened, and many are raised. Dale Bruner calls it a "preview of coming attractions." Already the death of Jesus has profound effects, reaching backward as well as forward. Matthew uses biblical apocalyptic imagery to say that with the death of Jesus the beginning of the end has come. Here we see a foreshadowing of the final triumph of the sovereign love of God at work through the vulnerability and apparent weakness of the crucified Jesus. And at last, for the first time in the Gospel, a human voice speaks the decisive truth: "Truly this was God's Son." At the beginning of Matthew's Gospel, gentile Magi pay homage to the newborn "king of the Jews." Now at the end of the story a gentile centurion pays homage to the one crucified under the title "king of the Jews" by declaring him "Son of God." The drama has come full circle.

If, as faith confesses, in the "cross of Christ" we see as nowhere else the "power and wisdom of God," what is the effect of entering the narrative world of Matthew where that power is so deeply hidden in weakness, vulnerability, and death? How does the narrative shape our sense of the power of God? On the most obvious level, it leads us to redefine power, not in terms of brute force, but in terms of the ability to achieve one's desired ends. Power expressed in coercive force can intimidate and force compliance, but it cannot liberate to love in freedom. Much of what to the world appears as "power" is little more than an attempt

1. Hans W. Frei, *The Identity of Jesus Christ* (Philadelphia: Fortress Press, 1975), p. 113.

to cover up impotence by violence. As Hannah Arendt has pointed out, force and violence are the alternative to *real* power on the part of those too weak to risk vulnerability.[2] From the perspective of the Gospel, the vulnerable but invincible love of the Triune God is the only power capable of turning us from the self-love that makes us rivals and enemies to the love of God and the neighbor for which we were created.

What does this mean for our understanding of the power of God? It means that the power of God is to be understood not as sovereign might but as the self-giving love that finds its most perfect expression in the Passion of Christ. The God rendered in the narrative of Scripture is not a God of unbounded omnipotence, if by that we mean the use of all the power at one's command. Rather, the "God and Father of our Lord Jesus Christ" is characterized by the willingness to be vulnerable, to take our sin and suffering into God's own divine life, "to bear our griefs and carry our sorrows." The power of God is the efficacy of God's holy love to redeem human beings without destroying our selfhood. There are depths of the human soul into which power simply cannot reach, so that if we are to be saved from our age-old love of power it will be by the power of love alone.

Gustaf Aulen summarized the matter well:

> Christian faith maintains that divine power is nothing else than the power of love. . . . The Christian faith, therefore, in spite of all appearances to the contrary, makes the affirmation that the sovereign power in the universe possesses the character of divine love. . . . If God's power were despotic, coercive, and violent, it would not be for faith the power beyond all power. Whatever the might of pure, external power may be able to accomplish, it cannot subdue human wills and set them free from the tyranny of egocentricity. Love cannot be induced by force. The hearts of men can be won only by the power of love.[3]

The same point is made more dramatically in a scene from *Moby Dick* in which, in the midst of a great storm at sea, Captain Ahab looks up at

---

2. Cf. William C. Placher, *Narratives of a Vulnerable God* (Louisville: Westminster/John Knox Press, 1994), p. 20.

3. Gustaf Aulen, *The Faith of the Christian Church* (Philadelphia: Muhlenberg Press, 1960), pp. 123-24.

the cross-shaped yardarms of his ship, the *Pequod,* tipped with St. Elmo's fire in the storm, and exclaims:

> I know thee, thou clear spirit. I know thee, and I know that thy right worship is defiance. I own thy speechless power, but to the last gasp of my earthquake life, I will dispute its mastery. Come in thy lowest form of love, and I will kneel and kiss thee; but come as power, and though thou launchest whole navies of full-freighted worlds, there's that in here that will defy Thee.[4]

The apparent powerlessness of God in Christ is able to move the human heart as no overt power can. Power can intimidate. Power can force conformity. But power cannot call forth the free response of love for which we were created.

One who knew as well as any the meaning of vulnerability was Dietrich Bonhoeffer. From a prison cell in Nazi Germany he wrote shortly before his execution:

> It is not by his omnipotence that Christ helps us, but by his weakness and suffering. . . . Man's religiosity makes him look in his distress to the power of God in the world; he uses God as a *Deus ex machina.* The Bible however directs him to the powerlessness and suffering of God; only a suffering God can help.[5]

There is much truth to that. And yet despite the fact that the "suffering of God" has become one of the dominant theological motifs in our time, we cannot relinquish the concept of the power of God altogether, as if all that we could say is that God is "the fellow sufferer who understands" (Whitehead). That kind of god would be, in the words of Woody Allen, "the ultimate underachiever." Perhaps very comfortable, well-pampered folks like us could settle for just a little "understanding," but not the vast majority of those who have ever lived and died.

4. Quoted in Paul Scherer, *The Word God Sent* (New York: Harper and Row, 1965), p. 173.

5. Dietrich Bonhoeffer, *Letters and Papers From Prison* (New York: Macmillan, 1953), pp. 219-20.

In his very helpful reflections on this whole issue of power and vulnerability, *Narratives of a Vulnerable God,* William Placher quotes Joan Northram, who says that if she found herself at the bottom of a pit with a broken arm,

> what I want and urgently need is a Rescuer with a very bright light and a long ladder, full of strength, joy, and assurance who can get me out of the pit, not a god who sits in the darkness suffering with me.[6]

Her point is well taken. We need more than merely a comforting little god who offers "understanding" in the midst of our suffering. We need a God who is in the midst of the battles of life with and for us with strength to redeem all our brokenness. We need not just a crucified God, but a crucified, risen, and exalted God, who in the end will achieve all of God's just and loving purposes for us and all of creation. We need, and have, a God who will give us "the victory through our Lord Jesus Christ." Otherwise love is impotent masochism, and the cross symbolized the final tragedy of life, not its redemption.

Albert Outler put it well in his "musings on providence." In the life, death, and resurrection of Jesus Christ we are encountered by no less and none other than

> God-with-us in life's turmoil and drudgery, unraveling and reweaving the strands of our memories and hopes, judging, thwarting, leaving us to suffer for our own misdeeds and those of others, and yet never forsaking us even in our suffering. God-with-us: endlessly patient, endlessly concerned, endlessly resourceful.

Outler says, "The ground of our belief that the battle is worth our best is not that God is *above it* calling the shots, but that God is *in it* sharing the blows — and that he is going to *win it,* for us and for our salvation."[7]

We cannot leave the Passion narrative of Matthew without taking note of the final scene before the resurrection. There the power of God in the crucified Christ comes to a head. Matthew alone says that the

---

6. Placher, *Narratives of a Vulnerable God,* p. 18.

7. Albert C. Outler, *Who Trusts in God: Musings on Providence* (New York: Oxford University Press, 1968), pp. 106-8.

chief priests and Pharisees came to Pilate, addressing him as "Lord" *(kyrie)* and asking him to secure the tomb, lest Jesus' disciples steal the body and claim that he had risen from the dead. Pilate grants them that one final impossible request. He says, "You have a guard of soldiers; go, make it as secure as you can" (Matt. 27:65). How secure is that? Can human powers keep down God's raising up? They may as well have ordered the sun not to rise in the morning. They make the tomb as secure as is humanly possible by sealing it with the Empire's own mark of power and setting a guard. But no human security system can stop the life-giving power of God. If it was necessary that the Christ should suffer many things and be killed, it was also necessary in the power of God that he be raised to life again and made Lord over all creation.

The power of God as rendered in the realistic narrative of the Gospel is vastly different from all the world's powers of force, intimidation, and violence. It is the ultimate efficacy of the vulnerable, yet invincible, love seen supremely in the cross of Christ. That divine love alone has power to call forth our free response of love and our whole-hearted participation in the promises and purposes of God. The power of God is not merely deeply hidden under what appears to be human weakness. It freely chooses weakness and vulnerability, because love by its very nature suffers with and for and in the suffering of the beloved. Every parent, every lover knows that painfully, yet also gloriously, well. We can speak properly of God's power only through the language of irony and paradox that holds together the vulnerability of holy love revealed decisively in the Passion of Jesus, and the power of that love that in the end will prove triumphant in the accomplishment of all God's just and loving purposes. To eyes of faith, the cross is the final revelation of the power of God that redefines for us the meaning and use of power until that day when the "kingdom of the world has become the kingdom of our Lord and of his Messiah, and he will reign forever and ever" (Rev. 11:15).

12. *When the Resurrection Community Reads the Passion Narrative*

ALBERT H. KELLER

Matthew's Passion narrative fascinates in the way a work of art fascinates. Recognizing that, then pondering what it is about the narrative that fascinates as it does, I find myself drawn into the text by the door of mystery rather than the door of rationality. The door of mystery opens into a space quite different from the analytical, circumscribed space of the modern, common-sense world, and into a time that is saturated with eternity — or, in the idiom of the narrative, resurrection. We cannot withhold rational inquiry from the drama and still be ourselves, investigating and reflective people that we are. Yet the source of fascination, in my view, along with the narrative's authority, lies beyond the line where rational analysis changes into something like what David Miller meant when he said, "The difficulty is that of a mystery rather than problem, like a rose in a poem by Robert Burns rather than a rose in a seed catalogue."

In this theological essay, I will attempt to show how Matthew's narrative performs the complex, transformative function just described. I will claim that the transformative dimension is intelligible only within the church, identified as resurrection community. The essay focuses on the account of the trial of Jesus before Caiaphas the High Priest (26:57-75), with reference to the civil trial in Pilate's court (27:11-31) and the Matthean account of the crucifixion.

How the Story Is Told

Matthew uses the word *synagein* to designate the gathering at the night trial, thus evoking the psalms of the suffering just one (Ps. 22:16; 86:14).[1] The legal trial takes place in Caiaphas' house and the account unfolds in forensic language. Authority and power rest firmly in the

1. Raymond Brown, *Death of the Messiah*, Vol. I (New York: Doubleday, 1994), pp. 402, 434.

hands of the High Priest, or so it would appear. False witnesses are brought forward to testify against Jesus, and then two witnesses (the requisite number in a Jewish trial) not tagged as false testify that Jesus was heard to say, "I am able to destroy the sanctuary of God and to build it in three days." Brown notes that the reference is to the sanctuary, not the whole temple. With textual undertones of the "suffering servant" of Yahweh, the trial of the one whom Pilate's wife will later announce as *dikaios*, the Just One, is underway.

Then the priest imposes an oath, a very solemn and absolute move. He puts Jesus under oath "before the living God" — an industrial-strength oath, in a Gospel in which Jesus has come out against the use of any oath at all — and demands of him, "Tell us if you are the Messiah, the Son of God." Now all the attention is riveted on Jesus.

This is the moment when Jesus — all the synoptic Gospels agree — goes apocalyptic. It is true that Jewish messianism was an end-time motif, and the addition of the "Son of God" title raises the stakes of the question even higher. Brown is not sure what Caiaphas could have meant by "Son of God," though it is very clear what the Christological title meant to the church at the time Matthew wrote. Whatever the historicity of this adjured question posed by the highest religious authority in Judaism (bearing in mind that there were no obvious eye-witnesses reporting to the writer), in the context of the narrative this is the decisive moment for Jesus to reveal his true identity.

Jesus does so by qualifying the titles "Messiah" and "Son of God," yet owning them with an authority that astonishes the High Priest. Jesus gives an idiomatic assent to the question and then adds a further qualification to Caiaphas' phraseology in the form of a citation of two very potent scriptural images:

> You have said so. But I tell you,
> from now on you will see the Son of Man
> seated at the right hand of Power
> and coming on the clouds of heaven.

The quotation cites Psalm 110:1, a royal psalm for the coronation of a king, in which the Lord says to "my lord" the king, "Sit at my right hand until I make your enemies your footstool." The psalm combines the figure of king with that of priest in the "order of Melchizedek," and ends with his decisive, violent victory and God's judgment against kings and nations. Universal, unending power and dominion is the theme. Even more daunting is the citation of Daniel 7:13, an apocalyptic passage in which a human being or "son of man" comes on clouds of heaven. "His dominion is an everlasting dominion that will not pass away" — a vision that even Daniel found terrifying.

When Jesus makes that response, the priest tears his clothes as a sign of grief or scandal and declares that blasphemy has been spoken, eliminating the need for witnesses' testimony. The assembly pronounces the verdict of death. They spit on him, strike him, and slap him, taunting him to "prophesy" (presumably as Messiah should be able to do) who it was that struck him.

Witness to Resurrection

Let us advance the hypothesis, then, that Jesus' apocalyptic saying is not an explanation or definition of messiahship; let us say a different kind of communication is happening. Matthew and his faith community believed that the series of events described retrospectively in the Passion narrative was the hinge of history. The writer's method of interpreting them drew upon (and likened them analogically to) the images of their ancestral, theological-historical tradition, and upon whole structures of consciousness and understanding projected into the future (eschatology), at the same time interpreting (and turning upside down) the constructed realities of their present situation, both temporal and spiritual. Images from the historical past, spiritual present, and eschatological future fuse into a synchronistic totality or wholeness that is not the same as what post-Newtonians call explanation or definition.

My point is this: Matthew's Passion narrative bears witness to resurrection even at the point where Jesus is seen most fully engaged with the engulfing darkness of death, with its moral and spiritual as well as biological dimensions. What does the church mean by "resurrection"? It was the Easter encounter with the risen Christ that brought the ineffable reality of resurrection most directly into the time and space in which the original human witnesses lived. The New Creation does not displace the old, but transforms it. It was the third day for the women at the tomb, but for Christ, as it came to be for the women too, it was eternity. They realized that the Risen Lord was inseparable from the crucified Jesus. An anonymous opinion piece in the *London Times* (4/2/99) makes this identification plain:

> In the light of Easter we see that love's redeeming work was indeed done through the Cross, not apart from the Cross. There the fight was fought and the battle won. The resurrection is no "descent from the Cross postponed for thirty-six hours for reason of effect," it is the declaration of a victory won on the Cross, and in the darkness and silence of death, and even in the hell of utter apartness from God. From there Christ rose again in triumph.

It is the testimony of Matthew's Gospel that if the "eternal now" is present even in the time of Jesus' trial and crucifixion (which he indicates by time-transcending images and apocalyptic utterances), as it is present on the "first day of the week" when the women come to the tomb, then we find that God's *eternal now*, or *new creation*, or *end-time*, or *resurrection*, or *Holy Spirit*, is present with us through every trial and even through death.

Does the theologian stretch too far, using all these discrete theological concepts to point to one reality? Through the door of rationality, probably so; but through the door of mystery, no. The writer Matthew leads us through the devices of language to realize something language cannot define, through the drama of time to realize something that transects time, through the localities of space to realize *something* that is not spatial except as it wills to become incarnated in our space. If we move into the historian's or scientist's domain to determine the limits of the possible, we miss it. But the narrative says the finite contains the infinite. It begins with Jesus, Matthew announces to us through every part of the narrative. And through Jesus it leads into eternity, into now — into *something* that is beyond definition.

[Homiletic insert: One day I expect to die. That is the judgment of this world. But because of my faith in Christ, no dread is connected to that judgment. *Something* is going to happen. It won't look like the signs of the resurrection of Jesus, because time and space will be no more — no reason to make it like a body eating fish any more! But those signs foretell it. God's presence in trial and suffering is a foretaste of that reality. And foretelling it also are the times when time has dissolved and I have been enabled to wholly live in the present, in the Now of God. Kenneth Scott Latourette intimated resurrection in this sense when he said once in an evening prayer group at Yale, "Thank you for letting me live with You another day of eternal life." He, like Matthew, knew more than he could tell.]

How the Church Reads Scripture

I have spoken of entering the narrative through the door of mystery. Matthew invites us to do that, I believe, by embedding concepts in a web of images that both cohere and conflict, creating both integration and cognitive dissonance — as in the story in which a prisoner in chains (probably blindfolded) claims the image of the God-empowered king and the apocalyptic Son of Man. Here is no rationalistic theology but a mystery of humiliation and exaltation, powerlessness and power, time and end time, coming into focus temporally and spatially in the trial and crucifixion of Jesus.

This door to Scripture opens only to those who engage in an ecclesial reading of the text. By that I mean that the church is a resurrection community. This fact of faith makes faithful church life the lens through which resurrection (the transforming dimension) becomes apparent in the text. Through experience within the full life of the church community — both coherent and conflictual, integrative yet always dissonant too, sacramental and mundane, suffering and joyful — the contemporary reader is in a position to appropriate the inner pattern, the profound undertones and the transecting flashes of resurrection, within the language.

This is what I mean by resurrection community. An *emotional* community is a group of people bonded by a shared, powerful emotion, such as those brought together by grief after a significant loss or by joy at an electrifying performance, or a team caught up in the passion of competing in a championship game. Sometimes experiences like that happen in a church, but they are not the defining element. To call the church a *resurrection* community is not to refer to any human feature, like great emotions or doctrinal correctness. It is to make the faith assertion that "we are a living community alive through the Spirit, that we share the very life of God," in the words of David Steinmetz. To call the church a resurrection community is to say that Christ is being formed in the church, gradually, dramatically, his revolutionary love, his benevolent rage, his dying to the world and rising by God's creative grace to life. Like no other community, the church is grounded in and enlivened by what is ultimate.

Resurrection is the Divine Mystery breaking into the reality we know in space and time. When that happens, it always configures Christ. I have suggested several words, each of which expresses part of the meaning of this event: new creation, eternal now, end time, resurrection, and Holy Spirit. The word or phrase most often used by Matthew (and by Jesus himself) to express it is *the kingdom of God (heaven)*. The church has the germ of the kingdom of God, the power of resurrection — the vital connection with the text, the ears to hear, the eyes to see. When the resurrection community reads the Passion narrative, then, like Matthew, it knows more than it can tell.

CHAPTER III

THE BINDING OF ISAAC (GEN. 22)

Introduction

Our next set of essays investigates readings from the Old Testament in light of their relation to the New Testament in the Holy Scriptures as officially recognized by the Christian church. In the particular set of passages emphasized in this project, we have seen the issue addressed clearly in the Matthean Passion narrative. "All this has taken place, so that the scriptures of the prophets may be fulfilled," Jesus pointedly reminded the crowds who were witnessing his arrest in Gethsemane (Matt. 26:56). If these cited prophets were not merely predictors or fortune-tellers, and the counsels of the one, true God are both coherent and unified despite their cultural and historical diversity, precisely how should pastor-theologians best describe the relation of the Old and New Testaments? More concretely, just how, if at all, may the story of Abraham's binding of Isaac illumine for Christians God's governance in the cross of Christ?

"Dialogue between the Testaments" opens the discussion by warning against the absolutization of the historical-critical method for interpreting the Bible. Human rationalism cannot be the final judge of Holy Scripture. Faith statements cannot be "gleaned from the Old and New Testaments without the faith element." The church can always benefit from the science of historical criticism, of course, so long as it serves but does not destroy the unique record of God's self-revelation. Creed, canon, and liturgy communally reinforce the Scriptures of the church to withstand the hegemonic dictates of secular methodologies. The community of believers has always eventually transmitted God's saving Word with both reverence and relevance. As the prophets creatively recast the law in the Old Testament, so the apostles "used, reinterpreted and applied" the entire Old Testament in its own Spirit-guided fulfillment within the New Testament. Mutual interdependence is everywhere apparent to the eyes of faith, not least in the binding of Isaac (Gen. 22), with its seminal intimations of Christ's later crucifixion and resurrection.

The selection entitled "The Music of Failure" offers a Christian reading of the binding of Isaac in witness to the resurrection. Prompted by the testimony of Hebrews 11:8-18, the pre-critical interpretations of Origen, Augustine, Chrysostom, Luther, and Calvin all took this approach. Our author emulates their lead, but prefers to stress "the unfaithful failures rather than faithful obedience of Abraham." For ultimately, at heart was "the faithfulness of God to his promises as the Lord of life" in both the birth and the binding of Isaac. Abraham's earlier failures necessitated God's testing of him; his obedience of faith at Moriah became the foundation for the covenant of blessing that was to be Israel's destiny.

"The Test" explores the classical Christian tradition's mediation of Genesis 22 to believers in the biblical and patristic theology of John Calvin. In "lucid brevity," Calvin depicts Abraham's basic test in terms of the potential destruction of human salvation in the loss of Isaac. How can the God of promise also be the God of such a command? Abraham's obedience of faith is grounded in confident trust and is also "bolstered by his confidence in the resurrection and his memory of Isaac's humanly impossible birth." Where such an interpretation is rejected (as even within the membership of the Pastor-Theologian seminar itself), the author proposes for interpreters a combination of "scholarship, faith, love, and a self-consciousness regarding their love-hate relationship with their own parents, their religious traditions, and even with God." Given the limits of human understanding, he holds that the benefit of the doubt should always be given to the Scriptures and to God.

The succeeding author's excerpt develops the narrative of the binding of Isaac in terms of "The Founding Vision of Covenant Community." Employing the findings of the historical-critical method to illumine the history of salvation, the writer emphasizes the theological context in the early chapters of Genesis: the Creator's lordship over creation, God's blessing of creation with humanity made in God's own image, and God's universal covenant with Noah preceding his saving covenant with Abraham. Sketching the scholarship of Levenson, Collins, Moberly, and Childs, the author develops a scriptural hermeneutic that traces the positive transformation of a "barbaric ritual into a sublime paradigm of religious life." It was this primal myth of the loss and return of the beloved son that was transfigured by both Jewish and Christian scriptural writers in dramatizing the decisive roles of Isaac and Jesus for their respective communities of faith.

A final contribution centers the Scripture's message and truth, as evidenced in both the binding of Isaac and the Passion of Jesus, in its true-to-life depiction of hopeful redemption in the midst of "Exile and Slaughter." The broader biblical witness speaks to all ages because all ages are in need of life as they face death, God's promises in the face of humanity's tragedies. At heart, the biblical message is that "God's people will face death and even then God will bless them." Its authority rests in the efficacious promise that God saves.

13. Dialogue between the Testaments

DEBORAH R. CLEMENS

Thesis

A main objective for the Pastor-Theologian Program has been to engage in pre-critical reading of Scripture. The purpose of this pre-critical reading is the hope that the meaning of God's Word, which may have been neglected for the sake of the rational historical-critical method of biblical study, can be experienced afresh in the community of the church.

The science of historical criticism has greatly expanded our knowledge of the history, setting, and character of the Word. The church will always benefit from it. Yet, the rationalistic principle (which has long predominated the discipline) that faith must be suppressed so that the objective meaning of the original intent of the biblical authors will not be distorted is fundamentally flawed. The error is in the assumption that any meaning can be gleaned from the Scriptures of the Old and New Testaments without the faith element. This is an error because the writings are faith statements. That is their primary purpose.

Textual and literary studies, along with archeological and interdisciplinary evidence, can all enhance biblical understanding. However, if done specifically to the exclusion of the faith, such practices take the heart right out of the living organism. They leave little but an empty shell or putrid corpse. The hermeneutics of suspicion is basically a by-product of this "scholarly" attempt to remove what some would call the "subjective" from the text. This prejudges faith as little more than human musings. If faith is, however, the apprehension of the transcendent, then it is fully objective. The object is the immutable God, who is Fact by which all other facts gain their significance and Truth through which all scientific proofs find meaning. God is apprehensible to human beings through the incarnation of God in Jesus.

Using the Bible to study merely the circumstances that surround the writings of the biblical passages (no matter how well researched and accurate) is, in the long run, useless. It is easy to understand how many can emerge from biblical studies with indifference, suspicion, and even contempt for the material when focused solely on the human factors behind the writing. When engaged through the eyes of faith, however, the same book is found to be life-giving and life-redeeming. Curiously, with eyes of faith even historical criticism can be revealing. In my understanding, the Pastor-Theologian project of 1999 is an attempt to utilize the Christian faith intentionally as the primary lens through which one engages the ancient texts, but it should not be assumed that this exercise is a reversion to biblical literalism or naive fundamentalism. The scientific tools continue to be important. However, they should be employed as supports to, not the means of destruction of, the faith tradition.

Using this principle, therefore, I see three primary ways in which we might approach biblical interpretation. One is the creedal method, which would initially allow the historical confessions of the faith community to bring clarity to the texts. The second method is the canonical method, which encourages a fluid dialogue between biblical passages in order to interpret any single passage. The third is the liturgical method, which reads the Word within the context of the liturgy and sacraments of a worshiping communion. All these are necessary and legitimate; none are mutually exclusive. In this exercise, I will use the canonical method to shed light on Genesis 22.

The Warrant

Before bringing Genesis 22 into a conversation with the New Testament, we first must ask what legitimizes the dialogue between these two Testaments. Opinions have varied through the ages as to how or if the sacred writings of the Jewish tradition and those of the Christian tradition can be connected. The apostolic church embraced the books of the law and the prophets as their holy texts. In A.D. 85 Marcion campaigned to reject the Hebrew Scriptures in their entirety because he denied seeing any similarity between the God known through Jesus Christ and the God of the Mosaic Covenant. During the classic Patristic period, Old Testament passages were used primarily as allegorical material. The historical context and the rabbinical interpretation were completely suppressed in exchange for fanciful interpretations. Old Testament passages were honored only for being hidden allusions to the Gospel message. On the other hand, John Calvin tended to emphasize the unity of the two covenants to such an extent that he saw no substantial difference between them. Finally in current times, with the heightened awareness of the pluralistic world in which we live and the sins of Western Christian triumphalism, some now argue that Christians have no right at all to interpret Hebrew scriptures, saying that they should be respected as Hebrew texts alone and left unhampered by Christian supersessionists.

Let us first consider the character of the Old Testament itself. Essentially the Jewish tradition embraces its canon under two broad categories, the law and the prophets. The law, or Torah, is the collected narratives of how God has worked for the salvation of his chosen. From the myths of creation to the grooming of the Promised Land, God has shepherded the people of Israel, brought them out of bondage, given them freedom, and held them in covenant with him. Cultic renewal services like those held by Joshua at Shechem (Josh. 24), and cultic feasts and festival observances such as Passover and Yom Kippur, were never believed to be just acts of remembrance of past events. They were public affirmations of the reality of the saving acts of God in the present. The nature of God, revealed in the stories of deliverance and covenant-making, did not change. As God called Abraham, God calls each generation of children to faithfulness. As God led the enslaved out of Egypt, God frees his people from bondage (Deut. 29). As God revealed his will in the giving of the Commandments, he holds his own accountable for their sins (Lev. 16:29) This Torah model can give us the first hermeneutical clue for legitimate interpretation of the ancient manuscripts: It is right and proper to engage the Pentateuch with the objective of recognizing God at work in the contemporary environment.

As for the prophets, the book of Isaiah may be illustrative. Whether by complementing or protesting the Torah, the prophetic materials move on to anticipate the promised future fulfillment of God's righteous rule of humanity. Indeed, God's eschatological future breaks into the historical present to give it direction and purpose. Isaiah speaks of more than just a revisiting of the glory days of Israel's past. He acknowledges the coming of even greater events than what has already been witnessed by even Adam, Abraham, and Moses. God is working his purpose out beyond history itself. God does not merely repeat the former blessings; on the basis of what he has revealed to his people and what he has already assured to them, we can know beyond a shadow of a doubt that there stands before us a transformation, a culmination, a completion yet to be expected.

There are other hermeneutical principles that can be applied from this prophetic confession. For example, Biblical historical events have eschatological significance. Worldly truths learned in the Hebrew communion have spiritual and universal consequences. By analyzing how God has interacted with the world in the past, predictions are indeed possible about God's next steps. The written words convey life. They necessarily point beyond themselves. The Hebrew Bible is by intent a light to all nations.

New Testament Application

The early church never stopped to question its right to use, to reinterpret, and to apply the Hebrew texts to its own particular situation. In fact, it is only because of these texts that the church knew any reason for existing. Not only were the books of the law and the prophets the Holy Writ that Jewish Christians had inherited, but they were understood to be the justification itself for the whole Christ event and therefore for the whole church's existence. Everything that happened in the salvific occurrences around the life, death, and resurrection of Jesus happened "in accordance with Scripture." Jesus himself declared as he was about to be bound and arrested:

> "Put your sword back into its place; for all who take the sword will perish by the sword. Do you think that I cannot appeal to my Father, and he will at once send me more than twelve legions of angels? But how then would the scriptures be fulfilled, which say it must happen in this way?" At that hour Jesus said to the crowds, "Have you come out with swords and clubs to arrest me as though I were a bandit? Day after day I sat in the Temple teaching, and you did not arrest me. But all this has taken place, so that the scriptures of the prophets may be fulfilled." (Matt. 26:52-56)

To what Scriptures was Jesus referring? Where is there a mention of the arrest, trial, conviction, and crucifixion of one man in the Hebrew tradition? Nowhere can we find such specific comments. In fact, the Deuteronomy 21:23 crucifixion is specifically mentioned as the one form of execution that is cursed by God. Yet the New Testament claims that Christ himself is the fulfillment of all revealed to the people of Israel before him (see John 19:36 and I Cor. 15:3-5, among others).

In the Matthew passage Jesus does give us a hint. The Scriptures he is appealing to are the writings of the prophetic traditions. The first apostles interpreted Isaiah's Suffering Servant, the one who would be led like a lamb to the slaughter, the one who would stand silent before his shearers, as a direct reference to the Passion of Jesus (see Isa. 53:3-12 and Acts 8:32-35). Jesus had identified himself as the realization of Isaiah's vision in his own preaching (compare Isa. 61:1-2 and Luke 4:18-19). There is little doubt that the comfort, deliverance, and salvation assured to Abraham and Sarah and promised by Isaiah were interpreted by the church as being fulfilled in Jesus.

The subject matter of both the Old and the New Testaments is the revelation of the one true God to human beings. Both Testaments understand the existential human crisis as the need to be freed from the powers of sin and death. Both agree that the intent of God's self-revelation to the world is for human deliverance. Therefore there seems to be a legitimate conversation to be had between the two Testaments. Even more so, there appears to be an organic connection linking them. Yet, at the same time, the Christian Scripture is not merely a sequel to the earlier writings. It is not the final chapter in the story of God's work among God's people. There are substantial and insurmountable differences between the two. In Christ, something totally new happened. In the coming of Jesus, something more has occurred. There is something more miraculous than the creation of the universe, the parting of the Red Sea, the healing of Naaman. What is promised in the Old has met completion in the New (see Jer. 31:31-34 and Col. 2:16-17). What was expected by Israel is accomplished by Jesus. The people of God knew themselves to be the elect because God had opted to reveal his true self to them. In Jesus, however, God not only revealed himself to humans, he did so in human flesh. Therefore in Christ God became one with all human existence. In the dispensation of the Holy Spirit, salvation is not only promised to us and grasped only through human subjectivism, but is implanted in us through the sacrament of Baptism.

Christians have no reason to claim superiority over their ancestors in the covenant, for the New Testament remains dependent upon the Old. Only through the history of revelation could the early church interpret the events of the Passion. Only by the law and prophets could Christians acknowledge the Resurrection (Luke 24:27). Christians cannot understand Jesus without first knowing the covenant with Abraham. At the same time, they cannot interpret Genesis 22 outside the Gospel message.

For this reason, Christians cannot speak of Genesis 22 without it being absorbed into the Resurrection. Abraham could not have ventured up Mount Moriah without the same conviction that life is in God's hands. There are many ways of assessing the binding of Isaac. If examined with the historical-critical method alone, it appears to be a horrendous portrait of the divine. If viewed from the Jewish perspective, it appears to be an example of human faith and obedience and God's assurance of the continuation of the covenant. But as Christians, we can read it only through New Testament eyes as an unquenched affirmation of the eternal efficacy of Christ, as an unapologetic Resurrection text.

14. *The Music of Failure*

THOMAS A. RENQUIST

Whenever we Christians read the Scriptures, these questions should be always in our minds:

— How does this reading point to Jesus Christ?
— How does this reading remind me of other passages of Scripture that can help to illuminate it?
— What does the church say about this reading?
— How does this reading challenge my world and invite me into a new world?

Huub Ooterhuis, a Dutch hymn writer, has captured well the transforming power of a Christian reading of Scriptures:

Words from afar, stars that are falling,
Sparks that are sown in us like seed.
Names for our God, dreams, signs and wonders
Sent from the past are all we need.
We in this place remember and speak
Again what we have heard:
God's free redeeming word.[1]

---

1. Huub Oosterhuis, "What Is This Place?" trans. David Smith, *A New Hymnal for Colleges and Schools* (New Haven: Yale University Press, 1992), No. 340.

In the section that follows I will use the questions listed above for a Christian reading of the Scriptures, applying them to a resurrection interpretation of the binding of Isaac in Genesis 22.

Resurrection in Genesis 22

Like Kierkegaard and the rest of the modern world, I am amazed at Abraham's faithful obedience in the binding of Isaac. It is a scandal, a stumbling block. Yet however much the story scandalizes me, I am absolutely convinced that this is, at bottom, a story about faithful obedience. It is not about our modern-day revulsion at a God some see engaged in child abuse, nor is it an ancient legend about how Israel was able to move beyond child sacrifice. It is about faithful obedience.

At the same time I have to admit, again like Kierkegaard, that I would have utterly failed such a test. So how did Abraham succeed? Was it because, as the author of the Epistle to the Hebrews states, Abraham "considered the fact that God is able even to raise someone from the dead" (11:19)?

Resurrection? In Genesis 22? That is what so many church fathers and reformers concluded.

> The Apostle, therefore, has reported to us the thoughts of the faithful man, that the faith in the resurrection began to be held already at that time in Isaac. Abraham, therefore, hoped for the resurrection of Isaac and believed in a future which had not yet happened. (Origen)[2]

> Yet Abraham is worthy of praise, because he all along believed that his son, on being offered up, would rise again. (Augustine)[3]

> Accordingly, Abraham understood the doctrine of the resurrection of the dead, and through it alone he resolved this contradiction, which otherwise cannot be resolved. (Luther)[4]

2. Origen, *Homilies on Genesis and Exodus* (Washington, D.C.: The Catholic University of America Press), p. 137.

3. Augustine, *The City of God*, Book XVI, Chapter 32.

4. *Luther's Works*, American Edition; *Genesis* (St. Louis: Concordia, 1964), pp. 4, 196.

Among the pre-modern witnesses, Chrysostom and Calvin are a little bit more reluctant to find resurrection in the binding of Isaac. Nevertheless:

> All this [the binding of Isaac], however, happened as a type of the Cross. . . . You see, it was necessary that the truth be sketched out ahead of time in shadow. (Chrysostom)[5]

> It may be that [Abraham], trusting in the providence of God, figured to himself his son as surviving even in death itself. (Calvin)[6]

Finding resurrection in Genesis 22 is at least understandable, given the fact that these Christian exegetes are following the lead of the Letter to the Hebrews. But what about twelfth-century rabbis?

> Down upon him [Isaac] fell the resurrecting dew, and he revived.
> The father seized him (then) to slaughter him once more.
> Scripture, bear witness! Well-grounded is that fact:
> And the Lord called Abraham, even a second time from heaven.
> (Rabbi Ephraim)[7]

> When the sword touched Isaac's throat his soul flew clean out of him. And when He let His voice be heard from between the two cherubim, "Lay not thy hand upon the lad," the lad's soul returned to his body. Then his father unbound him, and Isaac rose, knowing that in this way the dead would come back to life in the future; whereupon he began to recite, Blessed art Thou, O Lord, who quickens the dead. (Rabbi Judah)[8]

There is one other monotheistic religion that has its roots in the Abraham story: Islam. In fact, it was the *aslama,* the binding of Isaac, which gave that faith its name. Although it does not make a connection

---

5. St. John Chrysostom, *Homilies on Genesis 46-67* (Washington, D.C.: The Catholic University of America Press), pp. 21-22.

6. John Calvin, *Commentaries on the First Book of Moses, Called Genesis,* trans. John King (Grand Rapids: Eerdmans, 1948), p. 567.

7. Shalom Spiegel, *The Last Trial* (New York: Schocken Books, 1967), p. 30.

8. Spiegel, *Last Trial,* pp. 30-31.

to the binding of Isaac, *The Qu'ran* does include a section in which Abraham is taught about the resurrection:

> "How," said [Abraham], "shall God give life to this city, after she hath been dead?" And God caused him to die for an hundred years, and then raised him to life. And God said, "How long hast thou waited?" He said, "I have waited a day or part of a day." He said, "Nay, thou hast waited an hundred years. Look on thy food and thy drink; they are not corrupted; and look on thine ass: we would make thee a sign unto men: And look on the bones of thine ass, how we will raise them, then clothe them with flesh." And when this was shewn to him, he said, "I acknowledge that God hath power to do all things." (ii 262ff.)

But resurrection? In Genesis 22? The story itself does not speak of it. Could a belief in the resurrection have been the foundation that allowed Abraham to be successfully obedient to God's command? Hans Frei, who has encouraged many of us to read Scripture as narrative, issues a warning to this kind of typological or figural reading of Scripture:

> For a person, an event, a body of laws, a rite, etc., to be both itself and real in its own right, and yet stand for something else later in time and equally real which is to fulfill it, imposes strain especially on the earlier moment.[9]

And yet Erich Auerbach maintained that the *figura* is precisely the way that the biblical narratives depict reality:

> Doctrine and promise are incarnate in them [the biblical stories] and inseparable from them; for that reason they are fraught with "background" and mysterious, containing a second, concealed meaning. In the story of Isaac, it is not only God's intervention at the beginning and the end, but even the factual and psychological elements which come between, that are mysterious, merely touched upon,

9. Hans Frei, *The Eclipse of Biblical Narrative* (New Haven: Yale University Press, 1974), p. 29.

fraught with background; and therefore they require subtle investigation and interpretation, they demand them.[10]

The biblical author of the Letter to the Hebrews, as well as the premodern exegetes, did what was demanded of them: they saw a connection between the binding of Isaac and the resurrection. But how does one do that figural interpretation of the biblical story without imposing too much strain on the literal story? Frei distinguishes between *mimesis* (following the way things really are in the narrative) and creation:

> The only spiritual act is that of comprehension — an act of *mimesis,* following the way things really are — rather than of creation, if it is to be faithful interpretation.[11]

I would suggest that we take Auerbach's and Frei's advice and examine the background narratives that lead up to the binding of Isaac, following the way "things really are" in that narrative. At the same time let us keep in mind this formula offered by Nikos Kazantsakis: "Never return to success; return to failure." If we are so overwhelmed by Abraham's "success" at faithful obedience, let us return instead to Abraham's failures.

Here, of course, we have to pick and choose among Abraham's many failures. We could go back to Abraham's trip to Egypt and his cowardly act of passing Sarah off as his sister in order to protect himself. We even have two choices with that particular failure, because Abraham repeated his cowardice and did the same thing again with King Abimelech. Those failures of Abraham's were really threats to the promise, just like the binding of Isaac. Handing Sarah over to the harems of Pharaoh and King Abimelech set up the possibility that Sarah and Abraham could never make a child of their own . . . no child of the promise.

There was, however, another failure of Abraham that contained within it the seed of Abraham's later faithful obedience. Augustine points us in the right direction:

10. Erich Auerbach, *Mimesis* (Princeton: Princeton University Press, 1953), p. 15.

11. Frei, *Eclipse of Biblical Narrative,* p. 36.

Therefore the father [Abraham], holding fast from the first the promise which behooved to be fulfilled through this son whom God had ordered him to slay, did not doubt that he whom he once thought it hopeless he should ever receive would be restored to him when he had offered him up . . . thinking that God was able to raise him up, even from the dead.[12]

When God announced to Abraham that he would be a hundred-year-old father and Sarah would be a ninety-year-old mother, Abraham laughed. Yet in spite of Abraham's failure to believe, God still fulfilled his promise. It is the Letter to the Hebrews, of course, which describes that as a gift of life in the midst of death: Abraham, the one who was as good as dead (11:12), still had this life yet to come from within him.[13]

It was the faithfulness of God to his promises in the miraculous birth of Isaac, in spite of Abraham's own failure to believe them, that planted the seed of faithful obedience in Abraham at the binding of Isaac. If God was earlier able to turn around the death sign of sterility and barrenness, surely God would continue to be faithful to his promises and also be able to change a sacrificial death into life.

Minnesota poet Bill Holm calls this the music of failure. On an August afternoon, sitting on a slope high in the Rocky Mountains, he listened to the wind blowing through the aspen trees:

> Above me, wind does its best
> to blow leaves off the Aspen
> tree a month too soon, No use,
> wind, all you succeed in doing
> is making music, the noise of
> failure growing beautiful.[14]

Abraham's story is music, the noise of failure growing beautiful. It was precisely because of Abraham's failures at faithful obedience that God found it necessary to test him in the binding of Isaac. Specifically,

---

12. Augustine, *City of God*, Book XVI, Chapter 32.

13. It is interesting to note that Paul, too, in Romans 4:19, describes the sterility of Abraham with the same phrase, "as good as dead."

14. Bill Holm, *The Music of Failure* (Marshall: Plains Press, 1985), pp. 58-59.

it was Abraham's experience of God's providence in the birth of Isaac that was able to move Abraham toward a more faithful obedience when he was called to sacrifice Isaac.[15] It was the noise of failure growing beautiful: God's continuing providence changed Abraham from the one who failed to trust in the promises of God to the one who faithfully and obediently trusted in the God who promises.

Of all the pre-modern exegetes, perhaps Chrysostom was the most accurate when he described Isaac as a shadow of the truth. Certainly there is in this story no full-blown Christian doctrine of the resurrection of the dead; that would be a totally unsubstantiated strain on the literal story. But there is a life-affirming shadow in this story, a shadow pointing to a powerful God who had already affirmed himself as a God of life by overcoming Abraham and Sarah's infertility.

In the binding of Isaac, Abraham refused to submit to the contradiction of death, but instead put his obedient trust in the God of life. For us Christians who live today from the perspective of the New Testament, Isaac is a shadow of the resurrection truth. Is not God's power to raise Jesus — and us — from the dead the greatest evidence we Christians have of God's providence? The Passion and Resurrection of Jesus Christ is *the* failure growing beautiful. At the center of it all is a cross, an empty cross, and an empty tomb, the great sign of Easter — all of it reminding us of the success of failure.

15. The Test

JOEL E. KOK

Whoever, therefore, thinks that he understands the divine Scriptures or any part of them so that it does not build the double love of God and of

15. There might even be a playful hint of this connection in the Letter to the Hebrews when first it describes the birth of Isaac to one who was "as good as dead" (11:12), and later speaks of God in the binding of Isaac as being "able even to raise someone from the dead" (11:19).

our neighbor does not understand it at all. Whoever finds a lesson there useful to the building of charity, even though he has not said what the author may be shown to have intended in that place, has not been deceived, nor is he lying in any way.

Augustine, *On Christian Doctrine*

For many students of the Bible, Genesis 22 portrays God's rejection of child sacrifice and Abraham's "miracle of faith."[1] However, many of these same students would agree that Genesis 22 also frightens readers and could be twisted to justify abuse.[2] What readers make of Genesis 22 will have much to do with their relationship to religious traditions rooted in the Scriptures.[3] This makes Genesis 22 instructive regarding the church's crisis of biblical interpretation.[4] Genesis 22 poses inescapable questions that call biblical students who want to serve the church to practice a tradition-informed hermeneutic of love.

To demonstrate this thesis, I will use the work of John Calvin to provide an example of traditional Christian exegesis of Genesis 22. I will also raise some of the questions this traditional interpretation leaves open and then turn to the Jewish tradition to see what difference a hermeneutic of love could make for the church. Finally, I will offer a biblical model for pastoral biblical interpretation.

1. Herbert G. May and Bruce M. Metzger, eds., *The New Oxford Annotated Bible with Apocrypha: An Ecumenical Study Bible, Revised Standard Version* (New York: Oxford University Press, 1977), footnote to Genesis 22:1-19. *The New Jerusalem Bible* offers a similar footnote.

2. Terence E. Fretheim, *The Book of Genesis: Introduction, Commentary, and Reflection,* in *The New Interpreter's Bible,* Vol. I (Nashville: Abingdon Press, 1994), p. 499.

3. For an exploration of this, see Edward T. Oakes, Review Essay of *Natural Law in Judaism,* by David Novak, in *First Things,* May, 1999, pp. 44-51.

4. See Richard John Neuhaus, ed., *Biblical Interpretation in Crisis: The Ratzinger Conference on Bible and Church* (Grand Rapids: Eerdmans, 1989), and Carl E. Braaten and Robert W. Jenson, eds., *Reclaiming the Bible for the Church* (Grand Rapids: Eerdmans, 1995).

Orientation[5]

John Calvin did not aim at originality in his interpretation of the Scriptures. Instead, while concentrating above all on the mind of the biblical writer, he selected and modified what he judged best from the exegetical tradition he inherited.[6] Calvin's particular contribution to that tradition was not ingenuity but, rather, a style of writing characterized by "lucid brevity."[7]

According to Calvin, the book of Genesis reveals material that outstrips human capacity of understanding.[8] Therefore, interpreters must approach Genesis with "a sober, docile, mild, and humble spirit."[9] Calvin warns against presumptuous scoffers who question God's revelation to Moses.[10] The inspiration of the Holy Spirit establishes the authority, credibility, and purity of the Mosaic writings.[11] Within this framework, Calvin exegetes very effectively.

In interpreting Genesis 22, Calvin is guided by the idea of "teachability."[12] For Calvin, Abraham's test is not primarily a matter of carnal passions or even "paternal grief and anguish."[13] Such human affections are part of the picture, but they are subordinate to Abraham's grief that "in the person of his son, the whole salvation of the world seemed to be extinguished and to perish."[14] The drama of the story is that Abraham's "very piety and religion filled him with distracting

5. This structure was suggested to me by the structure of Walter Brueggemann, *The Message of the Psalms: A Theological Commentary* (Minneapolis: Augsburg Publishing House, 1984).

6. See David Steinmetz, "Calvin and Patristic Exegesis," in *Calvin in Context* (New York: Oxford University Press, 1995), pp. 122-40.

7. John Calvin, "Dedication," in *The Epistles of Paul the Apostle to the Romans and to the Thessalonians,* ed. David W. Torrance and Thomas F. Torrance, trans. Ross Mackenzie (Grand Rapids: Eerdmans, 1961), pp. 1-4.

8. John Calvin, *Commentaries on the First Book of Moses, Called Genesis,* trans. John King (Grand Rapids: Eerdmans Publishing Company, 1948), p. 57.

9. Calvin, *Commentaries on the First Book of Moses,* p. 57.

10. Calvin, *Commentaries on the First Book of Moses,* p. 58.

11. Calvin, *Commentaries on the First Book of Moses,* pp. 58-59.

12. I apply "teachability" to Calvin on the basis of his own conversion narrative. See John Calvin, *Commentary on the Book of Psalms,* trans. James Anderson (Grand Rapids: Baker Book House, 1984), xl.

13. Calvin, *Commentaries on the First Book of Moses,* p. 559.

14. Calvin, *Commentaries on the First Book of Moses,* p. 560.

thoughts."[15] God seems engaged in a personal contest with Abraham and has issued a command that was "in a certain sense, the destruction of faith."[16] According to Calvin, God "in a certain sense, assumes a double character" by seeming to disagree with his own self-revelation in a repugnant way.[17] God himself attacks Abraham with his own word — "the very sword, with which he had been wont to arm us."[18] The horror of God's test is that Abraham "conceives God to contradict Himself."[19]

Calvin emphasizes Abraham's certainty that this command comes from God and is not some "fallacy of Satan."[20] The fact that God addresses Abraham by name means "there may be no doubt respecting the Author of the command."[21] Moses emphasizes "the word 'said,'"[22] and, therefore, for Calvin, "all occasion of doubt is removed."[23]

Calvin also emphasizes Abraham's "true subjection" to God.[24] Abraham exemplifies true faith because "he, without delay, and without disputation, would subject himself to the hand of God."[25] Abraham's obedience is also bolstered by his confidence in the resurrection and his memory of Isaac's humanly impossible birth.[26] But the key is that Abraham "was unwilling to measure, by his own understanding, the method of fulfilling the promise, which he knew depended on the incomprehensible power of God."[27] For this reason, God holds up Abraham as "an example by which he might call us to a general trial of

---

15. Calvin, *Commentaries on the First Book of Moses*, p. 560.
16. Calvin, *Commentaries on the First Book of Moses*, p. 560.
17. Calvin, *Commentaries on the First Book of Moses*, p. 561.
18. Calvin, *Commentaries on the First Book of Moses*, p. 562.
19. Calvin, *Commentaries on the First Book of Moses*, p. 564.
20. Calvin, *Commentaries on the First Book of Moses*, p. 561.
21. Calvin, *Commentaries on the First Book of Moses*, p. 561.
22. Calvin, *Commentaries on the First Book of Moses*, p. 562.
23. Calvin, *Commentaries on the First Book of Moses*, p. 561.
24. Calvin, *Commentaries on the First Book of Moses*, p. 562.
25. Calvin, *Commentaries on the First Book of Moses*, p. 562.
26. Calvin, *Commentaries on the First Book of Moses*, pp. 563-64. Calvin shares this perspective with other traditional Christian exegetes, such as the author of Hebrews and Martin Luther. For an evaluation of how this perspective is at once anachronistic and correct, see Brevard Childs, *Biblical Theology of the Old and New Testaments: Theological Reflections on the Christian Bible* (Minneapolis: Fortress Press, 1993), pp. 334-35.
27. Calvin, *Commentaries on the First Book of Moses*, p. 564.

faith."[28] Although Abraham's test is particular to Abraham, in principle it also applies to all believers; Calvin wants us to observe "that God tempts his servants, not only when he subdues the affections of the flesh, but when he reduces all their sense to nothing, that he may lead them to a complete renunciation of themselves."[29]

Disorientation

Within our regional seminar, responses to Calvin's interpretation of Genesis 22 ranged over a broad spectrum. Some expressed appreciation for Calvin's ecclesial orientation and faith-grounded reasoning. Others, though, found Calvin authoritarian and fideistic. Troubled by questions regarding whether Abraham actually heard God correctly and whether Genesis 22 offered a trustworthy depiction of either God or faith, they did not find Calvin's call to subjection and resignation adequate.

The point to emphasize is that seminar participants posed these questions to Calvin's interpretation and to Genesis 22 itself not from the perspective of hostility to the Christian faith, but from within the household of faith. The question this raised, then, was not how the church should respond to "the autonomous scholar whose private ideological commitment is disguised as objective scientific research,"[30] but, instead, how the church should respond to criticism and differences that emerge from its own life together. Although our seminar meetings were congenial, they included disagreements over issues that have profound implications and have divided churches. It is not too dramatic to apply Jesus' words: "one's foes will be members of one's own household" (Matt. 10:36).[31]

---

28. Calvin, *Commentaries on the First Book of Moses*, p. 564.

29. Calvin, *Commentaries on the First Book of Moses*, p. 564.

30. Carl E. Braaten and Robert W. Jenson, eds., *Reclaiming the Bible for the Church* (Grand Rapids: Eerdmans, 1995), p. xi.

31. Perhaps this observation has some accord with Jenson's statement, "I have not tried to load the blame for the Bible's alienation from the church on secular scholars but on the clergy and other churchly scholars like myself. Nobody else lost the Bible but we, and nobody else can reclaim it." Robert W. Jenson, "Hermeneutics and the Life of the Church," in *Reclaiming the Bible for the Church*, p. 105.

Reorientation

Novelist Chaim Potok offers guidance for dealing fruitfully with the disagreements and even enmity that characterize the church's interpretation of Scripture. Potok's second novel, *The Promise,* continues the story of the two main characters from his more famous first novel, *The Chosen.*[32] Through such exemplary characters, Potok holds out ways for not only Jews but also Christians (and, presumably, members of other religious traditions) to struggle creatively with difficulties within their tradition and the controversies that arise from them.

With respect to Genesis 22, for example, obedience to the Scriptures' command to love both God and one another enables us to question the text and to fight with one another but to do so "for the sake of Torah," or, in the church, for the sake of Christ. Combining such love with the kind of psychological introspection and scholarly knowledge exemplified by Potok will make for a spectrum of interpretations that challenge the church constructively. Consider the difference it would make, for example, if all exegetes of Genesis 22 combined scholarship, faith, and love with self-consciousness regarding the character of their relationships with their own parents, their religious traditions, and even with God. Perhaps this would help us give the *benefit* of the doubt to alternative views, to the Scriptures, and to God.[33]

For pastor-theologians, however, the ultimate model for facing the tests involved in biblical interpretation is Jesus Christ, and particularly Jesus tested in Gethsemane. In Gethsemane, Jesus bore the judgment for us, who were God's enemies. He questioned the Father but, out of love, followed God's strange way of salvation and "was heard because of his reverent submission" (Heb. 5:7). Perhaps pastors who shape their studies into Gethsemanes will be heard not only by God but also by believers like Augustine, who, after many prayers and tears, was led to confess, "I would not have believed the Gospel, unless the authority of the Catholic Church moved me."

32. Chaim Potok, *The Chosen* (Greenwich: Fawcett Publications, Inc., 1967), and *The Promise* (Greenwich: Fawcett Publications, Inc., 1969).
33. For the notion of how the benefit of the doubt may apply here, I am indebted to Cornelius Plantinga, Jr., "Convocation Sermon 1996," Calvin College. Plantinga states, "'Love the Lord your God with all your mind.' It means giving God the benefit of the doubt because we know the limits of our understanding."

16. The Founding Vision of Covenant Community

SAMUEL H. SPEERS

In a seminar during this past year, clergy colleagues and I have been reading Genesis 22, the account of Abraham's readiness to sacrifice his promised son Isaac in obedience to God's commandment. As if to underscore this readiness of Abraham, commentators often refer to the text as the *akedah*, the Hebrew term for binding, that is used in verse 9:

> there Avraham built the slaughter site
> and arranged the wood
> and *bound* Yitzhak his son
> and placed him on the slaughter-site atop the wood.[1]

In perhaps unique ways, this troubling story poses crucial questions about how people of faith are to understand biblical texts that seem to portray values that are offensive to contemporary moral sensibilities. For people of faith who read Scripture as the witness that reveals the character of God, the dilemma the *akedah* poses is whether or not a people of faith today wants anything to do with a God who can command a father to sacrifice his son.

At its center, the text reveals that to satisfy the ultimate test of his devotion to and love of God, Abraham is required to show his readiness to give up his promised son. His deadly act of child-sacrifice is stopped only after Abraham has "stretched out" his hand against his son. As Jon Levenson has argued, Genesis 22 makes all too explicit that "Abraham will have his multitude of descendants only because he was willing to sacrifice his son who was destined to beget them."[2]

Levenson has worked to place this story that is so strange to our

---

1. Genesis 22:9. Unless otherwise noted, all translations are taken from *The Schocken Bible, Volume I: The Five Books of Moses* (Genesis, Exodus, Leviticus, Numbers, Deuteronomy), ed. Everett Fox (New York: Schocken Books, 1995).

2. Jon D. Levenson, *The Death and Resurrection of the Beloved Son: The Transformation of Child Sacrifice in Judaism and Christianity* (New Haven and London: Yale University Press, 1993), p. 13.

modern ears in its context, a culture "profoundly imbued with the conviction that the first-born son belonged to God."[3] In his close reading of biblical texts, Levenson argues that the story of Genesis 22 is part of a larger biblical theology underlying potentially disturbing passages like Exodus 22:29b, where God commands, "You shall give Me the first-born among your sons." Such passages (see also Mic. 6:6-8) point to a theology that insists that "first-born sons, like the male first-born of animals and the first fruits of the soil, belong to YHWH [God]"; these first-born are not the father's right or property, but God's.[4] As Levenson argues, this ancient theology includes an understanding that the God of Israel has the authority (if not requirement) to command the sacrifice even of children, who are understood to belong first and foremost not to their human father, but to God.[5] Crucially, Levenson argues, this passage is one of a number of texts that point to the actual practice of child sacrifice not only in the Canaanite cultures denounced later by the prophets Jeremiah and Ezekiel, but in ancient Israel itself.

As contemporary biblical scholars note, perhaps the classic expression of modern objections to this story is Immanuel Kant's:

> There are certain cases in which man can be convinced that it cannot be God whose voice he thinks he hears; when the voice commands him to do what is opposed to the moral law, though the phenomenon seems to him ever so majestic and surpassing the whole of nature, he must count it a deception. . . . The myth of the sacrifice of Isaac can serve as an example: Abraham, at God's command, was going to slaughter his own son — the poor child in his own ignorance even carried the wood. Abraham should have said to this supposed divine voice: that I am not to kill my beloved son is quite certain; that you who appear to me are God, I am not certain, nor can I ever be, even if the voice thunders from the sky.[6]

3. Levenson, *Death and Resurrection,* p. 177.

4. Levenson, *Death and Resurrection,* pp. 15-16, 35.

5. Levenson, *Death and Resurrection,* p. 16. In referring to "human fathers" here, I keep the masculine language in order not to efface the patriarchal context of the narrative.

6. Cited in John J. Collins, "Faith Without Works: Biblical Ethics and the Sacrifice of Isaac" (unpublished article, University of Chicago). I am very grateful to Professor Collins for sharing this forcefully argued essay. Kant's statement here is also

R. W. L. Moberly responds to such criticisms by revealing how Kant's critique, founded upon his project of establishing a universal moral law, is one that lifts the *akedah* out of both its historical and narrative context. If many contemporary biblical scholars agree, as Levenson argues, that child sacrifice was once a part of ancient Israel's cult, there is lively debate about how this historical scholarship helps church and synagogue better understand the passage. On this question of interpretation, the crucial contribution of Levenson's work is not its historical anthropology but its scriptural hermeneutic, which traces the positive transformation of a "barbaric ritual into a sublime paradigm of religious life."[7] To summarize briefly, Levenson argues that the rituals of child sacrifice that were once a part of ancient Israel's cult were rooted out in practice, even as the *"religious idea"* (italics his) related to one aspect of such barbaric practice — "the donation of the first-born son" — was never fully abolished, even after Jeremiah and Ezekiel, Deuteronomy and the Holiness Code made the practice of child sacrifice no longer acceptable.[8] Thus Levenson contends that the *idea* behind Exodus 22:29b — "You shall give Me the first-born among your sons" — is transformed into a sublime paradigm that has proved profoundly generative and dynamic. Levenson's work traces the development of this paradigm — what he calls the myth of the loss and return of the beloved son — and the ways in which it informed Jewish and Christian scriptural writers in their efforts to understand their beginnings.[9]

As Moberly argues in support of Levenson's work, such interpretive

---

cited in R. W. L. Moberly, "Abraham in Genesis 22 as a Person Who Fears God," manuscript of a chapter from a forthcoming book. As cited in Moberly, Kant's statement is from *The Conflict of the Faculties,* trans. Mary J. Gregor (New York: Abaris, 1979).

7. Levenson, *Death and Resurrection,* p. x; see also Moberly, "Abraham in Genesis 22," p. 53.

8. Levenson, *Death and Resurrection,* p. ix.

9. Levenson, *Death and Resurrection,* pp. 45, 36-37. Levenson argues, for example, that Christian understandings of the Eucharist as Jesus' last meal before his atoning death cannot be understood apart from the Jewish history of interpretation regarding sacrifice. Levenson writes, "Both the Jewish and Christian systems of sacrifice come to be seen as founded upon a father's willingness to surrender his beloved son and the son's unstinting acceptance of the sacrificial role he has been assigned in the great drama of redemption." See Levenson, *Death and Resurrection,* pp. 174-75.

transformation of problematic practice into "new forms of metaphorical and symbolic modes of understanding" is a process that is "deeply characteristic of scripture and the faiths rooted to it."[10] Such an understanding reflects, as Moberly and Levenson contend in similar ways, a confidence that religious traditions have within them the resources for critical and constructive re-interpretation of their own practice and self-understanding. Rather than abandon (or try to erase from memory) what appears to be objectionable, biblical imagination turns to historical practices it now finds unacceptable, and discovers within them metaphorical insights that continue to have power for the community of faith. Arguing that metaphor is the "natural key" to the continuing use of such problematic practices, Moberly asks, "Why else would texts depicting child sacrifice . . . be edited and preserved at key points within the compilation of Israel's scripture, when the 'literal' practices were obsolete, unless the texts were understood as able still to be implemented even if in ways different from those previously envisaged?"[11]

John Collins has noted the ways in which Moberly's defense of the continuing revelatory power of Genesis 22 is an argument against a modern tendency to offer anachronistic critiques of biblical practice.[12] Kant's objections to the *akedah*, for instance, in their search for universal moral principles, presuppose that modern judgments concerning child sacrifice apply as well to ancient Israel.[13] Yet Collins responds to Moberly's critique of Kant as anachronistic by arguing that "anachronism is a two-edged sword." Collins continues, "[Anachronism] defends the ancient story from judgment by modern moral standards, but only at the cost of rendering it irrelevant to modern ethics."[14] According to Collins, the crux of the matter for contemporary interpreters of the *akedah* is that "the story affirms that God can demand child sacrifice and that it is praiseworthy for a person to comply with this demand."[15] To those who might argue that Abraham did not actually

10. Moberly, "Abraham in Genesis 22," pp. 53, 54.
11. Moberly, "Abraham in Genesis 22," p. 55.
12. Collins, *Faith Without Works*, p. 13. Collins is citing Moberly, *Genesis 12–50* (Sheffield: JSOT Press, 1992), p. 43.
13. Collins, *Faith Without Works*, pp. 13-14.
14. Collins, *Faith Without Works*, p. 14.
15. Collins, *Faith Without Works*, p. 15.

commit child sacrifice, Collins notes, as Levenson also has, that what makes Abraham worthy of praise is precisely his readiness to sacrifice his child. For Collins, such readiness is what renders the *akedah* problematic for people of faith today: "The faith of Abraham cannot be divorced from the deed he was willing to do, and consequently it cannot be invoked as a positive moral example for the modern world."[16] For Collins, "honest critical reflection" reveals the *akedah* as a "cherished part" of our Jewish and Christian heritage, and a "thought-provoking moral tale." Yet such reflection also renders the *akedah* a tale whose values contemporary Christians and Jews can only find "difficult . . . to affirm . . . without serious reservation."[17]

Collins is willing to say that "the most cogent" response to Kant's critique comes from those who point to the literary nature of the text.[18] Such narrative interpretations note the difficulty and inappropriateness of asking how it is that Abraham knew the voice he heard was God's. Such contact with God is simply integral to the narrative, and unquestioned. What is at stake here is not whether or not God is the one who calls, but what God's command and Abraham's response reveal about the "character of God" and the "nature of human life."[19] Collins is also willing to say, with Moberly, that the question about the truth, or otherwise, of the story cannot be answered except by engaging with the beliefs and values that the story portrays.[20] Where Collins and Moberly differ is in their assessment of whether the values of this story, once engaged, can be accepted by contemporary people of faith.

For Collins and others reticent to affirm the *akedah's* continuing relevance, much of the problem lies in the ways that belief in a God who can (or more precisely *could*) command child sacrifice is dehumanizing. It is not necessary to follow Kant's project for a universal moral law to find the values underlying the *akedah* objectionable and even dangerous. Yet placing the *akedah* in the context of the whole of Genesis suggests that such readings isolate the climactic and undoubtedly haunting episode of the narrative from all that has led up to it. As I have tried to show, the story of the binding of Isaac puts in sharpest relief the

16. Collins, *Faith Without Works*, p. 15.
17. Collins, *Faith Without Works*, p. 15.
18. Collins, *Faith Without Works*, p. 14.
19. Collins, *Faith Without Works*, p. 14.
20. Collins, *Faith Without Works*, pp. 14-15.

themes that have been at work throughout the narrative — questions of vision and promise, covenant and obedience, blessing and creation. The question that the *akedah* thus presses to its furthest possible extreme is the question of what makes Abraham's unflinching devotion to God in the *akedah* not only not immoral, but profoundly human.

If the *akedah* presents a set of values that seem inhumane to contemporary readers, the communities of faith that look to Genesis as a faithful record of their ancestors' encounter with God — that is, as Scripture — have discovered in this seemingly unbearable story the devotion that founded a whole new kind of human community. Indeed the point of the story, as the lavish blessing of its conclusion makes unmistakably clear, is precisely that Abraham's unflinching devotion is what makes him worthy to found an utterly new family through which God has chosen to relate to the whole world. The text makes explicit the causal connection between Abraham's "awe" or "fear" of God in not "withholding" his son, his "only-one," from God, and the blessing he receives. The messenger says:

> By myself I swear
> — YHWH's utterance —
> indeed, because you have done this thing,
>> have not withheld your son,
>> your only-one,
> indeed, I will bless you, bless you,
> I will make your seed many, yes, many. . . .

(22:16-17a)

This astonishing blessing is both an echo and a crucial development of the blessing that Abram receives in his first call in Genesis 12. For if Abram's blessing is seemingly inexplicable in chapter 12, in the *akedah* Abraham's blessing is the direct result of his devotion to God.

17. Exile and Slaughter: The Authority of Scripture

ROBERT W. DAHLEN

The core issues of this project raise questions about the authority of Scripture. What is the message we hear from the Bible? Why is it true or authoritative? How do we faithfully proclaim it?

What Is the Message?

The assignments for our meetings have been to explore a rationale behind our proclamation of Genesis 22 and/or St. Matthew's Passion. Over the past months we have read many thoughtful, insightful, and helpful studies of these texts. The problem with so many of the studies is that they are too narrow. Rather than raise broad issues of how a given text opens themes that lead to the rest of Scripture, they examine a pericope and its specialized language and imagery in such a way that isolates the text and its hearers. For example, most of the studies on Genesis 22, from Calvin to the Qur'an, come to focus on Abraham and his great example of a faithful life. They then move on to show how today's believers are his children either through a physical or spiritual descent, all the while avoiding the chapters that immediately precede and follow Genesis 22. But issues of canon and the unity of Scripture cannot be avoided. A key reality that informs the hearing and proclaiming of any text is that all of us are members of a community that has heard and continues to hear the witness of Scripture beyond the narrow confines of a given pericope. (See the Formula of Concord, *De Compendiaria, Regula Atque Norma.* Teaching and dogma are subject to the witness of Scripture.)

Anytime we begin a study or proclamation of a text, we need to be aware of how that text relates to what precedes and follows it, even if it takes us all the way from Genesis to Revelation. In spite of having generations of academically trained pastors and teachers, the communities that I have encountered, be they Reformed, Lutheran, Roman Catholic, or Anabaptist, speak of the authority and unity of the Bible, Scripture, and tradition rather than that of selected pericopes. We certainly understand that the Bible is an anthology assembled in its present form over a thousand-year history, and most of us are guided in our reading and witness by the norms of so-called "canons within the canon," but the unity of the Bible still holds us. It is this unity of Scripture that will in no small way shape our witness.

I have become convinced that what holds the Bible together is the power of its words and the images they create. To be sure, the Bible is a mixture of rhetorical and poetic imagery, short stories, epic dramas, liturgies, sermons, exhortations, and legal matters. But through the centuries communities of faith have treasured the unity of the book.

The Canadian critic Northrop Frye argues, "Wherever we stop, the unity of the Bible as a whole is an assumption underlying the understanding of any part of it." He then goes on to explain that the unity of the Bible is not based so much on a unity of doctrine as it is a "unity of narrative and imagery and what we have called implicit metaphor. . . . If we 'freeze' the Bible into a simultaneous unity, it becomes a single, gigantic, complex metaphor, first by tautology, in the sense in which all verbal structures are metaphorical by juxtaposition; second, in a more specific sense by containing a structure of significantly repeated images."[1] Given Frye's understanding, questions I tend to raise concerning the basic message within a given pericope, such as our texts from Genesis and Matthew, revolve around an appreciation of significant repeated images.

I suggest that there are two structured themes or metaphors that emerge from Genesis 22 and St. Matthew's Passion. The first is one having to do with the slaughter or sacrifice of the beloved child. The second image is but a twin of the first and relates to the people's repeated entry into exile and all its dangers. However, these themes of exile and slaughter are not the end of the story. For when the Bible lifts up the first two themes a third will always emerge, namely the intensification of God's promises to the people. However, to see these images at work, we need to go beyond a narrow pericope study and be open to a broader biblical witness.

Slaughter and exile are not the last words in these stories. For

---

1. Northrop Frye, *The Great Code: The Bible and Literature* (New York: Harcourt Brace Jovanovich, 1982), pp. 62-63.

within contexts of death, the people receive a consistent pattern of promise and blessing from their God. In the Day of Atonement liturgies, even as the goats and bull die, the promise is that Israel will be atoned and become "clean before the Lord" (Lev. 16:30). After Cain has slaughtered Abel and is declared to be a wanderer and fugitive, the Lord marks him and promises him protection. Cain goes on to become the father of nations while his parents, who have lost their sons, are blessed once more with the gift of fertility. Seth is born to Adam and Eve, and the people come to call on the name of the Lord (Gen. 4:14-25).

God's promises to Abraham that are articulated in Genesis 12:1-4, 15:7-21 and 17:1-8 continue even as the shadow of death hangs over him and his family. The cries of Hagar's son are heard and the angel of God tells her to "fear not . . . for I will make of him a great nation" and shows her a well of water (Gen. 21:17-20). (It is interesting to note that the Bible's first use of the phrases "angel of the Lord" and "a God of seeing" are in Genesis 16, when Hagar flees Abram's household after being mistreated by a jealous Sarai.) The promise to Abraham and the nations is spelled out one more time at Moriah, when Isaac is saved at the last minute (Gen. 22:15ff.), and even after Sarah dies, the reality of Abraham's promised fertility is so powerful that it must be acted out again. The old man takes Keturah as his wife and has six more sons (Gen. 25:1-6). So it is that Abraham "died in a good old age, an old man and full of years," his sons came together, buried their father, and he was indeed the father of many nations (Gen. 25:7-9).

In their exile of Egyptian slavery Israel becomes a mighty nation, and as God remembers his promises to the patriarchs the Exodus begins. Ruth becomes the great-grandmother of David the king. And even as the exiles find it impossible to sing the Lord's song by the rivers of Babylon, the promise is that a road will be established in the wilderness and they will return (Ps. 137 and Isa. 40). Jesus is raised from the dead, and comes to the disciples, thus bringing into being the community that is the church. Blessings continue even under the shadow of death.

I have become convinced that this pattern of God's continued blessing and promise within contexts of exile, slaughter, and death is the significant repeated image of the Bible. Simply put, the message is this: God's people will face death, and even then, God will bless them. The question before the interpreter of the Bible now becomes one of authority: If this is the message, why listen to it, let alone proclaim it?

Authority and Reality — What Is True?

The authority of themes of exile and slaughter comes from two contradictory sources. The first is their brutal and honest presentation of human existence. The second rises out of the intensification of God's promises. In order to see the authority of the second source, a deep appreciation of the first is needed.

Themes of slaughter, exile, and death are repeatedly presented in the Bible in formal sacrificial and liturgical terms. Abel's murder, Cain's exile, and the sacrifice of Isaac are framed within scenes of worship, and can be seen as extensions of a life of worship and revelation that also includes bloody animal sacrifices. The prophets describe the destruction of the Davidic kingdom and the entry into Babylonian exile as a crisis of faith and worship as well as the result of political and economic injustice.

That the Bible moves from scenes of slaughter and exile to sections dealing with ethics, genealogies, and politics with such ease is a problem for modern readers. We are not at all comfortable with a liturgy of death and exile. Jewish readers of Scripture have gathered for worship without bloody animal sacrifice since the destruction of Herod's temple. Christians, while they may talk a great deal about the death and blood of Christ, have made his sacrifice a thoroughly spiritualized matter in the Eucharist. How then is this theme of exile, slaughter, and promise authoritative? Some examination of the nature of sacrifice is needed here.

In more traditional views of bloody sacrifice, slaughter, and exile, there is an exchange between humanity and the divine. The death of the sacrifice and the disposal of its remains through ritual consumption provide a way for communication between humans and the divine. For example, the Lord regards Abel's offering of a lamb, has no regard for Cain's first fruits offering, and somehow communicates this to Adam and Eve's sons (Gen. 4:3-5). The Lord is pleased with the odor of burning flesh when Noah sacrifices one of every clean bird and animal after the flood, and because of this scent promises never to interrupt the cycle of the seasons again (Gen. 8:20ff.). With Abraham's offer of Isaac, the Lord sees the patriarch's faith and knows something about him that God seems not to have known before (Gen. 22:12). In the Day of Atonement liturgies, the sins of the community are placed on the goats, the animals are destroyed, and in the process the people's sins are taken away (Lev. 16). The prophets look upon exile as the means by which God speaks to the people of their unfaithfulness.

There is, however, another way of talking about sacrifice, one that in my opinion has a deeper authority and reality than concerns about communication. Michael Wyschogrod explores issues of sacrifice. His comments are brutal and horrific:

> Sacrificial Judaism brings the truth of human existence into the temple. It does not leave it outside the portals. It does not reserve sacred ground only for silent worship. Instead, the bruiting, bleeding, dying animal is brought and shown to God. This is what our fate is. It is not so much, as it is usually said, that we deserve the fate of the animal and that we have been permitted to escape this fate by transferring it to the animal. It is rather that our fate and the animal's are the same because its end awaits us, since our eyes too, will soon gaze as blindly as his and be fixated in deathly attention on what only the dead seem to see and never the living.[2]

Here sacrifice is not seen so much in terms of communication between humanity and the divine as it is a simple description of reality. People die — they are slaughtered. People are in many and various ways driven from their homes — they are exiled. Wyschogrod goes on to suggest that Judaism was able to survive the destruction of the Temple and the end of regular sacrificial communications with her God because the people at some level came to see themselves as the sacrifice. Sacrifice and exile are not simply about communications between God and humanity. They are reflections on human existence.

How can anyone who has lived through the twentieth century think in any other terms! This century began with a spark in the powder keg that was the Balkans. It has moved on through two world wars, countless political and economic revolutions, genocides, and all the rest, and now closes with a return to exile and slaughter in the Balkans. During the eight days of this year's Holy Week, the little Northwest Minnesota community where I live had three deaths, two ice

2. Michael Wyschogrod, *The Body of Faith: Judaism as Corporeal Election* (New York: Seabury Press, 1983), p. 19.

storms, a flood, and multiple power failures that drove people from their homes. All of this is happening as an ongoing agricultural crisis drives a few more farm families from their grandparents' homes every year.

(My oldest daughter also reminds me that in 1998 the film *Titanic* was seen by millions, if not billions. It told the passionate love story of a poor exile and a young woman living in a gilded cage, and everyone who saw the film knew from the beginning that the boat would sink. For all its romantic drivel, sweet music, and special effects, it was the sinking of the ship and little else that made for any truth in the film. Never forget: the boat sank!)

All this is enough to lead rational folks to despair. This is the way the world is. It's not a matter of if our children will face bad times; the question is simply, When will it happen, and what then? My grandpa used to say that in this life we could face one of two realities: We can bury our parents or they can bury us, and we pray to God that it would be the former rather than the latter. Themes of exile and slaughter have authority because they are true. The witness of the Biblical themes of exile and slaughter is true and authoritative because it does not avoid humanity's darkest reality.

In response to this darkness, the apostle Paul raises the rhetorical question, "What then shall we say to this?" and without skipping a beat he goes on to speak of how God's promise is such "that even while we are regarded as sheep to be slaughtered . . . in all these things we are more than conquerors through him who loved us" (Rom. 8:36-37). God gives the community of faith the promise of new life and blessings even as that community dies. The Bible says that this was true of Adam, Eve, and their children, it was true of Abraham and his family, it was true for the people of Israel in and out of times of exile, and it was true for Jesus and his disciples. The promise is that this good news will be and is true for you and me.

There is an authority deep within this promise that breaks through the reality of exile and slaughter. Four thousand years after Abraham and Isaac mounted Moriah, a community of faith still gathers to hear how the Lord provides the lamb. The very fact that this community is still with us speaks of the power of God's promise. Even after Egyptian slavery, after the fall of the Davidic kingdom, after Babylonian exile, after the Roman destruction of Herod's temple, after two thousand years of persecution from all quarters, the community that worships the God of Abraham, Isaac, and Jacob still gathers around the witness of the book. This is the mystery of Israel's continued existence, and there is a source of authority here. We listen to this Lord, not because of the Lord's ontological definition as God, but because the Lord saves. Isaac was saved, Israel walked through the waters of the Red Sea, the exiles returned, and even after Pontius Pilate and the crucifixion, the community that was so scattered at the death of Jesus became the body that proclaims his resurrection to the ends of the earth. Biblical themes of slaughter and exile are countered by themes of return and resurrection, both in the witness of Scripture and in the lives and hopes of the people who gather around the book.

Proclamation — Where Do We Go from Here?

The type of biblical interpretation that I have proposed thus far in this paper says that the Bible is true because it offers words and images that mirror our present reality. In other words, the Bible is true because it describes us. At the same time the witness is true because we see around us signs of the promised return and resurrection. To be sure, some of these signs are subtle, hidden, easily ignored, or explained away. From the outside, the continuation of two or three thousand years of Biblical worship and witness can be rationalized as an accident of history. But the community of faith picks up the book, hears its message, and says, "This is about us — we are the people who know death and exile and at the same time we are here because of return and resurrection."

People can and do stand on their heads to avoid some of these issues. Most people are able to live their day-to-day lives without too much worry about death and exile. But this reality still haunts us to the core of our beings: death defines us. As so many of my colleagues in aging suburban churches are finding out, the issue is not *if* they will face death and exile, but *when*. The challenge before the preacher and student of the Bible is to show how God's promises of return and resurrection also define the people of faith. For to be defined by the promise is to open up to something new and significant even as we live under the shadow of death and exile. As St. Paul says,

101

We were buried therefore with him by baptism so that as Christ was raised from the dead by the glory of the Father, we too might walk in newness of life. For if we have been united with him in a death like his, we shall certainly be united in a resurrection like his. (Rom. 6:4-5)

PART TWO

HOLY CHURCH

CHAPTER IV

TRINITARIAN DOCTRINE

Introduction

In the Holy Scriptures, "faith" can mean either our trust in God or our beliefs about God. While theologically distinguishable, the two are practically inseparable in Christian piety. The community of faith, first in Israel and later in the church, developed doctrinal statements that publicly served to distinguish it from the confused or opposing views of others. Already in the Scriptures, neither pantheism nor polytheism could coherently co-exist with the awesome claim: "Hear, O Israel: the Lord is our God, the God alone" (Deut. 6:4). Moreover, in opposing "the Word became flesh and lived among us" (John 1:14), Gnosticism and Arianism fared no better in the early church. More elaborate creeds followed, coupled inseparably with the church's scriptural calling to "worship God in spirit and truth" (John 4:24), as well as to "proclaim Christ crucified" as "the power of God and the wisdom of God" (I Cor. 1:23-24). Therefore, doctrine, worship, and proclamation will constitute our major concerns in the remaining chapters of this book as central interrelated responses to the Holy Scriptures in the holy church.

Turning first to doctrine, the excerpt from the essay on "Matthew's First Thousand Years" provides us with a historical survey of major patristic trends in the church's interpretation of the Matthean Passion narrative, including homilies of St. John Chrysostom in the East and patristic commentaries assembled by St. Thomas Aquinas in the West. These authors and preachers were concerned "to identify the rules communally operative in affirming the soteriological significance of the narratives of Christ," given the sometimes conflicting readings to which the Gospels are susceptible. Testimony is presented on the one Christ, both divine and human, as well as on the salvation effected by this Christ in both his natures. The complex witness of decisive scriptural texts is documented and analyzed.

This development finds an articulate and normative expression in the scholarship of "Irenaeus on the Rule of Faith." This selection stresses "the necessity of establishing the vocabulary of a common Christian discourse" to guide the church in its life and mission in an increasingly pluralistic culture; it claims significant parallels between the first three centuries of the church's life and our own. Irenaeus explored the inner relation among the church's Scripture, tradition, and authority for maintaining the integrity of Christian witness. Challenged especially by the Gnostics, he attempted to demonstrate the unity and continuity of the church throughout the ages as grounded in the testimony of the Holy Scriptures and summarized in the church's "rule of faith." This is the very heart of the Christian *kerygma* itself, a trinitarian credo that governs how we Christians are to read the Scriptures and shape our lives.

Employing a similar hermeneutical norm, the next selection deals with "Christ's Self-Sacrifice and Ours." The author summarizes our Lord's ministry in fulfilling the Old Testament's "threefold office" *(munus triplex)* of Prophet, Priest, and King. This inter-testamental model has obvious importance in the interpretation of the Jewish-influenced Matthean Passion narrative. If the New Testament is characterized as "fulfillment," it is the Old Testament that can best depict the preparation of that which is being fulfilled. First, as High Priest, Jesus overturns the provisional temple sacrifice by his own eternal self-sacrifice. Second, as King, Jesus rules God's eternal kingdom, that is not of this world, in the power of the Spirit. Finally, as Prophet, Jesus speaks the Word of God's judgment and mercy with a power that comes from his unique personal authority as Son of God among us.

The solidification of scriptural narratives and exhortations into formal and potentially conflicting "Atonement Theories" is developed in our next excerpt. The author advocates a "metaphorical theology" holding that each of the particular theories' attempts to explain the truth of Christ's atonement is important but only partial, significant but in need of complementary reinforcement from other views that address other concerns. The Reformation positions of Luther and Calvin, along with the later views of Arminius, Socinus, Grotius, Ritschl, and Schleiermacher, are all grounded in varying degrees of dependence on the three dominant doctrinal theories of the atonement: Christus Victor (patristic), Vicarious Satisfaction (Anselm), and Moral Influence (Abelard).

Finally, "God and the Doctrine of the Atonement" concentrates on the repudiation of the modern liberal orientation of Schleiermacher in the Neo-Orthodox reformulation of Anselm's monumental "Why did God become human?" by Karl Barth. Under the rubric "The Judge Judged in Our Place," Barth develops the Genesis 3 narrative of the fall of Adam and Eve in four interrelated dimensions: (1) Jesus Christ becomes the *Judge* in our place; (2) Jesus Christ becomes the Judge *judged* in our place; (3) Jesus Christ received the *judgment;* and (4) Jesus Christ was obedient to God the Father who judged *righteously.* Thereby reflecting Pauline fidelity, he teaches that "in Christ, God was reconciling the world to himself" (II Cor. 5:19).

18. Matthew's First Thousand Years

JONATHAN L. JENKINS

Ours is not the first generation to face the challenges of preaching on Matthew 26–27. It might come as a pleasant surprise, nonetheless, to discover that the patristic church wrestled with the problems of interpretation in a manner notable for its sophistication and wisdom. Three old and distinguished commentaries on Matthew are translated into English. The *Homilies* of John Chrysostom[1] and the *Catena Aurea*, a collection of patristic commentaries assembled by Thomas Aquinas, are

---

1. John Chrysostom, *Homilies on the Gospel of St. Matthew, The Nicene and Post-Nicene Fathers*, Series I, Vol. X (Edinburgh: T & T Clark, 1888), available from Christian Classics Ethereal Library (www.ccel.org).

readily available on the Internet.[2] In addition, Chrysostom Press has recently published Blessed Theophylact's *Explanation*.[3]

These three commentaries are the legacy, not of academic inquiry, but of generations of pastors preaching to their congregations. They offer a wealth of insights: careful examination of the literal and historical account of the Passion, as well as discussion of its place in the biblical drama as a whole and of morals to the story. One very prominent feature is close attention to what came to be called Christology. At first glance, certain terms and concepts might seem to be outdated, but the questions posed are central to any sermon: How are we to understand the handing over of Jesus Christ in Matthew 26–27? What sort of oneness was there, and is there, between God and this mortal human being?[4] As we learn how such questions were resolved in the first millennium, perhaps we can find renewal for preaching today.

For orientation, consider an explanation that is typical of the commentaries: "The darkness was universal, not partial, as was the darkness in Egypt, to show that the whole creation mourned the passion of the Creator. . . . He said, 'Why hast thou forsaken me?' to show that He was truly man and not just in appearance" (Theophylact, 28:45).[5] It is good to bear in mind that such statements are intended as explanation, as a series of judgments by which the parts are to be rightly related to

2. Thomas Aquinas, *Catena Aurea (Golden Chain), Patristic Commentary on the Gospel of St. Matthew* (London: Parker & Rivington, 1842), available from Christian Classics Ethereal Library (www.ccel.org).

3. Blessed Theophylact, *The Explanation of the Holy Gospel According to St. Matthew* (House Springs: Chrysostom Press, 1997).

4. Cf. David Yeago, *The Faith of the Christian Church*, Part I (Columbia: Lutheran Theological Southern Seminary, 1996), Chapter Six, "Jesus of Nazareth — God Become Flesh."

5. Each reference is to the author quoted (here, Blessed Theophylact) and to the chapter and verse cited from *Matthew* (here, 28:45). Theophylact (b. 1050, Greek Archbishop of Bulgaria) rarely cites his sources, but his purpose clearly is to pass on the tradition of the Eastern fathers. Quotations from Chrysostom (b. 347, Bishop of Constantinople) are found in the *Homilies*. The other quotations are from the collection gathered by Thomas Aquinas (b. 1225, Dominican theologian). They are, in order of citation: Jerome (b. 342, translator and exegete); Hilary (b. 315, Bishop of Poitier); Remigius of Auxerre (b. 841, philosopher); John of Damascus (b. 675, theologian); Origen of Alexandria (b. 185, theologian); Augustine (b. 354, Bishop of Hippo Regius); Ambrose (b. 339, Bishop of Milan), and Gregory I (b. 540, Pope). Remigius should be thought of as medieval, instead of patristic.

the whole of what is understood. "Given the sometimes conflicting readings to which the Gospels are susceptible," J. A. DiNoia observes in a similar context, "these theologians were concerned to identify the rules communally operative in affirming the soteriological significance of the narratives of Christ. Their faith in the unity of God's salvific purposes induced these theologians to strive to discern and exhibit the inner coherence, consistency, and complementarity of the narratives about Christ."[6]

To generalize in this vein, we can discern a number of the "rules" at work in the commentaries. A statement such as our introductory example is, first, an explanation primarily conceived in terms *of* the text, in its unity with the whole of Scripture, the liturgy, and the life of the church as organized around her bishops. Its explanatory power is not drawn from another frame of reference, nor is its plausibility directly accountable to the "rules" of some other community of interpretation. Second, it is intended as an explanation of what is going on *in* the text, not ideas imposed *on* the text, and thus is open to correction *by* the text. Third, it is an explanation that moves *through* the text in order to set forth the same Good News *from* the text. The commentaries reflect the naive (and for the church, essential) confidence that it is possible to say what the text is saying, to preach Matthew's Gospel "in other words."

One Christ, Divine and Human

The Christological burden of the commentaries consists in answering the questions: who and what is Jesus Christ in Matthew's Passion? The response of the commentaries is unanimous and twofold. He is "God the Son" (Jerome, 26:38), the "eternal *logos* of God" (Hilary, 27:46). He is "the Son of Man," also, "because his human nature could suffer and die" (Remigius, 26:25). "You have him complaining that he is left to death, and thus he is man; you have him as he is dying declaring that he reigns in Paradise; and thus he is God" (Hilary, 26:46).

How do these two identifications fit together? What are the characteristics of each and how do they form one character in the drama? Fur-

6. J. A. DiNoia, O.P., review of John Meier's *A Marginal Jew*, *Pro Ecclesia* 2 (Winter 1993): 123.

thermore, what difference does it make to our preaching of salvation that Jesus, in being handed over to us in death, is "Son of God" and "Son of Man"? After we consider their explanations to these questions, we will examine the accuracy of the commentators' use of Matthew's titles. These commentaries are a reminder to preachers that Jesus is what God is, and he is what we are, "for the One Christ is both God and Human" (Damascene, 26:38).

The Passion is to be read, insist the commentaries, in recognition of Christ's divine nature. What the attributes of the divine nature are is presupposed. "Note his knowledge of things to come," for example, "how though about to suffer death within two days, he knows that his Gospel will be preached throughout the whole world" (Jerome, 26:13). Similarly, Jesus sent the disciples to "some person unknown to them, teaching them thereby that he was able to avoid his Passion. For he who prevailed with this man to entertain him, how could he not have prevailed with those who crucified him, had he chosen not to suffer?" (Chrysostom, 26:19). It is evidence of the wickedness of Judas that he "would not believe in the One who knew his heart" and "supposed" his action "was hid from Christ, deeming him man, which was unbelief" (Origen, 26:25). "As God, he foretells what will be" (Theophylact, 26:31). He displayed his divine foreknowledge and free consent to what was happening in order to "comfort" the disciples, so that they "might not think that it was through weakness that he suffered" (Chrysostom, 26:19). Likewise, he showed them that events were proceeding "as it is written of him," because "all that he suffered had been foretold by the Prophets" (Remigius, 26:25).

Today an exegete might question whether these actions are intended (in Matthew) to be evidence of divinity or even of extraordinary human knowledge. Is it necessarily divine foreknowledge that enables Jesus to make the prediction of his crucifixion (26:1-2) or only common sense? (Arguably, we might detect some resemblance to the "powerful acts" that indicate divine authority elsewhere in Matthew — cf. 17:24-27.) In any case, such signs of Jesus' divine nature are offered less as proof and more as illustration, that everything Jesus does and suffers derives from one of the Trinity. A "rule" for preaching could be formulated thus: we are to be telling the Passion story in such a way that *God* is the subject (who is never without his Son and the Holy Spirit) — doing and suffering these things.

"As he began to have fear and sorrow, he prays accordingly that the cup of his Passion may pass from him, yet not as he wills, but as his Father wills; wills, that is, not according to his divine and impassible substance, but according to his human and weak nature. For in taking upon him the nature of human flesh, he fulfilled all the properties thereof, that it might be seen that he had flesh not in appearance only, but in reality" (Origen, 26:44)

The commentaries affirm that Christ is fully human, in body, soul, and will. The Passion is not intelligible without this affirmation. "He was sorrowful and heavy in accord with the divine plan, so as to confirm that he was truly man. For it is human nature to fear death" (Theophylact, 26:39). "He was truly like us in all respects, but without sin" (Theophylact, 27:48). Jesus "desired food, drink, and sleep, by which life is supported, and naturally used them, and contrariwise shunned the things that are destructive of life. Hence in the season of his Passion which he endured voluntarily, he had the natural fear and sorrow for death" (Damascene, 26:38).

We might wonder if the "rule" is consistently applied in every instance, but we are reminded repeatedly that Jesus Christ is nothing less than a real human being. "Overthrown are the Manichaeans, who said that he took an unreal body; and those also who said that he had not a real soul, but his divinity in place of a soul" (Remigius, 26:38). The commentaries express ideas that could be read as a principle for sermons: the way *God's* personal identity comes to be established — for the Triune God and for the world — is biographical, as narrated in a course of events that is completed in death.

So who is Jesus Christ? Are his divine characteristics ever separable from what is characteristic of him as one of us? Is Christ "sometimes" only human and "other times" only divine? Does he have one, consistent identity and personality?

The point of the commentaries is to insist that Christ is only one character, a single actor of whom this drama is told. "Mark how he, that is ordained by the Father to be the Judge of the whole creation, humbled himself, and was content to stand before the judge of the land of Judea, and to be asked by Pilate either in mockery or doubt, 'Are you the King of the Jews?'" (Origen, 27:11). The person in question, the "self" who endures and does these things, is the Word of God. "Ah me! God is stretched out before man, and he, in whom not one trace of sin can be discerned, suffers punishment as a malefactor" (Chrysostom, 27:26). Such a statement is incomprehensible unless Christ's human existence is the direct, personal expression of the Son of God. "It was the Creator who suffered" (Theophylact, 27:51).

The explanations we are given are self-limited. They explicate what Matthew says happened, not the mystery of *how* the Creator could suffer and die.[7] "Although he died as man, and his holy soul was separated from his unstained body, yet his Godhead remained inseparate from either body or soul. Yet was not the one Person divided into two; for as both body and soul had from the beginning an existence in the Person of the Word, so also they had in death. For neither soul nor body had ever a Person of their own, besides the Person of the Word" (Damascene, 27:50). We are not to speak of Christ as having a "split" personality in Matthew's Passion, one time showing a "divine side" and another time a "human side" — perhaps even in opposition to each other. The Son of God's particular identity was — and for all the future is — enacted in and through the historical circumstances of his bodily life and death. A "rule" thus yielded for preaching is, we are never to speak of God as someone other than "the Father" of the crucified Jesus, nor are we to speak of "the Spirit" as someone other than the One who witnesses to and glorifies the crucified Jesus.

What Is Salvation?

The question of "who" and "what" Jesus Christ is, in Matthew, is linked directly to the question of what is accomplished in his Passion. What benefit is handed on to the church as Christ is handed over to death? An act of justice is required, explains one commentator, that is dependent on Christ's two natures. The "cause" or purpose of the cross "was that he might abolish with yet more justice the sentence of death which he had with justice passed. For as the first man had by guilt incurred death through God's sentence, and handed down the same to his posterity, so the second Man, who knew no sin, came from heaven that death might be condemned, which when commissioned to seize the guilty, had presumed to touch the Author of sinlessness. And it is no

---

7. Pointed out in Yeago, *Faith of the Christian Church*, p. 123.

wonder if for us he laid down what he had taken from us, his life, namely, when he has done other so great things for us, and bestowed so much on us" (Augustine, 27:50).

Interestingly, the "sentence of death" is not reversed by means of a payment of some sort, but because death committed the supreme act of "lèse majesté" when it "presumed" to "touch" Christ. Jesus Christ, it seems, has the perfect right to relieve death of its duties and office. As David Yeago observes, his *divine* "freedom" is precisely the freedom to die a *human* death which, being *divine*, overcomes death and sin in a way that no merely *human* death is able.[8]

What is more, the nature of salvation itself is defined by the two natures of Christ and his personal history. "Wherefore should we be offended that Christ came from the bosom of the Father to take upon him our bondage, that he might confer on us his freedom; to take upon him our death, that we might be set free by his death; by despising death he exalted us mortals into God, counted them of earth worthy of things in heaven? For seeing the divine power shines forth so brilliant in the contemplation of its works, it is an argument of boundless love, that it suffers for its subjects, dies for its bondsmen. This then was the first cause of the Lord's Passion, that he would have it known how great is God's love to man, who desired rather to be loved than feared" (Augustine, 27:50).

Augustine means that salvation is more than liberation from sin and death. The Passion is the enactment of God's personal identity in such a way that "mortals" are "exalted into" God, whose triune life is "boundless" love.[9] Preachers are to make it clear that Christ's death is much more than an impressive illustration of loving intentions that God has in any case, even without the cross. Salvation is communion *with* God in the freedom of love that *is* God through the story of the Son *of* God.

---

8. Yeago, *Faith of the Christian Church,* pp. 139-40.

9. In Augustine's doctrine of the Trinity, God is Love; "Father, Son, and Spirit" corresponds with "Lover, Beloved, Act of Love."

19. Irenaeus on the Rule of Faith

DAVID HENDERSON

As we conclude the millennium, the church finds itself in transition. Whether we speak of living in a post-Christian or post-Constantinian era, the challenges that confront the church in our time are many, and they are great. There is a crisis surrounding the church's identity, its mission and proclamation. Any number of social or ethical issues threaten to bring mainline denominations to schism. Among the laity, there is what may be described as a wholesale loss of commitment to, or confidence in, the national structures of denominations. There is a retreat into a kind of isolationist congregationalism with an accompanying loss of any clear idea of what it means to be a member of the holy catholic and apostolic church. Responses to the present situation confronting the church have tended to be ideological and polarizing. On one side, there is a reactionary move to a naive biblicism that neither deals honestly with the text nor speaks to the development of a coherent Christian worldview in the present context. On the other side, there is a detachment from the biblical witness itself that leads to a deconstruction of Christian identity.

In this seminar, we have struggled over the issue of how we might recover biblical authority in the life and work of the church. I suggest that at the heart of this discussion is the necessity of establishing the vocabulary of a common Christian discourse, by which we may achieve some minimal consensus with regard to who we are as church and by what and whose authority we live and move and have our being. I find it ironic that within the contemporary model of "dialogue" as a means of establishing communion, there persists a veritable Babel in our frenzied effort to erect monuments to our own ideological positions. Before there can be any recovery of unity, before there can be any renewal of the life and ministry of the church, we need a shared language. Much of the current division within our denominations exists due to failure to articulate clearly the parameters that establish our identity and purpose. We find ourselves either advocating or attacking particular positions without having first established the foundational terms of debate.

In our discussions this year, we have identified the need and desire to articulate what a "Christian reading" of the Scriptures might look like in an effort to recover biblical authority for the reform and renewal of the church. The canonical Scriptures, the formative texts for the church's life and identity, are the basis for the development of a common discourse. But the Scriptures are not read in isolation or detachment from the life of the church. They are to be read ecclesially, which means there are certain foundational presuppositions we bring to our reading that must be established prior to any debate on particular issues confronting the church. This prior move has been lacking in the current conflicts within our various denominations.

What has been termed "the Rule of Faith" is the set of hermeneutical presuppositions, derived from the canon itself, that have been employed throughout the history of the church in its effort to come to terms with what the church should teach and how it should live. The Rule of Faith is what the church has believed at all times and all places. It is not a static set of dogmatic assertions; rather, it is the very heart of the *kerygma* itself that informs how we read the entire canon of Scripture and allow Scripture to shape our lives. It is fundamentally Christological, insofar as the Rule of Faith points to the person and work of Jesus Christ as the hermeneutical key to our study of the entire canon.

It has become somewhat commonplace of late among historians to draw striking parallels between the first three centuries of the church's life and the contemporary situation. Issues surrounding how the church defines its life and mission in a pluralistic culture are not unknown in the history of the church. We are not so much entering new territory as finding ourselves in a period of transition to a context very much like the pre-Constantinian world. It is therefore instructive to examine how the church in the early centuries defined its proclamation and struggled to maintain its identity in an environment that was often hostile to the particularity of the Gospel message. Irenaeus, in his confrontation with Gnosticism, illuminates the relationship between Scripture, tradition, and authority, and how these function together to maintain the integrity of Christian witness.

With Irenaeus, we witness the beginnings of a canon of New Testament Scriptures. Irenaeus bears witness to the fact that, early on, this development posed a problem for the Christian interpretation of Scripture that was new in kind and of crucial importance in the battle against Gnosticism. Previously, the burden of Christian interpretation was simply that all of Scripture pointed to Christ as its end. The task had become more complex. Against the Gnostics, it remained to be demonstrated that the Hebrew Scriptures and the writings that contained the gospel formed a complete unity. This demonstration was needed to refute those who would recognize only those parts of the Old Testament that seemed to agree with the New, along with those who would remove parts of the New Testament according to their interpretation of its meaning. Above all, it had to be demonstrated that there was a continuity of the Scriptures from beginning to end along with a radical newness to the gospel.

For this last purpose, especially, a principle of non-literal interpretation was needed whereby the end could be seen in retrospect to have been in some way present in the beginning of the scriptural story. With Irenaeus, we see the development of a conception of the integral form of Scripture as a whole, along with the conditions that such a conception must fulfill. Irenaeus' understanding of Scripture as set forth in *Adversus Haereses* led to the employment of the "Rule of Faith" as a hermeneutical principle governing the whole of Christian doctrine and belief.

Irenaeus provides several descriptions of the "Rule of Faith." One of the most typical of these is given in Bk. I:10, 1, in the context of a discussion of the doctrinal unity of the church:

> The church, though dispersed throughout the whole world, even to the ends of the earth, has received from the apostles and their disciples this faith: [She believes] in one God, the Father Almighty, Maker of heaven, and earth, and the sea, and all things that are in them; and in one Christ Jesus, the Son of God, who became incarnate for our salvation; and in the Holy Spirit, who proclaimed through the prophets the dispensations of God, and the advents, and the birth from a virgin, and the passion, and the resurrection from the dead, and the ascension into heaven in the flesh of the beloved Christ Jesus, our Lord, and His [future] manifestation from heaven in the glory of the Father "to gather all things in one," and to raise up anew all flesh of the whole human race.

This trinitarian confession of faith, one of several found in Irenaeus and similar to others among the early church Fathers, purports to be the faith received from the apostles. As such, it is the faith that the church proclaims throughout the whole world. The church is one by virtue of its universal preaching of this faith. It was such a profession of belief that every catechumen recited before baptism, embodying in summary form the faith that the apostles had taught and committed to their disciples after them. This profession was substantially the same everywhere, although the actual phrasing varied from place to place. It was the indispensable guide in the understanding of Scripture and the ultimate warrant of right interpretation.

The church was not an external authority that could be the judge over Scripture, but was rather the keeper and guardian of that divine truth which has been deposited in Holy Writ. The Rule of Faith was intimately related to the sacrament of Christian initiation. It was the rule to which believers committed themselves, and into which they were initiated at baptism. This Rule of Faith was, for Irenaeus, nothing other than the truth that the apostles had deposited in the church and entrusted to her, to be continuously handed down by the succession of pastors, under the abiding guidance of the Holy Spirit.

Unpacking Irenaeus' version of the Rule of Faith, we may observe the following:

1. The church throughout the world confesses one God, almighty Father and Creator.
2. The church confesses one Jesus Christ. Contrary to Gnostic teaching, Jesus Christ is not a provisional mixture of radically different realities. He is one person, both God and man. He is the Son of God, but he is also the incarnate one.
3. The church confesses the work of the Holy Spirit. The Spirit was the one by whose means the prophets predicted the dispensations of God, the various events surrounding Christ's consummation of the Old Testament. Here we see that the Spirit establishes the identity between the Old Testament era and the New Testament. The essence of the Old Covenant is promise; that of the New Testament, fulfillment. Christ is the Lord of both the Old and the New. History is united under his lordship. The essence of Christ's redeeming work, as the article reads, is the recapitulation of all

117

things. This implies the resurrection of all humanity. Christ "reca-pitulates" not merely the soul or spirit; his work is universal and encompasses all flesh.

Such is the content of the apostolic faith, upon which common confession is based the doctrinal unity of the church, and through which the Scriptures, both Old and New Testaments, are interpreted. According to Irenaeus, without this doctrinal unity at the level of the Rule of Faith — that core set of beliefs regarding the Triune God and the person and work of Jesus Christ — the faith is distorted and cor-rupted. The church is the place in which this faith is constantly re-newed by the action of the Holy Spirit, and is thus constantly illumi-nating God's revelation to humanity.

20. Christ's Self-Sacrifice and Ours

GEORGE SUMNER

Just as Jesus has traditionally been considered with respect to his "threefold office" *(munus triplex),* so we will consider three themes in the Passion narrative itself. As Priest, Jesus is first of all the one who overturns temple sacrifice at the same time that he, in the language of Hebrews, offers, as the true priest after Melchizedek, the eternal sacri-fice. Before Pilate he promises to tear down and rebuild the temple in three days, a claim that helps to lead to the crucifixion itself. At the cli-max of the story, at the moment of Jesus' death, the temple curtain is rent in two, signaling the end of its role in the history of salvation. The story connects this closely with the rending of the grave, the beginning of eschatological release of new life out of death for the whole earth.

If one thinks of the purpose of sacrifice itself as just this release of the power of life, then this second rending has the effect of realizing the true and final sacrifice even as the provisional sacrifice of the Passover lamb in the temple is concluded. More generally, this is the effect of the narrative as a whole, that the sacrifice mandated by God is at once transformed and fulfilled even as its prior form comes to an end. The retelling of the narrative often takes place in a liturgical context, so that the hearer is engaged in a practice constituted by a story that at once undercuts any notion of offering therein, even as it describes the real and ever-present sacrifice. The narration of the story of the dying Jesus, High Priest, is for the telling and hearing church one of dissolution and reconstitution.

In our consideration of Jesus going to his death as the King, we can enlist the help of Hans Frei, who argues that the Passion narrative may be seen simultaneously as a transition for Jesus from power to powerlessness and a transition from intention to action, which is to say, a consistent enactment of his identity. Frei proceeds to tie this transition to the Chalcedonian confession of Jesus as God and human, for Jesus' transition to powerlessness is also the process by which "the initiative of Jesus disappears more and more into that of God" until his resurrected appearance, when the initiative is all God's, and the identity marking that initiative is all Jesus'.[1]

Now if we consider the resurrection as the final and complete manifestation of divine power, then several conclusions concerning human power follow. The risen Christ is believed to be present with the believers as they gather and hear. This power is tied to their recognition of this particular Jesus, made known in this story. No account of power, or access thereto, is possible independently of this present Jesus. At the same time, the terms in which power is spoken of utterly confound any human notion or calculus, since the act of divine power coincides with utter abandonment. Power is given to the church by the risen One precisely and only at the moment when the church realizes how alien and unalterable is its form in Christ: "the humiliation of God shows the super-abundance of His power, which is in no way fettered in the midst of conditions contrary to its nature . . . the greatness is glimpsed in the lowliness and its exaltation is not thereby reduced."[2] Here too, as the church gathers to pray, and then disperses to live its life in the world, its very act is systematically undercut and restored, on the basis of a strength that it can never reproduce nor even comprehend.[3]

1. Hans Frei, *The Identity of Jesus Christ; the Hermeneutical Bases of Dogmatic Theology* (Philadelphia: Fortress, 1975), p. 121.

2. Gregory of Nyssa as quoted in Hans Urs von Balthasar, *Mysterium Paschale* (Edinburgh: T&T Clark, 1990), p. 34.

3. The powerless King and the slain Priest merge if we consider the opening

The third office of Christ is that of Prophet, and here too, with respect to the fulfillment of the Word, the very course of the Passion story involves both the "plucking up and planting" of the listening church (Jer. 1). When Jesus counsels the disciples in the Garden to watch attentively, this advice is also addressed to the reader-disciple. Likewise, the command to take and eat a share of Jesus' death is at once a reminder that the disciples do not share that death, and, nonetheless, an invitation into its blessings — and all this pertains to the communing reader as well.

The narrative of the cross of Jesus generates Christian self-understanding in the patterns we have described. But no matter how subtle and dialectical we might describe these patterns to be, we must always bear in mind the danger of blunting their power precisely as we pay attention to it, for to intellectualize it is to domesticate it.[4] For each of these patterns, priestly or kingly or prophetic, conveys, at a most basic level, the profound affront to all thought, all system, all assimilation into human projects that is the cross. "But we preach Christ crucified, a stumbling block to Jews and folly to Gentiles, but to those who are called . . . the power of God and the wisdom of God" (I Cor. 1:23-24). The patterns of judgment and recognition we have mentioned ought, when properly understood, to point in the same direction: this cross is the end of human theorizing at the same time that it insists on being the beginning of all Christian reflection. In other words, the story of the cross constitutes identity in that it undercuts and renders provisional; it is the means of the divine breaking down, even as it constitutes and defines.

We can put the matter more positively: the narrative is so constructed that, in the moment we see Jesus dying as the active agent, the true Prophet, Priest, and King, in this very same moment of perception we know ourselves to be displaced, we perceive ourselves to be disqualified from these tasks. And this joyful and displacing perception is the way in which the story constitutes Christian identity. Now the next step is to see that the Christian life is so designed that the activities in which

---

scene of the Passion, the anointing in Bethany in the house of the leper. Jesus becomes king even as he is defiled, and this defiling requires, according to the Torah, the destruction of the house in which the defiled one, the man of sorrows, dwells (Lev. 14).

4. See Gerhard Forde, *Christian Dogmatics* (Philadelphia: Fortress, 1984), 2:79ff.

we take part are, in their form, what we cannot do: offering, ruling from twelve thrones, speaking God's Word.

Here an example may serve our purpose better. In the Cranmerian rite the celebrant stands before the people, and states that he or she is not and cannot do any sacrifice, that the one, true, and only eucharistic "sacrifice, oblation, and satisfaction" has been made, and that we are gathered only for a "sacrifice" of response to our blessed disability. This is a different and subtler response than either the notion that we can offer our gifts now (even with the qualifier of the empowerment of the Holy Spirit) or that we can simply refuse to take part in any such activity.

The liturgy acts out the self-understanding laid out in the scriptural narrative insofar as it presents itself as that "non-sacrifice" that follows from Jesus' sacrifice and engenders lives of "the sacrifice of praise and thanksgiving." The give and take, the dialectic of sacrifice and non-sacrifice, takes place as the liturgy acts out what it cannot in fact do. Its action is a counter-sign, as well as a pointer, that the ultimate counter-sign, the One greater than Jonah or Solomon, is here.

In the early church, the *Pascha* was a single celebration of the crossing over of Christ from death to life, a single narration encompassing death and resurrection. It is only in the light of the story's conclusion, the restoration to life of Jesus by the Father, that everything preceding, especially the crucifixion, must be understood. So in the wake of the resurrection, the disciples are given the gifts of the Holy Spirit and a taste of the future life in the close company of the Father and his Son, the wounded Lamb (Rev. 5). But the narrative would be misunderstood, and so too the personhood of Christians who hear it, if we were to suppose that what is taken away with one hand, the first part of the story, is simply given back with the other, its conclusion. For such a view would overlook the fact that the risen Christ alone holds the keys to Death and Hell (Rev. 1:18). He must give these gifts, and he gives them to the recently traitorous disciples. And the gifts are consistent with being led where one does not wish to go (John 21:18).

In short, these blessings too are inextricably linked to the Giver, and their handing-over equally inextricably located after the crucifixion with all that it implies about Jesus' followers. Only with these dramatic relations in mind can one have "humble access" to the true nature of the empowerment following the resurrection. In fact, the nature

121

of the story is such that the resurrected Christ, who hands us our personhood in communion with the Triune God, always does so from "ahead" of us, always gives us what we do not yet have but are called to reach for (Phil. 3:14), always assures that Christian personhood, defined by the crucifixion in terms of what it is not, is also defined by the resurrection, by who Jesus in his generosity already is.

It is only in this context that we can understand much that is written about Christian personhood in the image of God as derivative of the persons of the Trinity.[5] Theologians will sometimes derive human communality of human love from the Trinity. Likewise the Christian life is sometimes conceived as an invitation into participation in the triune divine life. Sometimes this is characterized as a "Johannine" as opposed to a "Pauline" perspective (though with considerable simplification of both authors). Such a view runs the risk of an easy triumphalism. All the "storm and stress," the costliness of God's redemption of us, seems to be jettisoned. This language of triune derivation and triune participation is, on the other hand, quite appropriate, so long as its location, linked to but subsequent to the crucifixion story, is borne in mind.

Maligning analyses of the contemporary church are tiresome, but this much is clear: ours is a church altogether open to Luther's critique of being a church befogged with a "theology of glory" *(theologia gloriae)*. Conversely, the decision to focus our attention on the Passion narrative so as to reclaim the Scripture for the church *(pro ecclesia)* implies that the church recover its "theology of the cross" *(theologia crucis)*.

---

5. See, for example, the rich and helpful treatment of the subject in Colin Gunton and Christoph Schwoebel, *Persons Divine and Human: King's College Essays in Theological Anthropology* (Edinburgh: T&T Clark, 1991).

21. *Atonement Theories*

JAMES KITCHENS

The final lines of the children's nursery rhyme, *Humpty Dumpty*, leaves poor Humpty in bad shape:

> All the king's horses and all the king's men
> couldn't put Humpty together again.

The church — at least from the perspective of most Christians in the pew and not a few pastors in the pulpit — is in similarly sad shape when it comes to its theology. The laity tries to grasp even a sliver of understanding of the disputes in our national governing bodies and ends up in despair. From a lay perspective it appears that no one can say, with any certainty, what a Christian is supposed to believe. Pastors have little better luck trying to make sense of the debates within the academy at the same time they are being forced into propositional corners by the doctrinal debates tearing apart most mainline American denominations.

Especially since the beginning of the modern era, the church has experienced an accelerating process of the fracturing of theology. In our hearts, many of us in the church fear that Robert Bellah and his colleagues may have indeed seen the future when, in *Habits of the Heart*, they conclude their interview with a young woman named Sheila by talking of "Sheilaism" as the ultimate form of individualized religion: each person living out of his or her own idiosyncratically developed faith.

The question I begin with, then, is this: using atonement theory as a case study, is there a methodological approach that can allow us to account for and incorporate the multiple perspectives we hear in any theological debate and yet still give us hope for an essential unity to the church's message about Jesus Christ? Is there a way to reframe the current conversation about atonement so as to take serious note of the critiques offered by contemporary theologians and yet find enough common ground to move into the future as one Body of Christ? If it is

123

possible to make such a case in the instance of the doctrine of atonement, then it could serve as a heartening case study for the church. It might shift our metaphor for theological reflection in the church from that of battlefield to that of dialogue among brothers and sisters equally dedicated to the cause of Christ.

In another way of stating the issue: if the dawning of modernity resulted in a conceptual "big bang" in general, and a theological "big bang" in particular, might the dawning of the postmodern era result in a corresponding "big crunch" in which the scattered shards of theological reflection might cohere into a unified (albeit more complex than before) understanding of the biblical narrative?

Starting with the Crucifixion

If we are to employ the scientific analogy of the "big bang" theory, we have to move behind the dawning of the modern era to find the "point of singularity" from which all theories of the atonement diverge. That point is, of course, the crucifixion itself, that point in human and salvation history when Jesus of Nazareth was executed in the first century C.E. in Palestine. All reflection on the meaning of his death as the Christ begins from that historical fact (we will here simply accept the historicity of Jesus' death on the cross, rather than argue for it). This does not mean that we should not take seriously the painful critique of the cross offered by some feminist theologians. It does, however, mean that we cannot jettison this most incontrovertible fact of the Christian faith — the death of Jesus on a cross — in order to take account of such critique.

While it took until the modern era for the church's reflection on the meaning of the death of Jesus on a cross to shatter so thoroughly, there were from the earliest days of the church divergent ways of talking about its meaning. The fact that the church preserved at least five different ways of talking about the crucifixion, Paul's epistles and the four gospels, is indication of that early divergence. Prior to the Reformation, these divergent understandings of the work of Christ coalesced into three dominant theories of the atonement: the patristic theory of the defeat of Satan, Anselm's formulation of atonement as satisfaction, and the moral influence theory of Abelard.

Reformation Refinements

Luther never attempts to develop a systematic theory of the atonement. He comes closest to doing so in his commentary on Galatians 3:13, wherein he links together the incarnation, death, and resurrection of Jesus:

> So in one person he joineth God and man together, and being united unto us which were accursed, he was made a curse for us, and hid his blessings in our sin, in our death, and in our curse, which condemned him and put him to death. But because he was the Son of God, he could not be holden of them, but overcame them, (led them captive) and triumphed over them; and whatsoever did hang upon the flesh, which for our sake he took upon him, he carried it with him. Wherefore all they that cleave unto this flesh, are blessed and delivered from the curse, that is, from sin and everlasting death. (Luther's *Commentary on Galatians*)[1]

More often, Luther is content to speak of a "happy exchange" or a "wondrous exchange" which takes place on the cross, "in which Christ accepts our sin and death, and we receive his righteousness and life."[2]

Calvin takes a more systematic approach to explaining the atonement in his commentary on the Apostles' Creed in Book II of his *Institutes*. Calvin proposes that Jesus offers atonement for sin as he exercises his priestly office:

> In the exercise of this office, Christ is both the priest and the sacrifice. He is the sacrifice, because no other fit satisfaction for sin could be found. And he is the priest, for no one else was worthy of the honor of offering an only-begotten Son to God.[3]

Calvin combines this sacrificial imagery, however, with images of penal substitution:

1. Quoted in Robert Culpepper, *Interpreting the Atonement* (Grand Rapids: Eerdmans, 1996), p. 95.
2. Culpepper, *Interpreting the Atonement*, p. 94.
3. John Calvin, *Institutes of the Christian Religion* (1536 edition), trans. Ford Lewis Battles (Atlanta: John Knox Press, 1975), 2.15.6.

He suffered, moreover, under Pontius Pilate, condemned indeed by the judge's sentence, as a criminal and wrongdoer, in order that we might, by his condemnation, be absolved before the judgment seat of the highest Judge. He was crucified, that in the cross, which had been cursed by God's law, he might bear our curse which our sins deserved.[4]

While Calvin, like Luther, combines images of sacrifice and penal satisfaction in his doctrine of the atonement (and does so with more moderate imagery than does Luther), later Calvinists disrupted that balance in favor of Calvin's legal arguments. Later Calvinist thought, therefore, came to be typified by a rather harsh doctrine of substitutionary, penal atonement.

Several of the more important developments in later Reformation-era doctrines of the atonement come in reaction to this hardening view. Jacob Arminius adapted the Calvinist position to give human will a more cooperative role along with God's grace in our salvation. "It always remains within the power of the free will to reject the grace bestowed," he wrote.[5] Faustus Socinus refused to believe that God demanded Christ's suffering and death as the price for God's forgiveness of human sin. Neither did he believe in Jesus' divine nature, but saw him simply as exemplifying God's work, thus shifting Abelard's moral influence theory away from Jesus acting by awakening sinful humanity's eyes to God's redeeming love and toward inspiring us to follow Jesus' example. Hugo Grotius attempted to counter Socinus' thought by developing a theory of atonement based on the idea of God as a moral governor who acts in the best interests of the realm's subjects, an idea that has had significant influence upon later Arminian theologians.

The Post-Reformation Period

While the theories of the atonement developed during the Reformation served the church well enough until the end of the 18th century, an in-

---

4. Calvin, *Institutes,* 2.16.5.

5. William Placher, *A History of Christian Theology: An Introduction* (Philadelphia: Westminster Press, 1983), p. 226.

creasingly central feature of theology through the 19th and 20th centuries was funding traditional (even biblical) terminology with nontraditional meaning under the influence of the thought of Immanuel Kant, at least up until the collapse of traditional liberal theology with the outbreak of World War I. Kant's understanding of human autonomy led him to do a complete about-face from his childhood Lutheranism and posit that human redemption is due to God operating through human moral reason, not through the justifying death of Christ on the cross.[6] God's saving activity takes place within the interior of the human life rather than in objective history. In Kant, therefore, theology largely drops its concern with objective reality and becomes much more subjective. Much of modern theological development has been built on the foundation of Kant's reliance on reason and human moral authority and his subjective approach to faith — or in reaction to it.

Friedrich Schleiermacher was perhaps the premier exemplar of a theology developed on the base of Kant's philosophical insights, so that his work may be thought of as typical of classically liberal theology. Following Kant's turn toward the human interior, Schleiermacher writes in *The Christian Faith* that his theology "is based entirely on the inner experience of the believer, its only purpose is to describe and elucidate that experience."[7] Rather than focusing on the historical event of the crucifixion as the foundation for his theory of the atonement, Schleiermacher focused on the "God-consciousness" he saw uniquely present in Jesus as the means of our salvation. Jesus' main work, according to Schleiermacher's doctrine of the atonement, was to transmit to the early Christian community "the consciousness of God which he himself possessed in a unique and exemplary manner." This leads Gunton to the conclusion that "although in Schleiermacher some of the language of Western atonement theology appears fairly prominently, *it ceases to mean what it once did*" (emphasis mine).[8]

Classically liberal theology was decimated by the evil unleashed during World War I. The two most thorough attempts to resurrect theology from its Great War ashes were made by Paul Tillich, who sought

---

6. Colin Gunton, *The Actuality of Atonement* (Grand Rapids: Eerdmans, 1989), pp. 4-8.

7. Placher, *History of Christian Theology*, p. 274.

8. Gunton, *Actuality of Atonement*, p. 12.

to redeem the liberal theology of Schleiermacher, and by Barth, who developed neo-orthodoxy to reclaim the unique self-revelation of God's purpose in Jesus as recorded in Scripture that he believed had been jettisoned by classic liberals.

22. God and the Doctrine of the Atonement

ADELIA KELSO

The atonement (the Good News) of our Lord Jesus Christ is shocking, continually shocking, and nothing in all creation can prepare us to see it. If we are not shocked by the atonement of Christ, we have not yet heard it clearly. I do not mean the kind of shock you have once and then you get over it — the kind of shock that comes initially as a shock and then becomes familiar, then routine, and finally boring. Christ's atonement is permanently shocking every time you encounter it afresh, and realize again as if for the first time that Christ is risen and Easter is true and therefore nothing in all human life and history is anything like the way it seems. A helpful articulator of this shocking, counter-intuitive atonement is Karl Barth, in the section of his *Church Dogmatics* entitled "The Judge Judged in Our Place."

Why did God become human? *(Cur Deus homo?)*[1] According to Barth, it was because "the great and self-sufficient God wills to be also the Savior of the world."[2] Jesus Christ did come to judge the world, but in order to do so the Judge became the one judged in our place.

---

1. Karl Barth, *Church Dogmatics* IV/1 (Edinburgh: T. & T. Clark, 1960), "The Judge Judged in Our Place," p. 212.

2. Barth, *Church Dogmatics* IV/1, p. 214. In reading this section, it is important to remember that "self-sufficient," for Barth, means God is from God's self; none of God's attributes depend upon us. It is God's grounding himself in himself. It does not have the more modern connotation of aloofness or aloneness. On the contrary, because God is grounded in himself, or in Barth's language, because God is free, God acts lovingly. Moltmann and others in the second half of the twentieth century elaborated on this issue of a "passionate" God.

What took place is that the Son of God fulfilled the righteous judgment on us men by Himself taking our place as man and in our place undergoing the judgment under which we had passed. . . . Everything happened to us exactly as it had to happen, but because God willed to execute His judgment on us in His Son it all happened to His person, as His accusation and condemnation and destruction. He judged, and it was the Judge who was judged, who let Himself be judged . . . in order that in this way there might be brought about by Him our reconciliation with Him and conversion to Him.[3]

Barth continues, "There and then there took place the strange judgment which meant the pardon and redemption of man the wrong-doer, the making possible of that which seemed to be contrary to every possibility."[4] Truly, it is better than we can imagine. Barth articulates this "for us" *(pro nobis)* in four ways.

1. Christ becomes the Judge in our place. Genesis 3 is important here. The serpent very craftily said, "Did God say, 'You can't eat from any of these trees'?" Eve said, "We can eat the fruit of the trees — except for the one in the middle, because when we do we die." The serpent said, "You're not going to die, because God knows that when you eat that one, your eyes will be opened and you'll be like God, knowing good and evil."

Certainly it is not particularly healthy to want to be like God, but what's wrong with knowing good and evil? Doesn't that help us make decisions? Doesn't knowing right from wrong mean we know how to live our lives and make judgments about things that come our way? How can the fall or sin have to do with knowing good and evil?

Barth says the desire to know good and evil is our desire to be our *own* judges. Our desire for a knowledge of good and evil is an evil desire, or as Barth put it, "in its root and origin sin is the arrogance in which we want to be our own and our neighbor's judge."[5] We want to decide between good and evil. We want to be the arbiters of what's right and what's wrong. We want to be the judges of the world, because then we

---

3. Barth, *Church Dogmatics* IV/1, p. 222. Barth also says, "There is, in fact, a complete reversal, an exchange of roles" (p. 226).

4. Barth, *Church Dogmatics* IV/1, p. 223.

5. Barth, *Church Dogmatics* IV/1, p. 231.

have control. "We find our consolation and refuge and strength in exercising it. In our supposed right to do this we all have our safe stronghold, a trusty shield and weapon in relation to ourselves, our neighbors and God."[6] That's what the serpent offered us in the garden, and we bit. As Barth said, "The fruit of this tree which was eaten with such relish is still rumbling in all of us."[7]

But Jesus Christ becomes the Judge in our place, and we are deposed. Our "safe stronghold is breached."[8] We are no longer in control. This is one aspect of the atonement for Barth: "To be a man means to exist under the occurrence of this judgment. Yet not . . . in the occurrence of the judgment in which man himself is the judge, but in the occurrence of the judgment in which this function is that of God Himself. It is this function of God as Judge which has been re-established once and for all in Jesus Christ. What we want to do for ourselves has been taken out of our hands in Him."[9]

2. Jesus Christ becomes the Judge judged *in our place.* Jesus Christ, in other words, confesses our sin of judging. (Here Barth calls Jesus Christ "the bearer and Representative," words that sound like earlier doctrines of the atonement.)[10] This began, for Barth, at Jesus' baptism, when he was baptized with the baptism of repentance. Jesus Christ has now become the unrighteous one and we have become the righteous. It is truly a switching of roles.

> [W]e may think of the darkness which we are told later came down at the hour of Jesus' death (Mk. 15:33), the rending of the veil of the temple (Mk. 15:38), the earthquake which shook the rocks and opened the graves (Mt. 27:51), as though — in anticipation of its own end — the cosmos had to register the strangeness of this event: the

6. Barth, *Church Dogmatics* IV/1, p. 232.

7. Barth, *Church Dogmatics* IV/1, p. 232.

8. Barth, *Church Dogmatics* IV/1, p. 232.

9. Barth, *Church Dogmatics* IV/1, p. 232.

10. One of D. J. Hall's arguments in *Professing the Faith* (Minneapolis: Fortress, 1993) is that "representative" might be a more useful term to describe Jesus' atonement in our era. Tentatively speaking, I am reluctant to agree with Hall because I believe Barth has already made use of this word. Perhaps upon a closer reading, it might become evident that there are important differences between Barth's and Hall's usage.

transformation of the accuser into the accused and the judge into the judged, the naming and handling of the Holy God as one who is godless.[11]

What are the results of Jesus being judged in our place? First, he shows us what our place *is*. We are seen for who we are: sinners. "In that God acknowledges us as sinners in Jesus Christ, His truth is the guarantee that we are such: that we are doers of that which is against Him."[12] Second, we must see ourselves as liberated creatures, as creatures whom God values. Third, we can no longer justify ourselves. We have now no place to stand from which to prove anything about ourselves. Self-justification is useless.

3. Jesus Christ received the judgment. This wasn't just any person who was crucified, but it was God himself acting in a particular person.

The gospels do not speak of a passion which might just as well have been suffered in one place as another, at one time as another, or in a heavenly or some purely imaginary space and time. . . . They speak of it as an act of God which is coincident with the free action and suffering of a man, but in such a way that this human action and suffering has to be represented and understood as the action and, therefore, the passion of God Himself, which in its historical singularity not only has a general significance for the men of all times and places, but by which their situation has objectively been decisively changed, whether they are aware of it or not.[13]

The Passion of Jesus Christ is "unique in kind."[14] It couldn't have been anybody at any time. It had to be this act at this time in this person. It's not just anybody who suffers, but God who suffers and dies. Because of this, theodicy questions are rendered obsolete; instead, the question is whether God has abdicated God's own deity.[15] If God has died, what's the point?

This is a good question, and Barth answers it by saying that God re-

11. Barth, *Church Dogmatics* IV/1, p. 239.
12. Barth, *Church Dogmatics* IV/1, p. 240.
13. Barth, *Church Dogmatics* IV/1, p. 245.
14. George Hunsinger's words in *How to Read Karl Barth*.
15. Barth, *Church Dogmatics* IV/1, p. 246.

veals his deity in God's own Passion. God reveals what it means to be God in his Passion. The definition of God is not a supreme being in the sense of humanity writ large, as Superman or the "Big Man in the sky" or being stronger or larger or faster than any human being. The definition of God is to suffer, be crucified, and die for people. In death, the reconciliation of the world to God happens, in "the redemptive judgment of God on all men."[16] Barth adds: "In this suffering and dying of God Himself in His Son, there took place the reconciliation with God, the conversion to Him, of the world which is out of harmony with Him, contradicting and opposing Him."[17] This is atonement: that God has intervened in person, that the Judge of the universe has become the judged in our place. In this we have our atonement.

For Barth this means sin itself was judged on the cross, and thus he can use the word "satisfaction," although Barth disagrees with Anselm in this usage. While agreeing that Jesus Christ suffered the punishment due to us, he does not allow that Jesus "'satisfied' or offered satisfaction to the wrath of God." The "decisive thing" for Barth "is not that He has suffered what we ought to have suffered," but "that in the suffering and death of Jesus Christ it has come to pass that in His own person He has made an end of us as sinners and therefore of sin itself by going to death as the One who took our place as sinners."[18]

The point is that we are no longer considered sinners, and that in Jesus Christ, God himself conquered sin. God must destroy sin in order to reconcile us to himself.[19] This is a radical change from what most Christians think of as atonement. This isn't against human beings but against sin itself! The decisive thing is that Jesus Christ makes an end of sin itself and of us as sinners — not that he suffered what we ought to. It is not that we are the center of all things and he took what should come to us.

4. Finally, Barth says that God, in being the judge, the judged, and receiving the judgment, has acted righteously. Righteousness is thus taking on sin and defeating it, and reconciling the world to God. Righteousness is not moral rectitude or self-righteousness, but an at-one-ment with human-

---

16. Barth, *Church Dogmatics* IV/1, p. 247.
17. Barth, *Church Dogmatics* IV/1, pp. 250-51.
18. Barth, *Church Dogmatics* IV/1, p. 253.
19. Barth, *Church Dogmatics* IV/1, pp. 254-55.

kind in all our misery (our constant proving of our own righteousness), such that sin is defeated and we are brought into relationship with God. The righteousness of God is God reconciling the world to himself. It is God-with-us.

This kind of "with us" is expressed in Philippians 2:1-11, in Paul's moving articulation of who God is, done under the rubric of obedience — the same word for the title of Barth's entire paragraph 59, "The Obedience of the Son of God." When Paul speaks about God here, he says that Jesus was obedient to God. Obedience is not a word we like very much. Most of us hear "obey" and feel as if we're caged in, marching in lockstep, doing what someone else tells us. Obedience can conjure up notions of blindly following orders, being both constrained to do things we do not want to do and, at the same time, abdicating all sense of ownership of our own actions. For others, obedience may mean doing what is right, doing what we know should be done. Most often we are obedient in order to get something. When asked what were the operative words at home growing up, a friend of mine replied, "Obey, and you shall be rewarded."

But what does Paul mean by obedience? Obedience can take different forms. Certainly Abraham's obedience was a type of what was to come in Christ. Barth says, "Jesus Christ was obedient in that He willed to take our place as sinners."[20] The obedience of Jesus Christ was that he became a sinner, he became THE sinner, in our place. He became, as Barth says, "the one great sinner . . . acknowledging that He is the one lost sheep, the one lost coin, the lost son. . . . [A]s the Judge [of the world] He is the One who is judged in our place."[21] Or, in the words of John Calvin's Geneva Catechism, "our Judge is our Advocate."

Obedience for Jesus consisted in "becoming sin for us," or as Paul says in 2 Corinthians 5:21, "For our sake he made him to be sin." He "confessed" our sin as his own. Barth says, "[He] confessed [our sin], [He took] upon Himself this guilt of all human beings in order in the name of all to put God in the right against Him."[22] His whole life was dedicated to "confessing" our sin for us. At his baptism he was baptized with the "baptism of repentance." God repented for us. And through-

20. Barth, *Church Dogmatics* IV/1, p. 258.
21. Barth, *Church Dogmatics* IV/1, p. 259.
22. Barth, *Church Dogmatics* IV/1, p. 259.

out his ministry he acknowledged there is one lost coin, sheep, son — the role he undertook at his cross. For Jesus, obedience was not blindly following orders, nor was it obeying to get a reward; it was obedience unto death, or as Paul says in Romans 5:6, it was "dying for the ungodly."

CHAPTER V

DIVINE WORSHIP

Introduction

Christian worship, as empowered by the Holy Spirit, centers on the adoration and praise of the Triune God. Both in judgment and in promise, the crucified and risen Head of the church, Jesus Christ, is present among us through the proclamation of the Word and the administration of the sacraments. Therefore, all authentic theology climaxes in doxology, as the fidelity, unity, and continuity of God's people throughout the ages are celebrated in the church's corporate worship. In joy and thanksgiving, the church's faithful publicly and regularly gather to be forgiven and renewed in the power of the apostolic blessing: "The grace of the Lord Jesus Christ, the love of God, and the communion of the Holy Spirit be with you all" (II Cor. 13:14). In exercising the awesome privilege of leading Christians in the communal hallowing of God's name, pastor-theologians have always found that the Holy Scriptures have a unique role to play in establishing norms for and informing the essential content of the sermons, ceremonies, prayers, hymns, versicles, and other edifying forms of the church's worship life, however elaborate or spare the ritual may be.

The first of our authors' selections on this subject, "Christian Worship as Blessing," sets the tone in its veneration of Holy Scripture. The written Word of God provides the perennial "support and energy" of the church as it keeps its public worship centered in God's incarnate Word, Jesus Christ. In the power of the Spirit, the exalted Christ is truly present to mediate adoration to God and salvation to humanity. Church worship also serves to communicate God's saving Word (1) as memory and discipline, (2) as poetry, (3) as awash in the liturgy, (4) as venerated, and (5) as Old and New Testaments. This "personal, communal, sacramental, enlivening, and eschatological" self-disclosure of God is to be radically contrasted with current perversions of human-centered entertainment, however sentimentally religious. In short, "it is on Christ's face that the church learns who it is."

In "The Baptized Imagination," the author seeks to "recover a Christian reading of Scripture" in its traditional and organic setting: the worship life of the local congregation. Wary of too programmed an approach, however, the writer champions all occasions where Scripture "may exercise its own power to baptize our imaginations" in order to foster a kind of holiness that "enables us to embrace the world in all its earthiness and imperfection for Jesus' sake." The church today is suffering a failure of the heart, a clouding of the imagination in its all-too-comfortable despair. Dostoyevsky's *The Brothers Karamazov,* and especially its Father Zossima, can point us to the Scriptures in order to revel in the mystery of creation and the mercy of Christ's cross. Divine power resides not in our theories about the Scriptures, but in our direct communion with the indwelling Holy Spirit within the Scriptures themselves. "The gospel leads us not away from the church but to the church" that is alive and at work in the world.

The next three excerpts from papers on this theme report on 1999 Lenten worship programs that were intentionally carried out in close tandem with concurrent sessions of the Pastor-Theologian seminars. The first, "Scripture in the Life of the Congregation," deals practically with the question of "how Scripture gets into the hands, ears, and lives of church people in the first place." This pastor shows how he integrated a holistic program of congregational life that was intentionally centered in Matthew 26–27 during the church season of Lent. First, the sermons in all worship services from Ash Wednesday through Easter Sunday were based on Matthew's Passion narrative in successive passages. Second, appropriate music presentations and art exhibits were arranged in church for added interpretation, not least in various portions of Bach's "St. Matthew Passion" that coincided with the Sunday readings. Third, a series of mid-week Bible studies was held based on the text appointed for the upcoming Sunday. Finally, a booklet of daily devotions on the entire text of Matthew 26–27 was prepared and distributed to all church members, with written prayers composed by public lay readers. This was total Paschal immersion.

A second author's excerpt on Lenten worship is "Living the Narrative in the Liturgy." Here the focus is on the scriptural narrative's liturgical rehearsal of Christ's atonement in Holy Week, and its climax in the ancient single liturgy of the *Triduum*, "Three Days," the continuous enactment of the Supper, the Crucifixion, and the Resurrection, covering Passion Sunday, Maundy Thursday, Good Friday, and finally the Easter Vigil. Special features of Holy Week worship involved supplementary musical, educational, and devotional opportunities. The Passion setting by Heinrich Schuetz was presented in its entirety in public worship. A Lenten series of adult forums and mid-week Vespers were also devoted to the two texts central to the Pastor-Theologian seminars. Finally, outlines and study guides of Matthew 26–27 were distributed to the congregation for Lenten home study devotions. The total program's underlying conviction was "that Christ's crucifixion is a word-event which happens in the life of the church through the telling of the story."

The third section explores the author's intention "to lead a group within the congregation during Lent 2001 in doing an in-depth study of the Passion narratives in the Gospels along with related Old Testament passages, which would be used in a Good Friday *Tenebrae* (Darkness) service as a means of demonstrating the value of a Christian reading of Scripture and showing how such a reading is enacted in worship." The text sketches the background and impetus for the project, an overall plan for the Bible study group, its anticipated outcomes, and the hermeneutical presuppositions guiding a Christian reading of the Scriptures (Christological, canonical, pneumatological, and epistemic).

23. *Christian Worship as Blessing*

THOMAS D. McKNIGHT

In recent decades, both the Protestant and Roman Catholic traditions have reaffirmed the centrality of Scripture in worship. A shared lectionary reflects this reality.

> In worship, Scripture both sets forth God's Word to us and offers us a language for speaking a word of our own to God. . . . To speak of Scripture as a sacramental word is to say that a worshiping community expects to hear God speaking a living word to it through Scripture. The community awaits a "fitting word" for its life before God.[1]

> The Church has always venerated the divine Scriptures just as she venerates the body of the Lord, since from the table of both the word of God and the body of Christ she unceasingly receives and offers to the faithful the bread of life. . . . For in the sacred books, the Father who is in heaven meets His children with great love and speaks with them; and the force and power in the word of God is so great that it remains the support and energy of the Church, the strength of faith for her sons, the food of the soul, the pure and perennial source of spiritual life.[2]

Worship Is Christ-Centered

From now on you will see the Son of Man seated at the right hand of Power and coming on the clouds of heaven.   Matthew 26:64

---

1. John Burgess, *Why Scripture Matters* (Louisville: Westminster/John Knox, 1998), pp. 104, 117.
2. Vatican II, *Dogmatic Constitution on Divine Revelation*, cited by Burgess in *Why Scripture Matters*, p. 45.

And what Christ is by nature, his Body the church is by grace, particularly in its worship, where his Spirit flourishes.[3]   Aidan J. Kavanagh

The story of Jesus fundamentally informs the pattern of Christian worship, and the person of Christ, through the Spirit, is at the heart of worship. The promises of the resurrected Christ inspire the hope through which the faithful anticipate the future. Jesus Christ is the subject of worship as he points to the value that God has set on the human race as the object of God's creating and saving love. Worship becomes blessing.

Christ continues to mediate God's blessing. "It is through his remembered, experienced and anticipated presence, concentrated in worship, that God reaches us. Jesus embodies not only the divine initiative but also the human response, not only God's grace but also man's freedom. He prays for us and includes the motion of our attempted self-offering as his own," in the words of Geoffrey Wainwright.[4] Christ, the Mediator, functions as the one who mediates human worship to God, and salvation from God to humanity. Christ is truly present in the new community that is always being born as the church. As man, Jesus was present in the limits of time and place. As God, Christ is present with us now.

Worship Is the Word . . .

But all this has taken place, so that the scriptures of the prophets may be fulfilled.
                                                                    Matthew 26:56

. . . As Memory and Discipline

I have a spotty education but am an incurable reader. Acutely aware of my ignorance, I read widely in theology, church history, monastic, litur-

---

3. Aiden J. Kavanagh, O.S.B., "Scriptural Word and Liturgical Worship," in *Reclaiming the Bible for the Church*, ed. Carl Braaten and Robert Jenson (Grand Rapids: Eerdmans, 1995), pp. 131-32.

4. Geoffrey Wainwright, *Doxology: The Praise of God in Worship, Doctrine and Life* (New York: Oxford University Press, 1980), p. 86.

gical and biblical studies. All of it has informed both my poems and the preaching that I've been asked to do in recent years. But at the first Bible study I attended with the women of Spencer Memorial Presbyterian Church, it was the sight of well-worn Bibles carried by the mostly gray-haired women, contrasting with my nearly new one, the Oxford Annotated, that my husband had given me for Christmas, that stunned me into silence. . . . Looking at the women, I felt as if I were seeing my own grandmother again. Her Bible, spine broken, binding cracked, that I had discovered when I moved into her house, looked very much like theirs. These women knew things about the Christian religion that I did not, the kind of things that are learned not through study but through a lifetime of faith, and the steady practice of both charity and prayer.[5]

Kathleen Norris

In weekly worship and communal Bible study, Scripture functions more as regular nourishment than as unforgettable feast. The "routine" hearing of Scripture each week in worship "sustains its power at other times to speak to us more personally and dramatically." Over time, the faithful, in charity and in prayer, themselves come to embody Scripture. According to John Burgess, "Scripture finally matters only to the extent that we ourselves become living commentaries on the reality of the risen Christ."[6]

Scripture becomes powerful when there is the real expectation, the "reverent confidence" that these words of Scripture set forth a Word of God for us. Burgess, in his book *Why Scripture Matters*, argues for the recovery of the practical discipline of reading and hearing Scripture as a Word of God. He speaks of the recovery of a kind of piety, and of the fostering of a different set of dispositions and attitudes toward Scripture.

. . . As Poetry

The struggle to recover Scripture is, in a sense, the struggle to recover poetry.[7]

John Burgess

5. Kathleen Norris, *Amazing Grace: A Vocabulary of Faith* (New York: Riverhead Books, 1998), p. 243.
6. Burgess, *Why Scripture Matters*, p. 95.
7. Burgess, *Why Scripture Matters*, p. 39.

Kathleen Norris argues that the church must recover incarnational language, language full of metaphorical resonance. This is especially so in worship. Bureaucratic jargon, central to our normal speech, robs language of power. Norris believes that what is needed are physical, concrete words and images "that resonate with the senses as they aim for the stars."[8] Such language does not so much convince its hearers of a certain point of view as it expresses truths that can be revealed most powerfully through metaphor. Hearing the lectionary readings with this expectation can be transformative.

. . . As Awash in the Liturgy

I do not think that a few verses of a severely edited psalm, a hymn or two, a brief sentence of Scripture for a preacher to muse on, and a sensitive "pastoral prayer" will be enough to reclaim the Bible and the liturgy for the church in its divine mission. The liturgy must be awash in Scripture, the divine presence must be worshiped in the beauty of holiness, the Word celebrated and declaimed above and beyond the limits of human politics and therapy.[9]

Aidan J. Kavanagh

The liturgy must be awash in Scripture, saturated with Scripture in order that the community's memory be exercised, challenged, and deepened. This happens throughout the order of worship, from the call to worship to the benediction. The Reformed tradition's use of the Prayer of Illumination prior to the reading of Scripture is but one example of this. In this prayer we are encouraged, through the Spirit, to listen for God's Word as Scripture even before it is interpreted in the sermon.

The Scripture is heard not just in the readings that precede the sermon and in the reflection upon the Word that occurs in preaching. The words and images from the Old and New Testaments are heard again and again in the collect, in the spoken prayers, in the silences, in the hymns sung, in the commission and benediction. Throughout all of this, worship "lifts up Scripture's character as sacramental Word." As John Burgess declares:

8. Burgess, *Why Scripture Matters,* p. 39.
9. Kavanagh, "Scriptural Word," pp. 136-37.

While preaching is the most obvious medium for setting forth this fitting word, a similar expectation may accompany the incorporation of Scripture into other parts of worship. For a Pentecostal church, Scripture may come most alive not in the reading prior to the sermon, but as it is incorporated into the language of prayer. For churches that focus on the Eucharist, Scripture may speak most powerfully as it is incorporated into the words of institution and eucharistic prayers.[10]

. . . *As Venerated*

The Bible has been the sacred book of the worshiping Christian community for centuries. It is still venerated in countless ways by different traditions. In Byzantine liturgy, the "lesser entrance" with the book of the Gospel is made with dignity second only to the "greater entrance" with bread and wine prepared for the Eucharist. Roman Catholics cense and kiss the Gospel when read. Protestants may bring the Bible in at the beginning of worship or leave it open on the table throughout worship.

From the early days of the church, Christians treated the Scriptures, especially the Gospels, with the same care that their Hebrew ancestors treated the Torah scrolls. In the synagogue, the congregation gathered around the Torah and waited to hear the Word of life, as God came to be present in the midst of them.

Those who hear these Gospel stories, according to Luke Timothy Johnson, are "invited to construct, in an almost kaleidoscopic fashion, an image of Jesus with many different and changing dimensions. . . . No less complex are the ways in which the words of scriptural texts are brought into new combinations and given new dimensions by the words spoken in worship . . . not only in the eucharistic prayer of thanksgiving and the community prayers of petition."[11] The Scriptures are read to proclaim the "Good News" — the grace and love of God as witnessed in the life, death, and resurrection of Jesus Christ. This "Good News" has been anticipated in the stories of the Old Testament and has been experienced in the lives of the post-resurrection New Testament faithful who have become Christ's disciples.

10. Burgess, *Why Scripture Matters,* p. 118.
11. Luke Timothy Johnson, *Living Jesus: Learning the Heart of the Gospel* (San Francisco: HarperSanFrancisco, 1998), p. 42.

The Scriptures are an unparalleled "good gift" — a true source of life. Too often, however, when Scripture is seen only as the way to discipleship, or only as the way to the mystery of God, or only as the ultimate source of external authority, Scripture is limited by our own partial understandings. We limit the way that Scripture can truly become an "audible signal of an inaudible grace."

Not only are the Scriptures heard — they can be experienced in new ways through dramatic presentations and through the use of powerful visual imagery. The cross, for example, when prominent in the worship space, can reinforce the Scriptural message in countless ways. And, of course, seeing the open Bible on the communion table reinforces the importance of the Word and Sacrament in a way that is different from what is heard.

. . . As Old and New Testaments

What are the reasons for reading the Old and New Testaments together in worship? Geoffrey Wainwright suggests four major reasons for including the Old Testament regularly in worship: (1) a reminder of the religious and cultural background of the historical Jesus of Nazareth; he was not "a docetic bolt from the blue"; (2) a recovery of the history of the God of Jesus with human beings over a far longer stretch of time than the New Testament can do; (3) a reminder of God's purposes for all of humanity — the universal scope of God's promises through Abraham, the Psalms, the servant songs, the apocalyptic visions, etc.; and (4) a means toward reconciling the church to Judaism and convicting the church of its hostility toward the Jews throughout all of its history.

What are the reasons for not considering the Old Testament indispensable to worship? Wainwright reminds us that the churches managed for a thousand years with scarcely an Old Testament lesson at the Eucharist. He argues that the absence of an Old Testament lesson (1) brings into relief the "radical newness" of the Christian message; (2) conveys a warning that the church needs to beware of limiting God's "saving history" to a particular nation, race, or culture, "be the culture as wide as historical Christendom itself"; and (3) leaves room for at least an occasional reading from another religious tradition. Wainwright contends:

143

It would be difficult to allow readings which appeared plainly contradictory to the Christian message; but the tentative use of matter which appeared at first sight harmonious with, or complementary to, the Christian scriptures would make a contribution to that exploration of relations which the contemporary trends toward a universalization of culture seem to demand of the religions.[12]

This contradicts the viewpoint of Luke Timothy Johnson, who argues that

> The most fundamental identity decision made by the church in every generation, therefore, is the decision to have these and only these compositions read aloud in the assembly as the Word of God, and to use these and only these compositions as the basis for debate within the community concerning fidelity to God's rule in present circumstances. Any effort to change the canon must be recognized for what it truly is: the desire to change Christian identity.[13]

The face of the church continues to be revealed through worship. If the church is faithful, it will continue to reveal the face of Christ to the world. As J. J. von Allmen writes,

> Worship is indeed for the church, while it waits for the Kingdom, the time and place par excellence at which it finds its own deep identity; the time and place at which the church becomes what it is. . . . [Yet] worship is not the time and place at which the church becomes aware of its own identity in the sense that it might be the time and place at which the church might discover in a purifying mirror its own image cleansed of every spot and wrinkle. It is not by looking at itself, even washed clean, that the church learns what it is. What makes the church first glimpse, and then see clearly, its true face is meeting with Christ and learning from him what sort of Bride it is that he loves. It is on Christ's face that the church learns who it is.[14]

12. Wainwright, *Doxology*, p. 27.
13. Johnson, *Living Jesus*, p. 31.
14. Wainwright, *Doxology*, p. 27.

24. The Baptized Imagination

THOMAS W. CURRIE

As a general rule, people, even the wicked, are much more naive and simple-hearted than we suppose. And we ourselves are too.

Fyodor Dostoyevsky, *The Brothers Karamazov*

In his autobiography, C. S. Lewis speaks of the "baptized imagination." Indeed, he insists that his own imagination was baptized into the faith before any other part of him was, and he implies that our imaginations play a larger role in our affirmations and loyalties than we often admit. It is our sense of beauty that needs to be converted as much as, if not more than, our moral or intellectual lives.

What baptized Lewis' imagination was a book by George MacDonald titled *Phantastes, a faerie Romance,* which he purchased to have something to read on a train. "The quality which had enchanted me in his [MacDonald's] imaginative works turned out to be the quality of the real universe, the divine, magical, terrifying and ecstatic reality in which we all live. I should have been shocked in my teens if anyone had told me that what I learned to love in *Phantastes* was goodness. But now that I know, I see there was no deception. The deception is all the other way round — in that prosaic moralism which confines goodness to the region of Law and Duty, which never lets us feel in our face the sweet air blowing from 'the land of righteousness.'"[1]

How are we to recover a Christian reading of Scripture? What is it that enables the church to be the place where the text of Scripture is authoritatively "performed,"[2] that is, where the plot of the narrative itself is not only acknowledged and received but also rehearsed and delighted in? I want to suggest that the recovery of a Christian reading of Scripture will occur not as the result of various projects, scholarly or pastoral, but rather through Scripture's own power to baptize our imagina-

1. C. S. Lewis, *George MacDonald, An Anthology* (London: Geoffrey Bles, 1955), p. 21.
2. The phrase is from Nicholas Lash, *Theology on the Way to Emmaus* (London: SCM Press, 1986), p. 42.

145

tions, allowing us to feel that "sweet air blowing from the land of righteousness" that enables us to embrace the world in all its earthiness and imperfection for Jesus' sake. Lewis, in recounting the effect of Mac-Donald's stories on him, speaks of a kind of holiness pervading this imaginative world, a holiness which, unlike that Romanticism that is all too eager to flee the mundane and particular in order to find some deeper spiritual truth, discovers instead in the smallest particulars the presence of the Kingdom: "But now I saw the bright shadow coming out of the book into the real world and resting there, transforming all common things and yet itself unchanged. Or, more accurately, I saw the common things drawn into the bright shadow."[3]

A basic presupposition of this paper is that what makes a Christian reading of Scripture difficult today is not a failure of Christian scholarship or even of ecclesiastical initiative, but rather a failure of the heart, a kind of *acedia,* or sloth, which has clouded the church's imagination and threatened us with that terrible form of despair that is bored with what is good, weary with what is beautiful, and indifferent to what is true. What is needed to combat this all-too-comfortable despair is not a list of things to do but a converted imagination that has discovered how extraordinary and sneaky God is ("like a thief in the night"), how subversive to our own agendas is his story, how happily and wonderfully self-forgetting are his gifts.

However, such a converted imagination is not something we can just conjure up, any more than we can re-invent ourselves. It is a gift for which we must pray. Still, what has mediated such a gift and sustained the life of the faithful for centuries is near at hand, even on our lips and in our hearts. Scripture itself brings us that gift in the strange story it tells, in the way in which it plants the seed of faith through its own particular narration. This story overcomes our own hopelessness and despair, subverting our cultivated weariness and even brilliant "explanations" while offering instead its simple gift of life to those who are caught up in a "culture of death."[4]

To illustrate the way in which Scripture converts our imaginations and invites us to a reading of its narrative as a means of grace (as op-

3. Lewis, *George MacDonald,* p. 22.
4. Pope John Paul II and others have used this phrase to describe a culture that no longer takes its bearings from the gospel story.

posed simply to a historical-critical puzzle to be solved), I recommend Fyodor Dostoyevsky's *The Brothers Karamazov*. To read this novel is to meet several characters who are struggling with, and often against, the reality that Scripture's story depicts. They find in the gospel both a threat to their nihilistic schemes of self-invention (Ivan) and, at the same time, the one weapon powerful enough to offer them hope in the face of despair (Alyosha, Dmitri). Strangely, it is Scripture's story that drives them to a deeper love for this world, indeed, for all of God's creation, enabling them to embrace even that misery and suffering they might otherwise only have held in contempt.

In many ways, the text for this novel might well be that passage from John 12:24, a text cited more than once in the course of its narrative: "Truly, truly, I say to you, unless a grain of wheat falls into the earth and dies, it remains alone; but if it dies, it bears much fruit." Father Zossima, the mentor and spiritual father of Alyosha Karamazov and one of the chief characters in the first half of the novel, cites this text often, clearly viewing his own life in its light. This is also the text, however, that Father Zossima believes accompanies and redeems the Karamazov family, foretelling both the suffering all the brothers will undergo as well as the redemption, the painful redemption, that will bring them to Easter's joy and light. When asked in another context whether such words can have been written by men, Father Zossima replies, "The Holy Spirit wrote them."[5] What enables him to be so confident in his reply is not his adherence to some doctrine of plenary inspiration but his conviction that Scripture's story is, in fact, the story of this world, the story of God's redemptive love for sinners, a love that is indeed full of suffering because it graciously resists our selfish conceits and burns away our even more selfish virtues. This sets us free for God, or to put it another way, it enables us to encounter true reality, an encounter that "sanctifies" us, however much it may hurt, so that we are gradually made like Scripture itself: holy, able to become a witness, able to tell the truth of God's intrusively happy grace.

Scripture captures our imagination through its power to evoke both our memory and our hope. Like the Deuteronomist, Dostoyevsky clearly believes that memory is the way we characteristically learn to

---

5. Fyodor Dostoyevsky, *The Brothers Karamazov*, trans. Constance Garnett (New York: Signet Classic, 1980), p. 285.

hope,[6] and that hope is what sustains us in the midst of despair. Part of the greatness of the novel consists in Dostoyevsky's refusal to reduce the mystery of human life to some ideological or scientific or homiletical explanation. Neither Father Zossima nor Alyosha offers schemes for the improvement of humankind. The only character who ventures in this direction is Alyosha's brother, Ivan, whose attempt to live without God leads, ultimately, to the murder of his father and the suicide of his half-brother and to his own madness. "Hell," Father Zossima insists, "is the suffering of being unable to love,"[7] a suffering with which all the characters are well acquainted, but which Ivan knows most deeply of all.

How might one recover a Christian reading of Scripture? We could do worse than to listen to Father Zossima's own sermon on the matter, a sermon in which he invites the priests and monks gathered around him to discover how an ecclesial reading of Scripture regularly baptizes the imagination:

> Friends and teachers, I have heard more than once, and of late one may hear it more often, that the priests, and above all the village priests, are complaining on all sides of their miserable income and their humiliating lot. They plainly state even in print — I've read it myself — that they are unable to teach the Scriptures to the people because of the smallness of their means and if Lutherans[!] and heretics come and lead the flock astray, they let them because they have so little to live on. May the Lord increase the sustenance that is so precious to them, for their complaint is just, too. But of a truth I say, if anyone is to blame in the matter, half the fault is ours.
>
> The priest may be short of time; he may say truly that he is overwhelmed with work and services, but still he must surely have an hour a week to remember God. He does not work the whole year round. Let him gather around him once a week, some hour in the evening, if only the children at first — the fathers will hear of it and they too will begin to come. There's no need to build halls for this, let him take them into his cottage. They won't spoil his cottage, they

---

6. See Alyosha's "Speech at the Stone" where he concludes: "What's more, perhaps, that one memory may keep us from great evil." Dostoyevsky, *The Brothers Karamazov*, p. 699.

7. Dostoyevsky, *The Brothers Karamazov*, p. 297.

will only be there one hour. Let him open that book and begin reading it without grand words or superciliousness, without condescension, but gently and kindly, being glad that he is reading to them, and they are listening with attention. Let him read loving the words himself, and only stopping from time to time to explain words that are not understood by the peasants. Don't be anxious, they will understand everything. The faithful heart will understand all![8]

A Christian reading of Scripture can find its true end only in the establishment of God's people and in the love that nurtures those people into a household of faith. That is why it can truly render the content of its story only in the context of its own "belief in God's people." And such "belief in God's people" is not pious optimism in the goodness of human beings generally or of Christians in particular, but the logical implication of believing in the God revealed in Scripture, the God of Israel and Jesus Christ. It is this God that compels us to reckon with "belief in God's people" as the first implication of the gospel's own story. If we miss that, we have missed the story itself. The gospel leads us not away from the church but to the church.

In his introduction to his book *Orthodoxy*, G. K. Chesterton tells of an Englishman who sets out in his own yacht hoping to discover an island in the South Seas. However, due to some navigational miscalculations, what he discovers is England. He sees his own homeland again, as it were, for the first time. The purpose of this paper is to suggest that the church would do well to undertake just such a voyage and see the Bible again for the first time. We should see it as a means of grace, as that narrative that links us with Israel and the church in Christ's story, giving us hope amidst a culture oppressed with itself. I do not argue that the Bible should be worshiped. But it should be venerated, much as an icon is venerated. The Bible should be lifted up as worship begins, raised high as it is brought into the sanctuary. It should be laid open on the communion table or altar, the central place around which God's people gather. As the Torah is to the synagogue, as it has even inspired dances when its cycle of readings has been completed, so should the Bible be to us, inspiring our imaginations and our worship. Then, when it is read in worship, we might see it again as for the first time, becoming

8. Dostoyevsky, *The Brothers Karamazov,* pp. 268-69.

like the little boy who grew up to be Father Zossima, receiving "the seed of God's Word" in our hearts and rejoicing in the understanding "of something read in the church of God."[9]

25. Scripture in the Life of the Congregation

DAVID D. MILES

Our topic this year was introduced with the following excerpt from a draft of the parallel Center of Theological Inquiry Scripture Project proposal:

> The conviction that generates the Scripture Project is that the church's life derives its coherence and inspiration from Scripture; therefore, Scripture should function as the church's chief guide both to intellectual understandings of the faith and to concrete practices of the Christian life. Unfortunately, Scripture rarely in fact plays this role in the "mainstream" churches to which members of the Project belong. Thus we confront a crisis in the interpretation and authority of the Bible in the church.

On the basis of this premise, I sought in my own project to go right to the heart of the issue by considering the ways in which Scripture can play a role in the life of the church. While it is easy to leap to questions of theology and interpretation of biblical texts, I was interested in the more basic and practical question of how Scripture gets into the hands, ears, and lives of church people in the first place. It seems to me that at least part of the crisis of biblical authority in the church stems from the fact that the texts themselves often do not occupy a central and lively place in the life of individual people of faith or in the life of the church. My aim, using the texts of Matthew 26–27, was to consider a number of different methods for creating a conversation between these texts and the congregation I serve.

9. Dostoyevsky, *The Brothers Karamazov*, p. 265.

Context

I have served as pastor of the Lamington Presbyterian Church for the last seven years. The church was founded in 1740, and most of our 550 members come from over 30 different rural and suburban towns in central New Jersey. The congregation is well-educated, middle to upper-middle class, and predominantly white. Because there has not been a long history, at least in the last half-century, of attention to the Bible in this church, I found a congregation that was basically biblically illiterate when I arrived. One of my primary goals, therefore, has been simply to introduce this church to the Bible and to the ways in which these texts may shape our understanding of the faith, our church, and our lives.

Approach

While the usual way in which biblical texts are heard in the church is in Scripture lessons during worship services, my aim was to provide a number of different ways for the text to engage the congregation. I chose the season of Lent, 1999 as an opportunity to work through the Passion story found in Matthew 26–27, and attempted to use a number of different methods to introduce the story into the life of the congregation.

Scripture Reading and Preaching

Since we do not follow the lectionary in our worship planning, I organized our journey through the Passion story by dividing up the text around the Sundays in Lent. Some members of our group pointed out that we were not regularly hearing Old Testament texts during Lent; it was my argument that while we need to hear from the breadth of the canon of Scripture over time, we do not necessarily need to do so each Sunday. Instead of preaching in a strict *"lectio-continua"* fashion, I preached on particular stories or characters in the Passion story, rather than dealing with each verse of the text equally.

It was suggested in our seminar group that the "point" of the Passion story is God's saving work through Jesus Christ, and that some of my sermons focused on the story from a more human point of view. This is an appropriate criticism of an approach that was deliberate on my part. Rather than making the same point over and over again for six weeks, my hope was to attempt to place us in the story from the perspective of the different human characters found in it.

Music and Artwork

While the visual arts traditionally have not played an important role in Reformed worship, I have been experimenting with using works of art based on biblical stories as a means of engaging the congregation with the story visually. I selected different paintings to be scanned on the computer and placed on the cover of the Sunday bulletin. While each painting does not speak to every member, I find that some of the works of art engage members in ways that a simple "hearing" of the text may not. I find that these works of art function as "visual exegesis" as the artist has made his or her own interpretive moves in trying to represent the story through his or her medium. Thus, the work of art provides another interpretive voice for the conversation.

Choral music plays a major role in our weekly worship, so I worked with our minister of music to connect the music with the texts as much as possible. We chose Bach's *St. Matthew Passion* as the primary musical text for Lent, and selected the portions from Bach's work that coincided with our readings for each Sunday. The congregation was able to hear the Scripture texts a second time as well as Bach's commentary on those texts through the accompanying recitations and arias. While Bach's musical interpretations represent only one particular perspective on the text, the work provides yet another medium to engage the congregation with the Scripture.

We found, through a great deal of verbal feedback, that these musical works not only helped the congregation hear more from the texts but that they listened more carefully to the music because they were familiar with the texts. We were somewhat surprised to find that even our youth commented that this part of the service was helpful to them in engaging the biblical story. Our minister of music also provided helpful notes on the music for the day printed in the bulletin to help the congregation be more aware of the musical techniques Bach employed in his interpretation of the texts.

Bible Studies

We offered Bible study classes each Wednesday in Lent based on the text that would be covered on the upcoming Sunday. There were two identical classes each week, one in the morning and one in the evening. Each class averaged fifteen people, and about fifty participated in the Bible studies overall. The format of the classes was to do a close reading together, hearing the different reflections of members and guided by historical and textual comments from me where relevant. The sessions were generally lively, with no shortage of discussion.

While I had some concern that those attending the Bible studies would consider hearing the story again on Sunday to be redundant, the opposite proved true: those who went to the Bible studies all agreed that they got more out of the sermon having spent more time with the text during the prior week. I also found it quite helpful to hear feedback on the previous week's sermon, as well as their reflections on the text prior to my preaching. My experience suggests that this kind of Bible study based on the upcoming Sunday preaching text might be valuable on a regular basis for both participants and preachers.

Devotional Readings

Finally, in an attempt to get every member involved with the text, we produced a booklet of devotional readings for each day of the season of Lent. After dividing up the entire text of Matthew 26–27 into brief units, I gave those texts to more than forty different volunteers to write a brief reflection or prayer based on that text. I was surprised that so many people were willing to take on the project and generally pleased with their responses.

While I have no statistical information as to how many members regularly used the devotional booklets during Lent, my informal survey leads me to believe that a large percentage of our members read the daily reflections on a regular basis. There were a number of positive results from these booklets. First of all, these readings and reflections provided a common experience of the Passion story for our members. At different meetings or church gatherings, I found that people often related the reading for the day to whatever we were talking about. I also found that the act of having church members write the reflections supported the often overlooked idea that every member of the church can offer his or her own valuable insights into a text, not just an ordained minister. Finally, I believe that these readings helped our congregation to become more immersed in the Passion story during the Lenten season.

Concluding Thoughts

It is easy for us to think that the crisis of biblical authority is solely one of theology and hermeneutics. While that may be true to some extent, I believe this crisis is also one of practice. While I am in no way interested in going the way of modern media in order to make the Bible "easy" for people who supposedly have a dwindling attention span, we do have to give more thought to how we bring together congregations and Biblical texts in ways that bring the texts to life for each new generation.

26. Living the Narrative in the Liturgy

ROBERT A. HAUSMAN

The recent exchange of articles between James M. Gustafson and William C. Placher in *The Christian Century* illustrates quite well the complexity of this year's seminar focus, the crisis of biblical authority in the contemporary church.[1] The exchange highlights difficult questions of

1. James M. Gustafson, "Just What Is 'Postliberal' Theology?" *The Christian Century* 116, no. 10, pp. 353-55; William C. Placher, "Being Postliberal: A Response to James Gustafson," *The Christian Century* 116, no. 11, pp. 390-92; and Gustafson,

historical relativism, pluralism, and natural science as interpreted by two theologians, both of whom I believe are sensitive to the crisis named above, but whose hermeneutics seem to yield little common ground for progress.[2] Nevertheless, they assume that pastors should be a part of solving the problems the scholars cannot solve. In another context, Robert W. Jenson, commenting on the alienation of the Bible from the church, lays the blame not on secular scholars, but "on *the clergy* and other churchly scholars like myself. Nobody else lost the Bible but we, and nobody else can reclaim it."[3]

What can pastors contribute to solving these problems? And what do their parishioners expect of them in practice? Most of my parishioners are aware of the complexities of our world; they do not expect their pastor to have all the answers to the questions that arise at the intersections of faith and the world. What they do expect is that I am able to give them a story that, while not provable in an empirical sense, is at least intelligible, coherent, and sustaining. Wherever they see challenges to their faith — from science, technology, philosophy, history, or fate — they want to know that their pastor can and will help them wrestle over these matters. They want help distinguishing sense from nonsense in theology. What counts in the end, however, is that within a community of faith, nurtured by Word and Sacrament, they are able to persevere.

Since I have experienced these expectations, I find myself attracted to theological proposals that give possible structure to my observations. For example, Ellen Charry talks about a "sapiental theology," or a theology more interested in the formation of the self than the emancipation of the self. She writes, "A pastoral or spiritual approach to doctrine is also interested in issues of coherence and intelligibility and moral responsibility. But it asks these questions not of the doctrine but of the life lived in light of the doctrine. Its concern is to demonstrate

---

"Liberal Questions: A Response to William Placher," *The Christian Century* 116, no. 12, pp. 422-25.

2. We hear the same old debate about the text absorbing the world, or vice versa.

3. Robert W. Jenson, "Hermeneutics and the Life of the Church," in *Reclaiming the Bible for the Church,* ed. Carl E. Braaten and Robert W. Jenson (Grand Rapids: Eerdmans, 1995), p. 105.

how the identity of God expressed by the doctrine maps a coherent, morally reasonable, unified, and godly — that is to say happy — life."[4]

Thinking of the identity of God not in terms of doctrine, but of story, Robert Jenson suggests a similar interest in coherence and a unified life when he talks about the *dramatic coherence* in the biblical story of salvation, a story of promise and fulfillment that drives towards a future in which God is all in all. Faith in such a God allowed Israel "to conceive a continuity of her own history through the discontinuities of her fate."[5] This same dramatic coherence of story challenges the church (paraphrasing Jenson) to find meaning in the repeatedly won conviction that God in his personal identity has been and will be the protagonist of her doings and sufferings, however apparently discontinuous.[6]

Finally, it seems obvious, in the light of the cross, that any story that coheres, any life lived fully, will show itself in sacrificial living. David Tracy chastises all of us when he asks, "Where, in all the discussions of otherness and difference of the postmoderns as well as the moderns and the antimoderns, are the poor and oppressed? These are the concrete others whose difference should make a difference. For through them the full and interruptive memory of the gospel is alive again among us."[7] It is one thing to talk about forming unified, morally reasonable, spiritually grounded lives; it is another thing to live them out in the public realm. I minister to a privileged suburban congregation; I also enjoy the "perks" of the Pastor-Theologian Program, which lives very well off the largesse of the Lilly Endowment. In both roles, I tremble.

Against the background of this kind of "pastoral thinking," I wish to turn to the life of my parish as a context for discussing the crisis of biblical authority in the church in the light of our chosen texts, the

---

4. Ellen T. Charry, "Spiritual Formation by the Doctrine of the Trinity," *Theology Today* 54 (October 1997):. 367-69. See also "Reviving Theology in a Time of Change," in *The Future of Theology*, ed. Miroslav Volf, Carmen Krieg, and Thomas Kucharz (Grand Rapids: Eerdmans, 1996), pp. 114-26; Ellen T. Charry, *By the Renewing of Your Minds: The Pastoral Function of Christian Doctrine* (New York: Oxford University Press, 1997).

5. Robert W. Jenson, *Systematic Theology*, Vol. 1 (New York: Oxford University Press, 1997), p. 64.

6. Jenson, *Systematic Theology*, p. 64.

7. David Tracy, *On Naming the Present* (Maryknoll: Orbis Books, 1994), p. 21.

akedah and Matthew's Passion. I begin with a quote from Robert Jenson: "the church's primal way of understanding the Crucifixion is that we live this narrative, that we rehearse the canonical story, in the context of Scripture's encompassing narrative and so that the rehearsing is a word-event in our own lives."[8] But how is this living or rehearsing done in the life of the church? First, Jenson suggests that it is done in the church's Good Friday liturgy. Then he expands his suggestion:

> Crucifixion and Resurrection together are the church's *Pasch,* her passing over from being no people to being God's people, her rescue from alienation to fellowship, her reconciliation. Only as this is enacted in the church as one event is the Crucifixion understood. One is — again — strongly tempted to say: what must happen as the fundamental explanation of atonement is that the ancient single service of the *Triduum,* "the Three Days," the continuous enactment of the Supper, the Crucifixion, and the Resurrection, covering Holy Thursday, Good Friday, and Easter Night, be celebrated.[9]

I wish to take Jenson's suggestion further and start already with Passion Sunday, following the liturgy through the *Triduum,* to find out what sort of story the church tells about God and about itself, and how that story might shape a full, Christian life. I need to note, first, that the texts referred to are from the Revised Common Lectionary, year A. In addition, I am a Lutheran pastor operating from an unabashedly Lutheran confessional position, so I will reflect Lutheran theology, liturgy, and hymnody. I wish also to note that, if we attend to all the propers for all the days and services of Holy Week, we are completely immersed in the larger scriptural context of the Passion. The Psalms of the Righteous Sufferer, the Servant Songs of Isaiah, Lamentations, the allegorical interpretation of Old Testament themes by the author of Hebrews — all these and more are appointed to locate the Passion within the story of Israel's relationship with God. Hence, we enter into the *Triduum* with the theme, "We should glory in the cross of our Lord Jesus Christ, for he is our salvation, our life, and our resurrection; through him we are saved and made free" (from the introduction to the

---

8. Jenson, *Systematic Theology,* p. 189.
9. Jenson, *Systematic Theology,* p. 190.

Roman rite). We are reminded of the close connection of cross and resurrection, as well as our participation in them. To quote Jenson again, "Crucifixion and Resurrection together are the church's *Pasch*, her passing over from being no people to being God's people, her rescue from alienation to fellowship, her reconciliation."[10]

Worship Planning

One of the first decisions our Worship Committee made in planning for Holy Week was that, on Passion Sunday, the choir would *sing* a setting of the Passion by Heinrich Schütz, rather than do the "reading in parts" that we usually do. Unlike the Bach Passions, this is simply the text of Matthew set to music, with a summary chorus at the end. There are no chorales or arias interpreting the text, just the music of Schütz and an occasional repetition of a word or phrase for emphasis. It was written as a liturgical piece and we planned to use it just that way. Still, it takes an hour to sing, making the whole service an hour and forty-five minutes long. Though this is not a congregation that expects only an hour-long service, this was still a stretch for us, so our strategy was to be direct and honest about the length, but to see it as an advantage — we were really going to learn Matthew.

We used the adult forums during Lent to discuss the passion of Matthew against the background of the whole gospel. This meant doing a little "tradition history," talking about the various settings of the material, looking at some of the usual historical cruxes, but most of our time was spent looking at the Old Testament foundation of the Passion, as well as surveying the gospel, looking at themes, patterns, and characters, and setting the Passion in that larger context.

Since only about twenty to twenty-five parishioners come regularly to forum, we also decided to make Matthew the core of our midweek Lenten services (vespers with a lesson or two and a ten-minute sermon). For psalmody I concentrated on the psalms that shape the Passion, but I chose for the theme the Great Commission, breaking it up into five sub-themes. Although I had not read Moberly at the time, I had read Otto Michel and Günther Bornkamm on this text, and they both treat it as a

---

10. Jenson, *Systematic Theology*, p. 190.

kind of hermeneutical key to the gospel as viewed from behind *(von hinter her zu verstehen)*. In other words, if we are doing some sort of "narrative theology," we assume that the *conclusion* of the narrative is central.

This is how I developed it:

1. *"All authority in heaven and on earth has been given me."* Here I talked about the tension in the narrative between who we know Jesus to be and how he is received, by authorities and by his Father. (I wish I had read Moberly by then, because I like what he does with the temptation account.) I dealt with the cry of abandonment and God's answer in the resurrection (I like Jenson's pithy summary: "the Crucifixion settled *who and what* God is; the resurrection settled *that* this God is.)

2. *"Go, make disciples of all nations..."* This is more than just the usual "sloganizing" mission text to be used in some triumphalist fashion. Making disciples is a process. They are not just called; they are instructed, trained, and sent. They are salt and light. They have their own discourse (Matt. 10); their fate is that of the Master; but they also get to call God "Father," and Jesus is their brother. I connected this with our call in baptism and its challenge (let your light so shine, etc.), as well as our parallels with the disciples in Matthew as those "of little faith." Finally, this was the place to connect with the universalizing theme of "all nations"; I talked about the movement in the gospel outwards (a shift at Matt. 13, according to Kingsbury) as represented by Gentile witnesses such as the centurion at the cross. This would be the place to get into Matthew's ecclesiology and the whole issue of supersessionism ("your house is forsaken"), but I could not go into that because of time (though we did do it in an adult forum).

3. *"baptizing them . . ."* Here I talked about Matthew as the gospel of the church, that we are baptized into a body, not into subjectivity or individualism (Robert Bellah's "Sheilaism," today's "mix and match" spirituality). That body has a history, tradition, and yes, even doctrine — assuming there is some sort of incipient Trinitarianism in the formula. Looking ahead to the Vigil, we will baptize children into the body of which we are members, and connect them to the head that is our head too. We will also share in the Eucharist, which is Christ's body for us, his "real presence" as the resurrected one.

159

4. *"teaching them to observe all things . . ."* This is the hard one for a Lutheran. Talking about the "greater righteousness," about fulfilling the law *(der Weg der Gerechtigkeit)*, tends to make me uneasy, but it has something to do with the life of faith as having a certain shape, certain models, certain priorities. It also challenges enthusiasm (that part I like) — "not everyone who says to me, Lord, Lord . . ." — as well as cheap grace, as done so eloquently by Bonhoeffer's *Cost of Discipleship.*

5. *"and lo, I am with you always . . ."* The final word from Emmanuel himself, God with us, who has known "godforsaken-ness" that we might not be forsaken. This text allows us to tie the gospel narrative together, from birth to resurrection, but it also sets that narrative in the larger narrative established "until the completion of the age" *(heos tes synteleias tou aionos)* (Matt. 28:20).

The Sunday before the Passion, we also discussed the text and music of the Schütz setting. A member of the congregation, who had written a dissertation on the piece, set it in its musical and historical context (Schütz was *Kapellmeister* in Dresden when he wrote it at age eighty-one!). We noted that Schütz, either intuitively or in simple recognition of the drama of the piece, seems to highlight musically what most biblical interpreters are saying about the text. He doubles or triples the various oaths, questions, and assertions that give strength to the development of the contrasting character (Peter's denial, Judas' "Is it I?", even Jesus' cry of dereliction becomes three times rather than two). He gives a major musical interpretation to the confession of the centurion, "Truly this was the Son of God." The motif of Jesus' blood comes through also in the special musical treatment of both the "blood money" and "his blood be on us and on our children."

In addition to the above, we also encouraged people to read the Passion story over at home and provided outlines and study guides for them to use.

27. The Tenebrae Service

DENTON McLELLAN

Proposal: To lead a group within the congregation during Lent 2001 in doing an in-depth study of the Passion narratives in the Gospels along with related Old Testament passages, which would be used in a Good Friday *Tenebrae* service as a means of demonstrating the value of a Christian reading of Scripture and showing how such a reading is enacted in worship.

Background and Impetus for Project

The service of Tenebrae is an ancient service of the church dating back to the fourth century. Traditionally held following communion on Maundy Thursday or preferably on the evening of Good Friday, the name *tenebrae* means "darkness" or "shadows," demonstrating the suffering of Jesus as candles are extinguished, one by one, following the reading of each lesson, until, at the end of the service, the church is left in total darkness.

On Good Friday of this year, our church revived the practice of a Tenebrae service after a hiatus of eight or nine years. It was a service structured according to readings of the traditional Seven Last Words from the cross along with parallel lessons from the Old Testament, interspersed with choral music and congregational hymns and symbolically dramatized by the extinguishing of the candles.

The service turned out to be one of the most moving and memorable Holy Week services we have conducted during my ministry in this parish. A number of worshipers expressed appreciation for the service and requested to know more about the tradition of Tenebrae while several left the service visibly moved by what had taken place. No doubt a part of the impact was due to the mood created in the service itself with the hauntingly beautiful choral music and Passion hymns, the dramatization of the Passion through the progressively darkened sanctuary, and of course the nature of the event we were remembering on that occasion.

The other element that accounted for the exceptional response was the narratives, read by members of the congregation and staff. Each set of readings was followed by a few moments of silent meditation and the response was profound. It appeared that many in the congregation heard the familiar Seven Last Words and lessons from the Passion narrative, as well as the Old Testament antecedents, in a fresh and powerful way.

In light of my reading for the Pastor-Theologian Program and our discussions in the seminars, I became interested in exploring how a Christian reading of Scripture could be done in a local congregation and, more specifically, how Scripture comes alive within the context of corporate worship and especially in a service such as Tenebrae. I therefore began to develop the idea of inviting a group of serious and intentional members of the congregation to an intensive Bible study, exploring in depth those passages that would be used in a Good Friday Tenebrae service next year.

Overall Plan for Bible Study Group

I anticipate that the group, carefully selected from the congregation, would meet weekly for six consecutive weeks for approximately an hour and a half each time. The basic material would be drawn from the Passion account in Matthew 26–27 but would also include reference to the narratives in the other three Gospels in order to provide a comprehensive overview of the suffering and death of Jesus. The last two classes would focus on the Seven Last Words from the cross and the parallel Old Testament passages that would be paired with them. The primary text for the study would, of course, be the Scripture itself, although I would also be guided by Raymond Brown's very helpful work on the Passion narrative. I would also likely share with the group some of the commentary from the Patristics and the Reformers. I would expect that those participating would commit themselves to the discipline of doing serious reading and study of the biblical texts and supplemental material. Readers in the Tenebrae service would be drawn from the study group itself.

Hermeneutical Presuppositions

Since a major object of the project would be to introduce members of the group to a Christian reading of Scripture, it is appropriate that I state clearly my own understanding of what constitutes such a discipline and practice. The following hermeneutical principles would undergird and inform my conduct of this project:

1. *Christological* — A Christian reading of Scripture interprets Scripture through the life, death, and resurrection of Jesus Christ. God's revelation in Christ is the unifying theme and reality that binds the Old and New Testaments together. This does not mean that the Old Testament is viewed primarily as a collection of prophetic tests that are fulfilled in the New, nor that Christian meanings are read into the Hebrew Scriptures in a way that violates the integrity and negates the original meaning of the text. It does mean that for the Christian community, all Scripture is judged by God's supreme revelation in Christ and is perceived to be the written Word that bears witness to Christ, who is the Living Word.

2. *Canonical* — A Christian reading of Scripture affirms that the locus of God's revelation is to be found in the authoritative canon of the Old and New Testaments. Without restricting the power of God's Spirit to reveal God's truth when and where He wills, it is within the church's accepted and authoritative canon of Scripture that we listen for God's Word, and that canon is the standard by which we judge all other truth claims.

3. *Ecclesial* — A Christian reading of Scripture can never be restricted to private reading and interpretation. The Scriptures are sacred writings that have come to us through the medium of a community of faith. While the right of individual interpretation of Scripture under the guidance of the Holy Spirit is a cherished principle of the Protestant tradition, we also are reminded in the Second Helvetic Confession that "The apostle Peter has said that the Holy Scriptures are not of private interpretation (II Peter 1:20), and thus we do not allow all possible interpretations." Therefore, the right of private interpretation must always be held in tension with the necessity of listening to the voice of the church through its creeds, confessions, and ancient rules of faith going back to the earliest times. In this project, we will demonstrate this practice of reading the text not merely as isolated individual believers but as those who are members of the body of Christ.

4. *Pneumatological* — A Christian reading of Scripture affirms that Word and Spirit are inseparable in interpreting and understanding Scripture. The Spirit does not reveal new truths that contradict or su-

persede God's Word revealed in Scripture. Rather, the Spirit bears witness to that Word already made known in Scripture. On the other hand, the Word in itself, apart from the Spirit, can and often does become a "dead letter," because it is the Spirit who not only first inspired the recording of that Word but also continues to be active in illuminating our understanding of it in the present.

5. *Presupposition of Faith* — Finally, a Christian reading of Scripture presupposes faith on the part of the hearer and student of Scripture. It is to those who are open and receptive to the Word that the Word is revealed ("They said to each other, 'Did not our hearts burn within us while he talked to us on the road, while he opened to us the scriptures?'" Luke 24:32).

Anticipated Outcome of Project

I would hope and expect to see some of the following results from the project proposed:

1. A satisfaction among members not only in the acquisition of knowledge and skills in interpreting Scripture, but even more, an excitement in discovering God's truth in a disciplined and prayerful study of the texts.
2. A recognition of the centrality of the Passion narrative in the larger story of salvation as recorded from Genesis to Revelation and a deeper understanding of how the Old and New Testaments relate to and inform each other.
3. An "ownership" in the Tenebrae service that would come as the culmination of having participated in the preparatory Bible study.
4. A sense of the presence and illumination of the Spirit that can be experienced through participation in the study. An appropriate prerequisite for this study might well be a willingness to be "surprised by the Spirit" in this experience of Christian reading.
5. Finally, I would see this short-term focused study as the harbinger and forerunner of continuing opportunities for similar types of disciplined Bible studies and Christian reading of Scripture in the future.

CHAPTER VI

CHRISTIAN PROCLAMATION

Introduction

It was the apostle to the Gentiles, St. Paul, whose ministry was marked by continual mission journeys and endless preaching, who likely summarized it best: "Faith comes from what is heard, and what is heard comes through the Word of Christ." Proclaiming the living Word of God is the Spirit-empowered means that couples the unconditional grace of God in Christ and its faithful human reception. Preaching ministers, declares St. Paul, are indispensable in a church that literally lives on and in the divine Word that comes through human words in both the Holy Scriptures and its ordained heralds: "But how are they to call on one in whom they have not believed? And how are they to believe in one of whom they have not heard? And how are they to hear without someone to proclaim him? And how are they to proclaim him unless they are sent? As it is written, 'How beautiful are the feet of those who bring good news'" (Rom. 10:14-17; cf. Isa. 52:7). So along with administering the "visible Word" of the sacraments, pastor-theologians boldly proclaim the "audible Word" of the sermons.

Therefore our first author's theological excerpt focuses on "Responsible Christian Proclamation." Challenging James Gustafson and other liberal Protestant theologians, the writer defends the uniqueness of "the reality of Christ in the world." Moreover, it is "the story of Scripture that gives shape to that reality" when the Bible is read by a Christian. Therefore, he argues, responsible proclamation is "about Christ and Christ alone." A lengthy doctrinal analysis ("God talk") on discerning the Word of God in a Christian reading of Scripture concludes with an interpreted series of daring affirmations concerning Christian proclamation rather as "God's talk": (1) the author of preaching is the Triune God; (2) the biblical Word is the essential element of preaching; (3) the church is founded upon God's grace; (4) the spoken Word is revelation; and (5) proclamation renews the church.

The next selection asks anew the psalmist's searching query: "How Can We Sing the Lord's Song in a Foreign Land?" The writer contends that the odd reality of the American church at the end of the 20th century is that of a paradox: "Though the 'what' of Scripture's presence is clear and undeniable, the 'how' is more and more contested." Even in the regional seminars of the pastor-theologians, what continually sparked debate was "'how' that [Scriptural] authority is grounded and exercised in the worship and ministry of the congregations." He proposes that the diverse approaches to Scripture likely originate more in our cultural communities of origin than in the nature of the scriptural text we hold in common. The real question is "the commensurability of the authority of various interpretations of Scripture." For finally, the purpose of the Scripture-event is not an academic interpretation but a personal transformation.

"The Cross: Its Particularity and Universality" presses the discussion still further with the related question, "What does the cross of Christ mean for us today?" Central to the writer's seminar experience was "the attempt to distinguish principles of translation that bridge the gap of time and space, and that relate particularity to universality." After exploring dimensions of meaning in the cross of Jesus (historicity, evangelist's intention, personal, communal, and cosmic significance), the author affirms that "the event of the cross/resurrection of Christ constitutes the normative focus of the church's proclamation." The current preacher's calling is not to "demythologize" (Bultmann) but to "re-mythologize," to discover and preach "those symbols and myths that are able to connect us with each other and the reality of that about which the biblical symbols speak."

The qualitative difference between lecturing to an audience and preaching to a congregation is explicated in "Preaching: Scripture and the Holy Trinity." The author identifies with the conviction that "the authority of the Bible stems from its self-authentication in the heart and mind of believers." The Holy Spirit employs the scriptural narrative to convey the reality of the crucified and risen Christ to listeners today. It is the Holy Spirit who testifies unto Jesus Christ and thereby incorporates us, through our faithful union with Christ, into the community of the Holy Trinity. The Trinitarian name reveals God's involvement in eternity. It is the preacher's duty and privilege to announce that "'God with us' is drawn into the very life of humanity and at the same time humanity is drawn into the very life of God."

Our final recapitulation calls for "A *Koinonia* of Pastors" to meet the current crisis in the church's life and mission. "If the bugle gives an indistinct sound, who will get ready for battle? So with yourselves" (I Cor. 14:8-9). Church renewal has always been grounded in scriptural renewal, in the life-giving work of the Holy Spirit effectively declaring that Jesus Christ is Lord of all. The institutional decline and decay of many of our churches is directly related to the widespread marginalization of the pastoral office "by the academy, a church bureaucracy, and a secular culture." Scripturally illiterate laity expect little from it, while scripturally distrusting pastors offer little to it. "When pastors abdicate their role as the primary leaders of Christian community and the primary readers of Christian Scripture, the pastoral office to which they are called becomes bankrupt." Neither secular structures nor ideological strictures will fill the bill. The ultimate solution is grounded in Scripture itself: "Acts 2:42 describes a uniquely Christian 'koinonia' (communion) which is formed around a devotion to the 'apostles' teaching.'" Pastor-theologians could also covenant together to arrive at a distinctively Christian and churchly reading of the Bible. They could reflect together on the claims of that same Scripture on the lives of pastors and their Christian communions. The Pastor-Theologian Program of Princeton's Center of Theological Inquiry deems this bold proposal to be worthy of your own prayerful consideration.

28. Responsible Christian Proclamation

PAUL D. MATHENY

Introduction

In a recent series of articles in the *Christian Century* (Vol. 116, nos. 10 and 12, 1999), James Gustafson criticizes the church for failing to answer the challenge of liberalism. Those not willing to accept Troeltsch's challenge to modern Christians should answer at least his questions. Gustafson argues that persons in congregations are disturbed by the cognitive dissonance they must experience between the modern sciences and the particularity of the truth claims of the Christian tradition as based upon revelation. He believes that, because Christianity is a "cognitive minority" in our cultural and intellectual life, we should have no epistemic privileges. We have inherited a world with a plurality of religious and cultural frames of reference, and so we should assume this context as our frame of reference and not that of biblical revelation. Many have left congregations exactly because pastors and theologians have failed to address the questions raised by our culture and their challenges to Christian tradition. It is the task of pastors to respond, even if they become liberals in the process.

If Gustafson is trying to advise pastors, then his challenge can be seen as an effort to critique Christian proclamation. It is valuable to reflect a moment upon this, for Gustafson's critique is a good expression of academic distrust of the tradition of the church. It raises important questions. Is the challenge that confronts pastors today the historical relativism Troeltsch worried about? Should pastors be concerned over their "rude" claims to have epistemic privileges, as if claiming such would be impolite? Is focusing upon the questions raised by our culture, its historical relativity, and its "dissonance" with the Christian tradition responsible?

Just what is it that pastors should proclaim, if we accept Gustafson's portrayal of our predicament as true? If we take historical relativism as the challenge to Christianity's claim to particularity that Gustafson claims it to be, then whatever we proclaim would be relative to our context. Anything radically new that may have happened in the world external to our context would be insignificant, except as history or as a claim to be history. Scripture's relevance would be stuck in the frame of reference we now assume as our cultural and intellectual context.

Do both the liberal and the preacher face the same dilemma? No! The Christian preacher, I would argue, has a way out of this dilemma. The Christian preacher is not stuck. The object of his preaching is something radically new. The biblical story relates the actual coming of God into the world in Jesus Christ. It is not the story of how God chose to be revealed in history, but of the reality that God came into the world. The categories and framework that Gustafson proposes fail, as all liberalism does, in that they cannot allow the reality of Christ in the world. Their "world" is the reality of their own experiences and thoughts within modern intellectual and cultural history. Because their categories for understanding the world are taken totally from their cultural context, they cannot allow the story of Scripture to give shape to reality. They cannot read the Bible as a Christian. In this one belief, they fail to responsibly advise pastors concerning what they should proclaim. Responsible proclamation for a pastor, I will argue, is about Christ and Christ alone.

A Christian reading of the Bible is necessary for the church's very existence. A liberal reading of the Bible cannot help us. If the Bible is not the central source for the church's self-understanding, the church ceases to be the church. The Bible exists for the church, and the church exists as a witness to the same witness the Bible gives: to the God of the Bible in Jesus Christ.

Affirmations of a Theology of the Proclaimed Word

We are accustomed to referring to theology as "God talk." Yet it is not in theological essays that God talks to his community; it is through proclamation. As such, the first task of a theology of preaching is to identify the God we confess. If we assume that a Christian reading of the Bible can communicate the truth about God, then the God we confess is the God we read in Scripture, the Triune God: Father, Son, and Holy Spirit. It is through a Christian reading of the Bible as Scripture that we are able to do this first task. The second task is to identify God's relationship to us. If a Christian reading of the Bible can communicate the truth about God, then we are those whom God addresses in Scripture — those who are confronted with the salvific action and grace of God. Preaching is concerned with God's action for us and with us as witnessed to in Scripture.

In the end, the question must be raised as to how it is possible to conceive of proclamation as being "God's talk." This is the litmus test for its truth. From a Christian perspective, the question of what happens when the Word is proclaimed is the pivotal question for all theology. How to judge what happens when the Word is proclaimed may be summarized in some basic affirmations concerning oral Christian proclamation.

a. The Author of Preaching Is the Triune God

For the theology of proclamation, the first question addressed is, "Who is God?" Christians confess that God is Father, Son, and Holy Spirit. Preaching addresses this reality. What is proclaimed is the Word of God, the good news of the Gospel. Through it we receive the promise of salvation and the call to repentance and to faith. The focal point is always Jesus Christ. Jesus Christ is the only reason that God is speaking to us and the only reason that we preach to others. God's self-disclosure takes priority over everything else. If we give priority to solving the problem of our culture's cognitive dissonance, we have nothing to contribute to its resolution.

b. The Biblical Word Is the Sine Qua Non of Preaching

The faith that we may discern the truth about God from a Christian reading of the Bible is the essence of Christian preaching. Although biblical texts are connected with historical events, the focus is not on these events but upon God. It is God who spoke and speaks in history. God acted and acts in history. God acted and acts with God's people. God's actions are not available to historical reconstruction or philosophical construction. They occurred in history for us. The promise to which we cling and from which we preach is that God will again act in history with the community of faith. As this community of faith, we confess that the Bible, which contains the Scriptures of the Old and New Testaments, is the Word of God.

Added to this we recall the analogy between God the Son and the written Word of God — the Old and New Testaments. The sermon that is preached is God's Word and the Bible is God's Word. The sermon can be God's Word because it is based on the biblical narrative that points directly to God's acts in Christ. The Scriptures are God's Word, because we find therein the true voices of believers pointing to the Word made flesh. Jesus Christ is the authority witnessed to through human words.

Biblical witness, however, is not a static witness, not a mere record of past events. Instead it is a living voice. The Apostle Paul recognized this about the gospel and proclaimed it in Galatians 1:11-12. It is as a living, breathing voice that it brings life to the church. This living voice is none other than Christ himself.

c. The Church Is Founded upon Grace

When revelation is proclaimed, the church should understand that it rests on the foundation of witnesses individually called to be apostles. The church needs to understand that it does not live for itself alone; its life is not its own, nor does it rest on its own foundation. The church is founded solely on the unique action of God accomplished in Christ. The church is founded on the overflowing of God's grace made present in Jesus Christ our Savior, who is the fulfillment of the law. This is the gospel. The church is the community of faith gathered for the purpose of revelation. The church is the place where the biblical story lives. In the church, God has spoken and still speaks. There we are given our mission and our vocation. Proclamation's task is to witness, not to offer an apology for Christian faith.

The church must recognize that it is subject to and founded upon a call. The church itself does not proclaim a religious frame of reference. The church's perspective is God's perspective. It is the church's task to discover God's will and to live it. Preaching is the proclamation of the church's obedience to the task it has been given by Christ.

Once again, the question of humanity's sinfulness and disobedience is central. How can a congregation made up of sinful people participate in the holy work of God? How can a sermon become not only a proclamation, and therefore revelation, to the church and at the same time be a proclamation of the church? This is accomplished in the work of the Holy Spirit. Through the Holy Spirit, the sermon becomes the Word of God. The preacher is a member of the Body of Christ. Likewise, the members of the congregation are members of that same body. Therefore, the sermon is a proclamation of that body, made to the body. The sermon, as proclamation, becomes a proclamation of the church as a whole.

d. The Proclaiming Church Is a Confessing Community

The church is central. Both the belief in proclamation as the Word of God and the belief in the Bible as the Word of God are confessions, statements of faith that have validity only within the living community of faith. It is only in the church that proclamation has its rightful place, because proclamation is bound up with the church's existence, vision, and mission. Proclamation conforms to revelation, or it is not proclamation. The Bible provides the entire framework for Christian proclamation. Therefore proclamation is a particular concrete event that takes place in the context of the life of the church. It is a concrete event occurring in history. It does not deal with an idea of general significance that could arise at any time in any place. It deals with a relationship with the living Christ alone.

e. The Spoken Word Is Revelation

What is the nature of proclamation that is so tightly bound up with the worshiping congregation? Proclamation is nothing other than revelation. The living God is revealed in the Scriptures. The living God is proclaimed in the sermon and the sacraments. The task of the pastor and the church is to faithfully read the Scriptures and listen to God's Word, so that God, in Jesus Christ, can be heard.

God's purpose, both in Scripture and in proclamation, is revelation. God bears witness to revelation and intends for us to do so as well. The fixed point of all proclamation is revelation. God has revealed God; the Word has become flesh. God has taken on human nature and has put on sinful humanity. Humanity has gone astray like errant sheep, but we are called back home. Indeed, in Christ, God goes and searches for us until we are found. Finally, God has sacrificed Jesus Christ on the cross for our sins. In his death on the cross, Christ has borne our sin and our punishment for us. We have been redeemed and reconciled to God in Christ. To believe means to recognize that this is so.

We must carefully distinguish between who is being revealed and who is revealing. It is not the case that the pastor reveals God. Only God can reveal God. God has done so in the past (Epiphany) and will do so in the future *(Parousia).* God is the actor. Whatever happens through proclamation is an act of God. Revelation is a self-contained process in which God is the subject, God is the object, and God is the means by which God is revealed. Only God can provide truth that God exists. Proclamation is an act of God in Jesus Christ through the Holy Spirit.

What now can be said about the content of preaching? The content of preaching must be the fact of God's sacrificial gift to humanity. This gift was not only given to humanity at one specific point in the past, but is also present now and in the future. This fulfillment of revelation is the redemption that awaits us. The life of faith is not merely focused on something that has happened in the past. The life of faith is oriented toward the *Parousia,* the return of Christ. Preaching, therefore, moves in an atmosphere of eschatological expectation. Preaching is obedience in listening to the will of God. It is the exercise of sovereign power on the part of God and obedience on the part of humanity.

f. Proclamation Renews the Church

It is only as a result of proclamation that the church is continually being built up anew. The church is renewed every time the Word of God is proclaimed to it and by it. Proclamation evokes response. The response of the community of faith is decision, repentance, renewed faith, and the strength to go out into the world to proclaim the good news. Through faith we are inaugurated into a new, transforming life and are given the strength to constantly turn from our old ways. Only by the grace of God can the church go out and work in the world. This is the work of reconciling the world to God through Jesus Christ.

173

In the New Testament, preaching is not seen apart from the function of the apostles. The apostolic function is fundamental to the foundation and the existence of the church (see Matt. 16:18-19; 18:15-20). Those who are called follow in Christ's footsteps. They are called to their mission and must continue to act as the apostles did, because the pastor is the successor to the apostles. This is the true meaning of the priestly function of the ministry.

Final Remarks

Having argued for the possibility of a true Christian reading of the Bible, I outlined the various affirmations of a theology of proclamation above. Basic to these affirmations is the belief that a theology of proclamation necessarily contains within it the elements of a confession of faith. The questions addressed are the same. Who is God the Father, Son, and Holy Spirit? Is a Christian reading of the Bible truthful? Who is the church? How is God made known to the church? It is only when we realize that God is the primary actor that we can talk of our proclamation as responsible proclamation. It is God who proclaims, God who is the subject of proclamation, and God's community who hears God being proclaimed. Only when we realize this can the community of faith become the witnessing community and be sent into the world to proclaim the Good News. Only then can the church be the church God has prepared it to be.

Post-Christendom Christianity is faced with the challenge that the Reformers and early Christianity faced. It is the challenge of proclaiming the gospel to a world distant from the power of the biblical narrative. This essay suggests that the church is stuck in a reaction to pluralism, so that it continues to rely upon biblical interpretation that is alien to the Bible as Scripture. Since the eclipse of the biblical narrative by historical criticism, proclamation has been married to the interpretation of history. This marriage is now facing a divorce. Without significant revision, historical criticism can no longer help us. Today academic scholars such as James Gustafson continue to call us to wed historical methods and biblical exegesis for the purpose of interpreting contemporary life in theoretical terms. We listen to this call at our own peril. Certainly their expectation is a very serious one. Our response should be just as serious. As Karl Barth said over seventy years ago, the church has the theology that it earns.

29. How Can We Sing the Lord's Song in a Foreign Land?

CHARLES D. VALENTI-HEIN

If there is a single thread holding the worshiping church together at the beginning of the twenty-first century, there can be no doubt but that its basic fiber consists of the words of Christian Scripture. The past five hundred years have seen seismic changes in the structures of the various Christian churches. There have been numerous revisions and revolutions in liturgical practice within and among the confessional branches of Christianity since the Reformation. The number of prayers written and offered would defy compilation. But in each and every reform, revision, or recasting of the Christian liturgy you would find the reading of Scripture and the influence of biblical imagery on prayers and meditations.

The odd reality of the church in this age, however, is that it seems that the single thread of unity has increasingly become a source of anxiety. Though the "what" of Scripture's presence in the life of the church is clear and undeniable, the "how" is more and more contested. In an attempt to address this rising concern for the role of Scripture in the church, the Center of Theological Inquiry, through the generosity of the Lilly Endowment, sought to bring together pastors from various theological and confessional backgrounds to engage in serious and disciplined conversation regarding issues of the authority of Scripture in the church.

In regional gatherings, the central focus of the work of those groups has been two rich and yet difficult texts from Christian Scripture: the story of the binding of Isaac found in Genesis 22, and the narrative of Jesus' Passion as told by Matthew 26–27. In each case, proper and diligent attention has been paid to the text, with many fruitful observations, some theological reflection, and a fair share of contextual discussion. It has become abundantly clear, at least to this participant, that there are several functional approaches taken to the text, and varying degrees of comfort with the presuppositions that may inform each individual's preferred approach to Scripture. In spite of this diversity of approaches and variation of presuppositions, the central question that sparked debate has not been *whether* Scripture functions as an authority for the church, but rather *how* that authority is grounded and exercised in the worship and ministry of congregations nearly two thousand years after the last of the words were written, assembled, and edited into a form generally recognized by the Christian churches to be sacred.

Complicating this pluralistic approach to Scripture within the church is the added reality that the surrounding cultural influences that feed and inform the life and work of the church are, at least in contemporary terms, increasingly secular. Though this notion of "secularism" is slippery at best, what it seeks to elucidate is that what a seminary professor named as the "intractable, intangible" questions that form the center of religious discourse are marginalized in the larger world of public debate. What claims attention is that which is tractable and tangible, with what Kant might have called the "noumenal realm" relegated to private reflection and parlor games. The fundamental issue, for those interested in questions generically regarded as "religious," is that it is difficult to carve out the context for a "sacred" conversation in a "secular" environment. The problem is only compounded when one introduces what is purportedly a "sacred" text as an authority.

In this context, while a clear focus on the text of Scripture itself may be gratifying and enlightening, it may be important to assure that sufficient attention is paid to the backgrounds and foregrounds that have informed various readings and discussions of the text. David Tracy illumines some of the issues involved in this move from the text to its context in his book *The Analogical Imagination*. The second sentence (p. xi) sets the question: "In a culture of pluralism, must each religious tradition finally either dissolve into some lowest common denominator or accept a marginal existence as one interesting or purely private option?"

The simple fact is that the pluralism manifest in this particular group of pastor-theologians is modest when considered on a global scale. All of us at least would affirm a centrality for this text — a presumption that would not hold in the larger context of this age on the North American continent. Yet even in this context, in which the text we share enjoys an assumed prominence, the perceived diversity of opinions regarding *how* this text may function in the various communities threatens to drive the conversation toward lowest-common-denominator or private options for interpretation from which we will share the fruits, but not the assumptions, of our labors. The questions I would like to examine in this reflection, then, are what it is that informs our unique choices of the criteria by which we tend to approach the text, and what the conditions would be under which we are willing to treat the text as "authoritative," if at all.

I would suggest that if we examined the diverse approaches to Scripture that exist around the table when a group of pastor-theologians gather, the reason for that diversity would lie more in communities of origin than in the nature of the text we hold in common. Simply put, what a congregation wants and needs from the text in Grand Rapids, Michigan, may not be exactly the same as what is desired or required in a "Gen-X" congregation in the Twin Cities, or in God's real home town of Goodrich, Minnesota. The real reason we come at the text so differently is that we come at it from such different directions and with such different questions that to do otherwise would violate the trust of the communities that have called us to the ministry.

What this simple realization leads me back to is the question of whether the really important question we need to deal with is the "authority of Scripture," or if it is rather "the authority of *interpretations* of Scripture." To put it to a finer point, is the real question the *commensurability* of the authority of various interpretations of Scripture?

In order to approach this question of commensurability, however, it may be important to pay close attention to the problem not only of the variety of "publics" but to the variety of criteria for authoritative claims that dominate each of those arenas. In particular, I would suggest that in order to move between these various publics, and the competing methodologies they endorse, it may be valuable for the theologian who finds the conversations between these publics important to search for different analogies for the theological project than those that dominate one or another of those realms. Specifically, it may be that for theology to negotiate successfully the challenges of authoritative appeal to Scripture, we would do well to seek to understand our fundamental relationship to the text less in terms of arguments and more in terms of "performance."

A word of caution is required at the outset. There is a danger in the use of the language of "performance" to assume that then the audience is largely passive — that the interpretation of Scripture is something done "for" people, rather than something in which the people are engaged. To get to the nuance of performance I recommend, I would encourage a creative recovery of a term from the thought of Martin Luther, who writes of the object of biblical interpretation in terms of *"enarratio."*

In his *Brief Instruction on What to Look for and Expect in the Gospels,* Luther writes, "When you open the book containing the gospels and read or hear how Christ comes here or there, or how someone is brought to him, you should therein perceive the sermon or the Gospel through which he is coming to you, or you are being brought to him. For the preaching of the Gospel is nothing else than Christ coming to us, or we being brought to him."[1] What is clear for Luther is that the goal *(telos)* of interpretation of the text is not a reasoned argument regarding abstract truth; instead, interpretation is an event in which one *encounters* the living Word of God. Exposition of Scripture, therefore, is not a matter of "commentary" on a written page, but it is a matter of "enarrating" — i.e., of bringing the text to life in the hearing of the people. Kenneth Hagen elucidates Luther's sense of this in his work on Luther's approach to Scripture: "'Enarrare,' for which there is no simple English equivalent, means to speak, to tell, or to set forth in detail. A public context is connoted. Therefore, it means to speak in public in detail. 'Enarratio' includes 'narratio,' which means to narrate, but involves both 'detail' and 'public.' 'Enarrare' means to take out (to narrate) and to apply. In other words, this process takes theology out of the text and applies it in public."[2]

When speaking of the authority of Scripture in relation to "performance," then, what we really acknowledge is that the reality of the biblical witness is not, and cannot be confined to, its written occurrence,

---

1. *Luther's Works: Galatians,* American Edition (Minneapolis: Fortress, 1964), pp. 35, 121.

2. Kenneth Hagen, *Luther's Approach to Scripture as Seen in His "Commentaries" on Galatians, 1518-1535* (Tübingen: Mohr, 1993), p. 50.

but can be understood only in the context of its public enactment, as it is read, preached, or discussed in a particular context. But the criterion for judging a great performance may be different from the criterion by which the public or the academy certifies as appropriate the appeal to a source as "authoritative."

The simple way to navigate these thorny questions — the way Tracy suggests has become prevalent in modern times — is to collapse them all into matters of personal taste. It is certainly possible simply to throw up our hands and insist that the one "right" interpretation is the one that appeals to *us,* and should we be so fortunate, to those we've met along the way whose tastes are more or less congruent to our own. The problem with such an approach is that it negates the important *public* aspect of the text that is captured in Luther's sense of *enarratio.*

Might it be that the real problem of the authority of Scripture in the modern church is not really a crisis of the authority of Scripture at all, so much as it is a crisis of pride on the part of interpreters, and a failure on the part of the contemporary church to take seriously enough the fundamental and glorious diversity that constitutes the church at the dawn of the twenty-first century? Might it be that what we're really arguing is for our own comfort, and not for Scripture at all?

As a starting point, I would suggest two strategies for overcoming these entwined challenges of individualism and pride that confound attempts to place Scripture in the life of the church. First, it is necessary to recover the communal ground for all appeals to authority in general. As the church, it is important to appreciate that this communal ground is itself a composite of several "publics," to use Tracy's terms. We cannot claim the communal ground for Scripture unless its various public manifestations in worship, study, and mission are shared.

Any approach to Scripture, then, must be mediated by sensitivity to context. It must simply be acknowledged that a community of scholars within the context of the modern university will approach the text differently from a community of attorneys, or a community of farmers, or a community of immigrants. In each case the various publics from which the community is gathered and to which the individuals within the community may be accountable will, at least in part, dictate the place of the text in the gathering of the community as it worships, as it studies, and as it takes the Word back into its surrounding world. It must be clear, however, that this sensitivity to context does not entail a

Balkanization of Christianity, such that the text can be read *only* at the lowest level of communal agreement, or that any and all reference to the text must be taken to be idiosyncratic and therefore incommensurate when one leaves the immediate sphere of interpretation. Such dangers, however, can be avoided if the community of interpretation is clear that the text is not a possession of the community, but that the community itself is constituted by and a possession of the text.

The second strategy I would suggest in order to meet the entwined challenges of individualism and pride rests in the understanding that insofar as the *telos* of interpretation is best understood not in terms of rational argument but rather in terms of artistic performance, the mark of authority may best be understood as an appreciation of interpretation as process, which can finally be judged only within the various perspectives that merge each time Scripture is invoked in the gathering of the faithful. One of the implications of this thought is that *final* authority, if such a notion has any merit whatsoever, must be understood as a dynamic *relationship* by which the text, with all its surplus of meanings, is brought to bear in a particular context, motivating a community of faith to respond to God's unique call to that time and place in continuity with the historic witness of the church throughout the ages. This relational sense of authority bears the insistence that, finally, the text of Scripture is an *event* in which the lives of believers are called beyond all normal and familiar categories of knowing, because the point of the event surpasses the capacities of human knowing. Indeed, the purpose of the Scripture-event is not to interpret the ancient text, but to bring the listener/reader to life in a way that is truly transformative.

A "good" or "bad" performance of the text, then, is not simply a matter of personal preference, but may be measured by the extent to which the meeting of text and believer is a catalyst to authentic response to the life-changing faith that Christians know and claim in Jesus Christ. Such interpretations will not *foreclose* possibilities for Christian life in the world, but *disclose* possibilities by which a particular people in a particular place and time can become a part of a witness that transcends and completes our particularity.

30. The Cross: Its Particularity and Universality

PAUL A. WEE

What does the cross of Christ mean for us today? How can the particularity of the historical event of crucifixion be preached and taught as having universal significance, that is, significance for all people at all times?

These questions lead to an inquiry about the principles which underlie the "translation" of the text into contemporary idiom. Various principles are assumed in such a translation, whether or not the preacher-theologian is aware of them. The attempt to distinguish principles of translation that bridge the gap of time and space, and that relate particularity to universality, has been at the center of lively debate during the pastor-theologian gatherings in the Southeast Region.

Three Dimensions of Meaning

There are several levels of meaning implied in the cross of Jesus, among them the following:

a. *The historicity of the event itself — what "really happened."* I believe this is an important element of our understanding, even though we must recognize the difficulties in describing with accuracy the historical circumstances surrounding the death of Jesus (for example, the limits of our knowledge of the period and the overlay of tradition that can obscure historical fact). Nevertheless, a reliable modicum of historical fact illumines meaning and prevents reduction of the Passion to a type of Gnosticism or mythology unrelated to the realities of life. The insistence on such a reliable modicum (Jesus lived, was "crucified under Pontius Pilate," left followers) implies, however, that one of the most basic affirmations of faith rests in part on a probability.

b. *The meaning of the event — that is, "what the evangelists intended and conveyed to their audiences," as Raymond Brown put it.* This is the heart of the proclamation, the *kerygma* (gospel) of the early church and the church through the ages. The proclamation of the gospel is central to the Passion narratives of all the evangelists, although it is evident that each writes from a different perspective, reflecting the needs of the community. Mark, for example, emphasizes the anguish of Jesus, his bearing of the cross, and his forsakenness by God. Luke emphasizes God's uplifting presence throughout the Passion. Matthew is concerned with the fulfillment of Old Testament prophecy. As with the various atonement theories, vicarious satisfaction (Anselm), moral influence (Abelard), Christus Victor (Aulen), each of the Passion narratives has meaning and relevance for a particular time and place, without necessarily contradicting each other or violating the integrity of the event itself.

Already within the New Testament context the cross was understood in terms that go well beyond the historical fact of the death of Jesus. The early church believed that Jesus was the Christ of God, and that this act manifested the depths of the reconciling love of God for the creation (Eph. 3:18-19). The crucifixion also expressed the submission to the demands of the law (Phil. 2:8) for the purpose of releasing the sinner from the law's condemnation (Gal. 3:13; Col. 2:14; II Cor. 5:19; Eph. 2:16). It also expressed the divine victory over the powers of evil. In the life of the Christian, the cross represented the call to a way of living in which one was willing to suffer for the sake of Christ (Matt. 10:38; 16:24).

c. *The universal significance of the Passion of Christ — that is, the meaning of the event for the lives of all people.* Can it be said that there is something in the cross that discloses or reveals the power of transformation that is expressed in this event and yet transcends it? In my ministry, I have attempted to ask this question from a strictly empirical standpoint as follows: what are the factors in the dynamic of human interaction that are able to produce healing, hope, and reconciliation out of situations characterized by despair and alienation? At the risk of oversimplifying complex phenomena, my answer to this question is, (1) the willful subjection of one's self to the condition of alienation by becoming vulnerable, by being willing to suffer for the other, and (2) the acceptance of the other unconditionally, in spite of the other's hostility and hatred, including projected self-hatred. In my experience, these are the fundamental characteristics of a dynamic that is able to effect healing and wholeness in situations of daily life (such as the relationship between wife and husband, or between groups in conflict). Such experiences have deepened my understanding of the meaning of cross and resurrection. They have provided me with an understanding of the power of grace that is at once rooted in the historical event of Jesus Christ and at the same time transcends that event.

Joseph Sittler once suggested that Jesus is not the inventor of grace, but rather its incarnation. It is because of the historically-rooted event of the cross and resurrection of Jesus Christ that such moments in contemporary life take on their deepest meaning and receive their healing power. It belongs to the task of the church catholic, and to the vocation of the pastor-theologian, to discern such moments in contemporary life, identify with them, and point them to the source of their healing power in the event of Jesus as the Christ.

The Normative Focus

Just as the event of the Exodus constituted the normative focus of the Old Testament faith in God's deliverance from forces of bondage and death, so the event of the cross/resurrection of Christ constitutes the normative focus of the church's proclamation. It is only in light of the cross/resurrection event that the life and ministry of Jesus can be understood in its fullness. Speaking of the resurrection, John Knox *(Jesus, Lord and Christ)* claims that "it was not the final miracle of a series, but the first. It was not accepted because of earlier miracles, but earlier miracles were accepted because of the resurrection. For the resurrection was the moment when not only the spiritual lordship of Jesus began, but when also the whole earthly life was 'transfigured' before his disciples."

The resurrection would, of course, mean nothing apart from the Passion that occasioned it. Indeed the two are so integrally related that the very language that speaks of two events rather than one leads to an unfortunate confusion. It is the cross/resurrection that is miracle, a sign-event in which is disclosed the one power that bears the transforming power for human life.

For the church, furthermore, it is through the event of the cross/resurrection that the dramatic events of Old Testament history find their full significance. The meaning of the creation of the world at the beginning of time is grasped only through the Word *(logos)* that becomes flesh in Jesus Christ (John 1). The full significance of the Passover and Exodus is now understood in light of Jesus, the Passover lamb, who is brought to Calvary to be sacrificed for the sins of the world. The prophets are now understood, not only in the *Sitz im Leben* in which they first appear, but also in the Christ who comes as fulfillment of the prophetic hope. For Matthew in particular the words of the prophets find their fulfillment in the life and Passion of Jesus the Messiah.

For the life of the church today it can be no different. The primary norm for its life and its ministry of proclamation, witness, and service is the cross/resurrection of Christ. It is the focal point of the church's announcement of the good news of God's free grace to bring transformation to individual and social life. The cross/resurrection is at once a sign of God's identification with the brokenness, injustice, and oppression that characterize the human condition and a disclosure of the power of suffering love that overcomes it. Without the cross/resurrection at the center of our preaching, we fail to discern the pretension and idolatry at the heart of our individual and collective existence. We fail to tap the one power that is able to overcome guilt, sin, and the many forms of bondage, including political and economic oppression, freeing us to know salvation and wholeness.

Furthermore, the symbol of the cross/resurrection represents the call to follow Christ wherever the path leads, whether we are acting voluntarily or under compulsion. This is the meaning of the story of Simon of Cyrene, who becomes a model of the life of discipleship for the church. Yet to say that Simon is a model of discipleship is not to say that he is, in himself, an example to be emulated, either literally (walking around with a wooden cross) or figuratively (being willing to suffer for Christ, to bear the burdens of others in Christ's name). Rather, Simon's action takes on significance only in the light of the central event of the death and resurrection of Jesus. In light of God's gracious action in Christ we, like Simon, are called — even compelled — to suffer for Christ's sake and to follow him into new life.

Re-mythologizing: The Task of the Preacher/Teacher

The process of reinterpreting historical events in light of the present needs of the community begins in the Passion narratives themselves.

Matthew's account of the Passion is written in the context of the destruction of Jerusalem. In one sense the rending of the veil represents a re-visiting of the crucifixion in light of God's punishment of the leaders of the Temple, a punishment that is taking place some forty years after the crucifixion. The desolation of the Lord's house represents a retelling of the account of the crucifixion in order to express its meaning for the contemporary church.

In dealing with these symbols today, the preacher needs to be aware of the extent to which the original meaning has been corrupted and determine whether such corruption has rendered inadvisable the use of the symbol itself. Given the fact that the community determines the meaning of symbols, this task belongs to the whole church. Still, each pastor must decide, for example, if the term "miracle" (in the face of Miracle Ear, Miracle Gro, Miracle Whip, and the conventional exclamation "It's a miracle!" for anything astonishing) can be interpreted in a way that is able to express the biblical meaning. St. John's use of "sign" for miracle instead of "wonder" or "power" indicates that the problem is not a new one. In a sense, every sermon represents an effort to recast the ancient message in terms that are understandable today. The challenge is not to demythologize (reducing to an abstract principle or propositional truth) but to "re-mythologize," that is, to discover those symbols and myths that are able to connect us with each other and with the reality of that about which the biblical symbols speak.

Here the arts come to the aid of the preacher. Movies such as *Good Will Hunting, The Virgin Spring, West Side Story,* or *Amistad* might help us rediscover the essence of the message that is expressed most decisively in the cross and resurrection of Christ. These are not substitutes for the historical event of the cross/resurrection of Jesus, nor do they convey the fullness of its biblical meaning. They are, rather, contemporary images that provide insight into the dynamic of human transformation rooted in that power that finds its clearest focus in the story of the cross/resurrection of Jesus Christ.

31. Preaching: Scripture and the Holy Trinity

SONJA M. HAGANDER

Questions of Audience

As I read Matthew, I cannot but help think of my ministry's campus context in the middle of a city. What would the words of these two chapters do to the Muslims crowded into Starbucks a block away? What will the words do to the freshmen students who come from within a Christian faith tradition, and yet now after their first college religion course doubt (they claim) the existence of God, after learning that God's creation of the world in six days might not conform to their understanding of six literal days? The college audience varies incredibly. For example, I cannot assume when I preach that even the word "passion" is understood as having anything to do with the Passion story itself. Some may know it of course. Others will never have heard it before in reference to Jesus' Passion.

For the preacher, the truthfulness of the Bible, then, must have something to do with language and the use of language. We cannot get beyond language; it rules us. Language creates reality. The Bible, then, becomes self-authenticating. By this I mean that by reading the Bible we do not "gain access" to some foundational Truth. I believe that we cannot "get outside" of language in the Bible or anywhere else. The Scriptures are not saving in and of themselves. They are a witness to Christ as Savior. God's promise is presented to us in the Word. I trust Scripture to bring people to faith in its particular proclamation and particular contexts with the power of the Holy Spirit.

I like Roy Harrisville's statement that "the authority of the Bible stems from its self-authentication in the heart and mind of believers. At bottom, the Scriptures of Old and New Testaments derive their authority as sole and final rule for faith and life from their power to evoke assent and trust, to wring a 'yes! yes!' from deep inside their readers and hearers."[1] Not only does the Bible function authoritatively in the community

---

1. Carl Braaten and Robert Jenson, eds., *Reclaiming the Bible for the Church* (Grand Rapids: Eerdmans, 1995), p. 48.

186

of faith, but it may also function as Scripture, with God grasping individuals through the story of God's revelation of Jesus Christ, outside the community of faith as well.[2] We become receivers of Truth, not searchers for Truth. So in my academic context, the Word has power not only among those students and faculty that are Christians but also among those who have never heard the gospel. Behind this fact is a certain doctrine of the Trinity or Holy Spirit that seems worth exploring here.

The Holy Spirit and Scripture

Behind my thoughts on Matthew's Passion, I have in mind the Trinity as community. The shape that comes to mind is a circle, with the Father, Son, and Holy Spirit as points on that circle. In creation, that circle is opened and God goes forth into the world. This image is similar to Irenaeus' "two hands of God." The goal of all creation is a gathering into community, closing the circle of the Trinity. I Corinthians 15 may be read in this light. "When all things are subjected to him, then the Son himself will also be subjected to the one who put all things in subjection under him, so that God may be all in all" (v. 28). God is the complete community, gathering in all of creation.

Before the closing of the circle, we must attend to the open hands in the world. Irenaeus' view of the Spirit and Son as the two hands of God is very clear in John, when Jesus discusses the promise of the Holy Spirit: "The Advocate, the Holy Spirit, whom the Father will send in my name, will teach you everything, and remind you of all that I have said to you.... When the Advocate comes, whom I will send to you from the Father, the Spirit of truth who comes from the Father, he will testify on my behalf. You also are to testify because you have been with me from the beginning" (14:26–15:27). We, then, are pressed to name that Spirit of life in the world as the Spirit of Christ. The Spirit then is the gatherer and sender, creating community and mutuality, which already exists in the Trinity, and sending us to name life in the Spirit as life in Christ. Then the naming re-creates community.

---

2. This also means that the audience at Augsburg College is making and hearing many arguments for Truth, whether they be voiced in the language of Biology, Philosophy, or Theology, for example.

The Gospel of Matthew is helpful in setting the stage for Spirit-talk. It clearly shows God's mission taking up all of creation. Jesus is part of this mission, conformed in action to God's will in the world. This is reminiscent of Jürgen Moltmann's emphasis on the goal of the Trinity: "The interactions between Christ and the Spirit must be understood as forces of historical movement and should be seen in the light of their goal."[3] Matthew's Passion narrative carries with it a strong sense of urgency and relentlessness. This mission of God in the world is like God responding to the different voices and calling us to respond in mutuality. Jesus is killed as King of the Jews.

It is important to note that his construction does not separate the Spirit of God the Father and God the Son. To do that would be to slip into Modalism or Montanism. This construction is also faithful because it takes seriously the Nicene Creed and Scripture. It also does not remove emphasis on Christ as the saving event.

The Christian tradition has been extremely concerned with the tension of unity and diversity in the Trinity. Today is a time, like other times in history, when it is common for people to make claims on God, Christ, Spirit; it is also a time in which it is common to disclaim God, Christ, Spirit. The Trinity is torn apart and each person is used for better or worse. We live in a time when the Trinity is viewed by some as three gods. It is presumed in the readings of some feminist theologies that God as Father is patriarchal, supporter and infrastructure of systematic violence to women. In the readings of liberation theology, only part of society may claim Jesus as their Christ. And for the "touchy-feely types," the Spirit is a breath that only some may hold for themselves, creating separation rather than unity among peoples. This is the present danger of separating the persons of the Trinity. On the other hand, it is also common, in keeping the unity of the Trinity, to create a static God, separate from our daily lives. This God is a mysterious one that has no creative action in this world, in history.

This view of the Holy Spirit speaks to the audience at Augsburg College. The Holy Spirit as the breath of life and the creator of hope challenges present-day individualism. The power of the Holy Spirit is the power that calls us into being. We are not called into being as sepa-

---

3. Jürgen Moltmann, *The Spirit of Life: A Universal Affirmation* (Minneapolis: Fortress Press, 1993), p. 223.

rate individuals, but into community. Life, however, does not guarantee community; plenty of people live without a sense of community. The Holy Spirit, though, has the power and authority to name life as life in Christ. This truly is the living Body of Christ, the Christian community that is outside any borders or margins that we know. "If the Trinity is a community," according to Moltmann, "then what corresponds to it is the true human community of men and women. A certain depatriarchalization of the picture of God results in a depatriarchalization and dehierarchalization of the church too."[4] We are created in the image of God. What is at stake, then, is how we view ourselves. The Spirit as the breath of life acts to make us in the image of God, and if God is a community as expressed in the Trinity, then living in the image of God means relating to one another.

The Trinity

The doctrine of the Trinity originated in order to answer the questions of who God is and what God does: "The doctrine of the Trinity originated as an explanation of how God's relationship to us in the economy of salvation *(oikonomia)* reveals and is grounded in the eternal being of God *(theologia)*."[5] Slowly, early theologians began to make a distinction between these two perceptions — the economic and immanent Trinity became differentiated. Luther and Calvin show this separation. They both begin with soteriology, with the cross. In their view, the gift of God is revealed in the work of Christ; yet there is some of God that we still do not see, that is hidden. For them, this is the wrathful God that must be appeased. Contemporary theologians have reoriented trinitarian thought. The economic is the immanent. What God does reveals the totality of who God is. This is a much more Hebraic sense. So God is by nature relational in the three persons of the Trinity and with the world.

God "for us" through the events of time and place ends up as God crucified on the cross. The way of the cross is God's ultimate act of self-

4. Moltmann, *Spirit of Life*, p. 160.

5. Catherine Mowry LaCugna, *God for Us: The Trinity in Christian Life* (San Francisco: HarperSanFrancisco, 1991), p. 8.

revelation and self-giving. God in Jesus knows the misery of suffering and death and utter despair: "My God, my God, why have you forsaken me?" was his cry. The trinitarian name reveals God's occupation; God is involved in salvation history. In the act of the cross, God exposes the despair and the suffering that are all part of the human condition, and says that "wherever you are, I am with you." In the cross, God stands in solidarity with all who suffer and mourn and die. What was thought to be alien to God is now part of who God is as God.

The trinitarian name reveals what God is up to. God is involved in salvation history. The trinitarian name also reveals the relational nature of God. God is in relationship within the Trinity and with the world such that "God with us" is drawn into the very life of humanity, and at the same time humanity is drawn into the very life of God. God is not in isolation; the life of God is not a non-temporal, impersonal reality, as the Hellenistic world suggested. For if God is affected by our lives, then God must be a God in time, not above it. If God is affected by our lives, then God must be dynamic, not static. If God is affected by our lives, then God must be intimately personal. As the life of God changes such that God becomes "God with us," it is the Spirit that provides continuity. It is the Spirit that draws God and humanity into longed-for hope. The Spirit calls, gathers, enlightens, and sanctifies us into a future in God.

In thinking about the Trinity, I draw from the field of psychology and semiotics, specifically Julia Kristeva, a French theoretician. She transforms language theory from that of a study of word pattern to a study of the speaking subject.[6] The emphasis is no longer on a system, but on a living, breathing human being. No longer do we have a universal language, but a process between speaking subjects. This combats Kermode's lack of faith in speech having anything to do with meaning. Applied to the Trinity, this allows for creativity in the powers of the Father, the Son, and the Holy Spirit. They no longer have only one way of relating to humanity and creation, but speak in order to realize the goal, rejecting the static and the systematized. Emphasizing the speaking subject reveals the power and give-and-take in the relationship.

I also draw upon the thoughts of M. M. Bakhtin, a twentieth-

---

6. Toril Moi, *Sexual/Textual Politics* (London: Routledge, 1985) provides an excellent critical overview.

century Russian linguist/theoretician.[7] A main thrust of Bakhtin comes in his term *"heteroglossia."* This term means that in literature one may find meaning in listening for the many voices of the text, not just the dominant one. Oftentimes this is revealed in the voices of the margins. More than one voice defines the whole. This is helpful in discussing the Spirit. If we stretch, and think of the Father, Son, and Holy Spirit as voices, not one voice can fully define the others. We must listen to all the voices. How they speak is not defined essentially. And, if we remember the origin of the Trinity as community and the goal of Trinity as community, then we, as drawn into life by the Spirit, are able to listen to the many voices of others with confidence.

32. A Koinonia *of Pastors*

ROBERT RICE

The Crisis

Two decades of infighting over issues such as human sexuality and a three-decade hemorrhage of membership, which has recorded the loss of our children to secularism, give evidence of a deep crisis in the Presbyterian Church. Numerous articles have been written and not a few studies undertaken to analyze the denomination's present condition and to offer solutions that will save us. Many have proposed cultural and theological factors that have brought us to this point. Yet in all of the argument and analysis, I have not heard anyone asking whether or not the changing role of the pastor in the Presbyterian Church has contributed in any significant way to our present predicament.

My sense is that over the last several decades the pastoral office in this denomination has become increasingly marginalized. And while this is certainly not the only reason and probably not the primary rea-

7. His works may be found in M. M. Bakhtin, *The Dialogic Imagination,* trans. M. Holquist (Austin: The University of Texas Press, 1981).

son we find ourselves where we do at the beginning of the twenty-first century, it is certainly a factor that has contributed to the present crisis. It has possibly served to exacerbate the conditions that have been thrust upon the denomination by a changing cultural climate, rending the church less capable of dealing constructively with the momentous societal changes it has faced since the 1950s.

I offer the following thoughts not as a definitive analysis of the current crisis in my own denomination, but in hopes of beginning a conversation in the church about the role of the pastor as a spiritual leader in a long-term caring relationship with a worshiping community. I offer my own observations as a child of the Presbyterian Church, having served as pastor for over twenty years in four different regional bodies and four congregations ranging in size from one hundred to one thousand members.

During my tenure as an officer in the church, it has seemed to me that the traditional role of the pastor has come under attack from several quarters during the period that roughly corresponds to the numerical decline of our denomination's membership. Over the past several decades, the pastoral office has become increasingly marginalized by the academy, a church bureaucracy, and a secular culture. Pastors themselves have been willing accomplices by abdicating their role in the church as the primary readers of Christian Scripture and as the primary leaders of Christian community.

Bureaucracy

When I graduated from seminary, I accepted a call to a small congregation. The leader of the regional body of which I was a part and his associate had both been successful pastors and were respected as such by their peers. What they brought to their positions was an intimate knowledge of congregational life and an understanding of the joys and challenges faced by the pastors of the churches in the body.

In subsequent moves across the country, this model of regional leadership proved to be an exception rather than the rule. At some point in time, the title of the executive was changed. Corresponding to that change, the regional bodies have become less inclined to fill that position from the pool of clergy who have distinguished themselves as pastors in local parishes. Instead, we have tended to hire those whose résumés highlight the managerial and administrative gifts of a CEO. Increasingly, lay members of the denomination have been hired in these positions, creating another level of separation between pastors and the higher judicatories. The regional bodies understandably have come to look for leadership among those whose primary involvement and passions in the church have been at the regional or national level, but this appears to have been done at the expense of recruiting those with gifts and experience in the pastoral ministry of the local church. Assuming that governing bodies serve the local community of faith, not the other way around, and assuming that the "life" of the church flows out of worshiping congregations, it seems to me that we should be looking for our regional and national leaders primarily among the ranks of successful pastors.

Because of the felt lack of the pastoral wisdom and presence on the staff of presbytery, there has in recent years been a move in a number of such bodies to call someone to be a pastor to pastors. Unfortunately, instead of revisiting the old model that appears to have worked in the past, the church has pursued a therapeutic model of ministry at the regional level. As a result, staff pastors have been called who are given no administrative or executive clout, thereby separating out functions that are not separated, for good reason, in the life of the local parish.

During the last several decades, the Presbyterian Church has become more bureaucratic and less pastoral in its polity. (I use the word "bureaucratic" in a descriptive, not pejorative way, and the word "pastoral" as it relates to the office, not in the therapeutic sense.) This, it seems to me, has resulted in two significant changes in our life together. First of all, it has meant that the ways we have decided to live together have become less informed by the wisdom of Scripture and the character of worshiping communities, and secondly, it has meant that we have come to place the emphasis on functional rather than relational aspects of being the church.

Nowhere has the fallout of this bureaucratic shift been more evident than in the transitional period between installed pastoral leadership in local congregations, the time in which congregations are most vulnerable to bureaucratic pressures and tendencies. Few would argue that the increasing length of time that elapses between permanently installed pastors in Presbyterian churches is a good thing. And yet we continue to prolong a painful process with ineffective and burdensome requirements that take a tremendous toll on worshiping communities. I suspect that if a study were done on the impact of interim periods on the membership of local congregations, it would show a direct correspondence between the length of the interim and membership loss. My own experience suggests that two- to three-year interim periods expend significant spiritual capital in congregations, taking a toll on membership, finances, and energy.

In the name of process and proper order, we have limited the options of local congregations in the calling of pastors over the last two decades, while at the same time levying on them increasingly burdensome requirements that serve to thwart congregational initiative. It is not at all clear to me that doing away with the office of assistant pastor and ruling out the possibility of associate pastors (and, to a limited extent, interim pastors) taking another pastoral position in the same church have made for either stronger congregations or for more successful pastoral relationships.

The recent institutionalization of interim pastors reflects a marked change in our denomination's understanding of the pastoral role as it relates to the nature and purpose of the interim period in congregations. The use of the title "pastor" as a designation for such a temporary office sounds a dissonant chord to what has been traditionally understood as a long-term caring relationship with a congregation as spiritual leader. In addition, the underlying assumption that there is a task that should be accomplished in the interim between installed pastors in every congregation, one that can best be accomplished by a "trained" interim pastor, hardly bears out in my own experience.

Academy

While my own institutional memory is admittedly limited, it is my understanding that forty to fifty years ago seminary faculties consisted primarily of pastors who had served local congregations with distinction. These persons had also pursued academic degrees, and at some point in their career they were asked to join the faculty of a seminary. In addition, there used to be a consensus that the primary purpose of the seminary was to train pastors for service in the local parish.

Today, pastoral experience is hardly a requirement for seminary faculty and it is not necessarily assumed that the seminary is educating its students for work in a local parish. Rich insights into the rhythms of congregational life and strong pastoral passions are no longer passed from professor to student in the classroom. Even in the field of practical theology, the final bastion of pastoral theologians on seminary campuses, pastors rarely fill teaching positions. My impression is that courses in pastoral care and administration are taught from a decidedly non-pastoral perspective. Ironically, even many who teach preaching have learned their trade in the academy and not in the daily grind of the parish. They have little or no experience of weekly preaching and worship leadership, and a limited understanding of the pastor's role in a worshiping community.

Many if not most professors in our seminaries no doubt have a strong Christian faith and are actively involved in local congregations, but their education, experience, and passions are with the academy and not the parish. While in many ways the interests of the academy are similar to the parish, at some point there is necessarily a divergence between the two. Nowhere is the difference between the presuppositions of each more apparent and critical to the life of the church than in the reading of the Bible. Worshiping communities read the Bible as "Scripture," while the academy, for good reason, does not. It is surprising to me that little attention has been paid to the difference between the hermeneutical presuppositions of each. Instead, it seems, congregations and seminaries have naively assumed that an academic reading of the Bible is synonymous (or at least closely related) to the act of reading the Bible within a worshiping community.

Several years ago, when I graded the ordination exams of seminary students, a large number of candidates were consistently stumped on the Bible Exegesis exam by the requirement to move from an exegesis of a passage to the creation of a rudimentary sermon. Many appeared unable to connect their exegesis with the sermon, which in their case was arrived at by a completely different way of reading the text. It was as though the exegetical tools handed the student in seminary seemed to unearth a wealth of insight that was useless for preaching. At the time, instead of questioning the relationship between the requirements of the academic exercise and the demands of the pastoral exercise, I assumed like everyone else that the difficulty those candidates experienced in connecting the two on their exam reflected solely upon their incompetence.

From committees on preparation for ministry to conversations with seminary faculty, regional staff, and pastors in local congregations, I hear expressions of concern about the readiness of recent graduates for ministry in the parish. Admittedly, if there is a crisis in the formation of young pastors, the seminary should hardly be expected to bear the full responsibility for it. The impact of local congregations and our present culture during formative years probably is more determinative of the spirituality and character of young people than the three years they spend in seminary could ever be. Yet in the formation of pastors, seminaries do have a key role to play. For example, this past year the congregation that I serve called as an associate pastor a recent graduate of a denominational seminary. She was at the top of her class academically; she is a bright and able theologian; she has a strong personal faith; but she was utterly overwhelmed by the normal demands placed upon her as a pastor and strikingly unfamiliar with the rhythms of congregational life. Her seminary training had hardly prepared her for the task before her, requiring neither an exposure to the very practical elements of worship and administrative leadership nor helping her to begin to think theologically about the life of a worshiping community.

Because many who are working with candidates and young pastors sense that we need to be doing something more to prepare them for ministry in the local church, a number of different solutions have been put forward. In response to the lack of a pastoral presence on the campus, seminaries have followed the lead of the university and hired chaplains to attempt to fill the gap. More recently seminaries have added courses in spiritual formation and direction. However, while these solutions may give students a handle on their personal spirituality, they do little to prepare them for the uniquely communal spirituality of congregational life. I have heard leaders in the seminary and in the church wish aloud that candidates for the pastoral ministry could be required to take internships, or even better, externships for licensure. I have heard some conversation about encouraging professors to take a sabbatical year with a congregation. But no one is suggesting that pastoral experience be required of seminary faculty. One can hardly expect the seminaries alone to remedy what appears to be a crisis in pastoral formation. Still, I cannot help but wonder if the attrition of pastoral theologians among the ranks of seminary faculty has not contributed to the present crisis.

Culture

The marginalization of institutionalized religion by modernity has been well documented. In his book *Society and the Sacred*, Langdon Gilkey observed that science and technology have become the new high priests of Western culture. Instead of trusting religion to address the fundamental ills that come from inside the self and arise from our finitude, Western culture has placed its trust in the promise of science to control external threats. Whether we trust ourselves to medicine or psychological counseling to fix what is wrong, the modern impulse is not to look for help in the wisdom and mystery of religion but instead to trust the knowledge and control of science. In addition, for those for whom the religious life *is* important, as Robert Bellah reports in *Habits of the Heart*, the tendency in our culture is to understand religion as a private and purely subjective endeavor. It is not uncommon even for active church members to think of the forms and substance of the faith as a buffet, from which they feel free to pick and choose according to their personal likes and dislikes.

This cultural shift has had an inevitable impact on pastors, particularly in mainstream Protestant churches. Small-town congregations, which in the past have provided a pulpit for the vast majority of pastors and a training ground in community for young pastors, are drying up as fast as the "mom and pop stores" in these same towns. In many ways, pastors of local congregations no longer have the status in their communities or even among their parishioners that they once did. Only pastor "superstars" who serve large congregations seem to command attention, and even then not always for the Gospel message, but for what our culture prizes — numbers and power.

Pastors no longer appear to be valued by society for their deep insight into living and meaning, but instead primarily for their ability to officiate at rites of passage and for perfunctory prayers. On matters of life and death, relationships and ethics, pastors are regularly passed over for pop psychology and secular expertise, from funeral directors to family therapists. Counseling, which used to derive its power from pastoral experience, has been co-opted and reshaped by a therapeutic culture, so that even the term "pastoral counseling" no longer refers to that which flows out of the Scripture and life of a worshiping community. Increasingly pastors are expected to be entertainers and managers with a friendly face. They struggle to be faithful to their calling in the fragile communities they serve. People come to church for therapy instead of community, and in times of disagreement or discomfort they mirror the "fight or flight" reflexes of the larger culture.

Pastors

A strong pastoral presence in the denomination is critically important to its future vitality. This is not to say that the offerings of the academy and the bureaucracy are not vital to the church as well. Certainly not all pastors are qualified to serve as denominational leaders or on seminary faculties. However, when these two domains lose the leaven of pastoral experience, their contribution to the church is greatly diminished. And when pastors abdicate their role as the primary leaders of Christian community and the primary readers of Christian Scripture, the pastoral office to which they are called becomes bankrupt. On the one hand, pastors relinquish their position in the greater church by belittling their own unique perspective, participating without question in the present patterns of denominational dysfunction and deferring to the opinions of "experts." On the other hand, some abandon their pastoral responsibility by disengaging from duties and debates outside of the local church, which appear at best to be a waste of valuable time and energy and at worst are destructive to the witness of Christ's church.

Pastors appear all too eager to defer to the expertise of seminary and university faculty when it comes to the interpretation of Scripture. Current scholarship has much to offer the church, and pastors who take their responsibility as interpreters of Scripture seriously will always have an ear to what the academy is saying. But much that interests the academy has little to do with and often does not edify Christ's church, nor does its wisdom necessarily arise from the truth of Christian doctrine of the pages of Scripture. After all is said and done, it is the responsibility of pastors, not the doctors of the academy, to break the bread of Scripture for the church. Pastors have a unique calling to assist the Christian community in interpreting its Scriptures, and we fail the church and its Lord when we relinquish our role in that regard. We have a sacred responsibility as persons who have been set apart by the Spirit through the voice of the church to lead the community of faith through the reading of its Scriptures.

A *Koinonia* of Pastors

As one who has a deep love for the denomination into which I was born and by which I was nurtured, I take no pleasure in the thought that our present way of being the church (at least at the regional and national level) cannot keep us together, much less sustain us. Admittedly, denominationalism has a short history in Christendom. Christ's church will survive and even thrive without its present organizational structure. As H. Richard Niebuhr observed in *The Kingdom of God in America*, Christian movements invariably go the way of old wineskins as patterns of faith and community change. When these structures and forms are no longer able to mediate the vitality of God's presence, the Spirit always breaks out in new and fresh ways. While our present ways of being the church may not survive the next century, and while the winds of the Spirit will blow where they will and there is little we can do to control them, still it is incumbent upon those of us who have been called to the pastoral office to be faithful in our present context.

In this regard, we might look to the description of the church in the second chapter of Acts for insight and guidance. Acts 2:42 describes a uniquely Christian *koinonia* that is formed around a devotion to the "apostles' teaching." That this would hardly describe how we live together in regional and national settings, or even to a large extent in our local congregations, is an indictment upon those of us who are called to be the primary leaders of Christian community and the primary readers of Christian Scripture. It would seem to me that as pastors, we might best serve the church by intentionally modeling such a *koinonia* ourselves. I cannot see this happening within the bureaucratic or academic structures of the Presbyterian Church, which are presently informed by a different imagination. Still, it is conceivable that it could be brought about by pastoral initiative. I imagine that such pastor-initiated gatherings were the basis of the beginnings of my own denomination itself, in the creation of both organizations and schools for training pastors.

To a certain extent, there is already *koinonia* among pastors. Most pastors get together socially with other pastors, and some meet regularly in the discipline of study groups. However, becoming a community of pastors informed and formed by Scripture for the sake of the larger church will take a greater level of commitment and intentional effort. Instead of reflecting the current groupings of like-minded members within our denomination, a *koinonia* of pastors would have to pursue the more difficult path of reaching across the sub-sets that divide us in our denomination. Obviously, there will be some in the denomination who have a greater loyalty to sectarian agendas than to the larger Christian community (I Cor. 1:12), but I suspect most would welcome *koinonia* formed by a devotion to the reading of Scripture.

The initial task of such groups of pastors, it would seem to me, would be to arrive at a common understanding of what marks the general outlines of a Christian reading of the Bible. A second task flowing from the first would be to reflect on the claims of that same Scripture on the lives of pastors and their Christian communities.

If the portrayal of the church in the second chapter of Acts provides any clue for a Christian reading of the Bible, it assumes first and foremost a Christian identity of the reader. The Christian discovers her or his identity in the person of Jesus Christ as witnessed to in Scripture and experienced in the life of the church. A Christian reading of the Bible means to read it as the Scriptures of the church, as one who has recognized God's claim in Jesus Christ through baptism and who lives out that claim in Eucharistic fellowship.

I would suggest that the primary reason Christians read Scripture is in order to ascertain the mind of God, through its witness to Jesus Christ as God's Son. Scripture's authority is not contingent upon any other truth or authority but is intrinsic to its relationship to the community of believers as the church's Scripture, primarily as it witnesses to the Lord of that same community. Its authority is rooted in the experience of a people's encounter with God. Scripture records the apostolic witness to the one whom we believe most fully reveals God and most clearly shows us our true self.

Our reading is therefore not self-referential but Christ-referential. Scripture's authority is relational, functioning much as a parent or as family stories within the Christian community. Since the goal of reading Scripture is to know the mind of Christ as witnessed to in the text, a Christian reading is not concerned with getting behind the text in order to determine "what really happened" (as if that were possible), nor does it compress the unique witness of the different books of the Bible into a uniform consistency. This is not to say that historical or source criticism cannot provide valuable insight into the meaning of the text, or that Christian doctrine has no place in the interpretation of Scripture; it is simply to say that Christian identity is shaped by the Christ of the canonical text.

Our identity as Christians is further formed by Christ's church, as together with the greater Christian community we wrestle with the implications of what it means to live in obedience to the Christ who is witnessed to in Scripture within the context of our present experience. While one may experience the mind of Christ through a private reading of Scripture, the book of Acts portrays the reading of Scripture as a communal act. In reading Scripture together, we most nearly discern the mind of Christ within the varied landscape of the text, and are most able to discern Christ's call to us within the present challenges of culture and history. The corporate reading of Scripture has its institutional expression through the creeds and confessions of the church. Furthermore, the church recognizes among its members those with particular gifts for discerning the mind of God through the voice of Scripture. These persons are set apart by the church for the pastoral office as the primary interpreters of its Scripture through preaching, teaching, and pastoral care.

The only hope that I see for the renewal of my denomination is to be found in the reclamation of the pastoral office. My hunch is that this will occur when pastors reclaim their role in the denomination as the primary readers of Scripture and leaders of community. I imagine that such a transformation would happen if pastors committed themselves to one another in a *koinonia* shaped by the reading of Scripture and colored by the Christian virtues of humility and charity.

LIST OF PARTICIPANTS

1998-1999
Pastor-Theologian Program

Center of Theological Inquiry
Princeton, New Jersey

Resource Theologians

George Hunsinger
Princeton Theological Seminary
Princeton, NJ

Alexander McKelway
Davidson College
Davidson, NC

Robert W. Jenson
Center of Theological Inquiry
Princeton, NJ

Dennis Olson
Princeton Theological Seminary
Princeton, NJ

Donald Juel
Princeton Theological Seminary
Princeton, NJ

William Placher
Wabash College
Crawfordsville, IN

George Lindbeck
Yale Divinity School
New Haven, CT

David Steinmetz
Duke University Divinity School
Durham, NC

James L. Mays
Union Theological Seminary
Richmond, VA

List of Participants

Scripture Project Theologians

Gary A. Anderson
Harvard Divinity School
Cambridge, MA

Brian E. Daley
University of Notre Dame
Department of Theology
Notre Dame, IN

Ellen F. Davis
Virginia Theological Seminary
Alexandria, VA

Richard B. Hays
Duke University Divinity School
Durham, NC

L. Gregory Jones
Duke University Divinity School
Durham, NC

Robin Darling Young
Catholic University
Washington, D.C.

Regional Seminar Conveners

Cynthia A. Jarvis — Northeast
The Presbyterian Church of
Chestnut Hill
Philadelphia, PA

Ephraim Radner — South Central
Church of the Ascension
Pueblo, CO

Bruce Rigdon — North Central
Grosse Pointe Memorial Church
Grosse Pointe Farms, MI

John Stapleton — Southeast
St. John's United Methodist Church
Aiken, SC

Virgil Thompson — West
Bethlehem Lutheran Church
Spokane, WA

Pastor-Theologians

Elizabeth Audette
Rockland Congregational Church
Rockland, ME

Robert C. Ballance
Highland Park Baptist Church
Austin, TX

Byron C. Bangert
First Presbyterian Church
Bloomington, IN

Joseph Bassett
The First Church in Chestnut Hill
Chestnut Hill, MA

Joseph Carle
Chapel Hill Presbyterian Church
Blue Springs, MO

John Christopherson
The Christus Collegium
Bozeman, MT

Deborah R. Clemens
Frieden's United Church of Christ
Sumneytown, PA

Jennifer Copeland Cox
Monaghan United Methodist
Church
Greer, SC

Richard R. Crocker
Central Presbyterian Church
Montclair, NJ

Thomas W. Currie
First Presbyterian Church
Kerrville, TX

Robert W. Dahlen
Goodridge Area Lutheran Parish
Goodridge, MN

F. Harry Daniel
Second Presbyterian Church
Little Rock, AR

Jeffrey C. Eaton
Emmanuel Evangelical Lutheran
Church
New Brunswick, NJ

Barry A. Ensign-George
Springville Presbyterian Church
Springville, IA
Lynn Grove Presbyterian Church
Mt. Vernon, IA

Pamela Fickenscher
The Spirit Garage
Minneapolis, MN

Douglas Fletcher
Westlake Hills Presbyterian Church
Austin, TX

Shirley Funk
Lake Edge Lutheran Church
Madison, WI

Sonja M. Hagander
Campus Ministry at Augsburg
College
Minneapolis, MN

Robert A. Hausman
Lutheran Church of the
Resurrection
St. Paul, MN

David Henderson
St. Paul's Episcopal Church
Steamboat Springs, CO

Scott Hoezee
Calvin Christian Reformed Church
Grand Rapids, MI

Joy Hoffman
Logan Memorial Presbyterian
Church
Audubon, NJ

Phillip Jackson
Incarnation Episcopal Church
Houston, TX

Jonathan L. Jenkins
Holy Spirit Lutheran Church
Lancaster, PA

Albert H. Keller
Circular Congregational Church
(UCC, PCUSA)
Charleston, SC

Adelia Kelso
Northminster Presbyterian Church
Pearl River, LA

Ray Kibler III
Lutheran Bible Institute
Irvine, CA

James Kitchens
Davis Community Church
Davis, CA

Joel E. Kok
Trinity Christian Reformed Church
Broomall, PA

Donald Mackenzie
University Congregational UCC
Seattle, WA

Paul D. Matheny
First Christian Church
Conroe, TX

Harold McKeithen
Hidenwood Presbyterian Church
Newport News, VA

Thomas D. McKnight
St. John's Presbyterian Church
Berkeley, CA

Denton McLellan
Germantown Presbyterian Church
Germantown, TN

Allen C. McSween, Jr.
Fourth Presbyterian Church
Greenville, SC

David D. Miles
Austin Presbyterian Theological
Seminary
Austin, TX

James Miller
First Presbyterian Church
Tulsa, OK

Bruce K. Modahl
Grace Lutheran Church
River Forest, IL

Kenneth Olson
Zion Lutheran Church
Lewistown, MT

Rush Otey
First Presbyterian Church
Pensacola, FL

Thomas A. Renquist
Lord of the Hills Lutheran Church
Aurora, CO

Robert Rice
First Presbyterian Church
Norman, OK

John Rogers
Covenant Presbyterian Church
Charlotte, NC

John Rollefson
Lord of Light Lutheran Church
Ann Arbor, MI

John Rosenberg
St. Paul Lutheran Church
Vancouver, WA

Charles Rush
Christ Church
Summit, NJ

Jill Sanders
Colesburg United Methodist Church
Colesburg, IA

Charles Smith
Rocky Mount District
Superintendent
The United Methodist Church
Rocky Mount, NC

Samuel H. Speers
Rockefeller Memorial Chapel
Chicago, IL

Erik Strand
Edina Community Lutheran Church
Edina, MN

Laird Stuart
Calvary Presbyterian Church
San Francisco, CA

George Sumner
Trinity Church
Geneva, NY

Hamilton Throckmorton
Barrington Congregational Church
(UCC)
Barrington, RI

Charles D. Valenti-Hein
Memorial Presbyterian Church
Appleton, WI

Douglas Vaughan
First Presbyterian Church
Wilmington, NC

Barry Vaughn
Episcopal Church of St. Matthew
San Mateo, CA

Joseph Wahlin
Holy Shepherd Lutheran Church
Lakewood, CO

Anita R. Warner
Advent Lutheran Church
Morgan Hill, CA

Paul A. Wee
Church of the Reformation
Washington, DC

Ken Williams
Rockland Community Church
Golden, CO